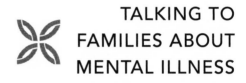

TALKING TO
FAMILIES ABOUT
MENTAL ILLNESS

TALKING TO FAMILIES ABOUT MENTAL ILLNESS

What Clinicians Need to Know

IGOR GALYNKER, MD, PhD

W. W. Norton & Company

New York • London

Manufacturing by Quad Graphics, Fairfield
Book design by Bytheway Publishing Services
Production manager: Leeann Graham

Library of Congress Cataloging-in-Publication Data

Galynker, Igor I., 1954–
  Talking to families about mental illness : what clinicians need to know / Igor Galynker.
— 1st ed.
      p. ; cm.
  "A Norton professional book"—T.p. verso.
  Includes bibliographical references and index.
  ISBN 978-0-393-70600-0 (hardcover)
  1. Families of the mentally ill.   2. Mentally ill—Family relationships.   3.
Communication in psychiatry.   4. Interpersonal communication.   5. Physician and
patient.   I. Title.
  [DNLM: 1. Mental Disorders.   2. Physicians—psychology.   3. Communication.
4. Professional-Family Relations.   WM 62]
  RC455.4.F3G33 2011
  362.2—dc22   2010035001

ISBN: 978-0-393-70600-0

W. W. Norton & Company, Inc., 500 Fifth Avenue, New York, N.Y. 10110
www.wwnorton.com
W. W. Norton & Company Ltd., Castle House, 75/76 Wells Street, London W1T 3QT

1 2 3 4 5 6 7 8 9 0

To Richard and Cynthia Zirinsky
with my deepest gratitude

To the memory of
my father, Ilya Galynker,
and my grandfather, Herzl Zack

CONTENTS

PART IV. REAL-LIFE ISSUES

EXPANDED TABLE OF CONTENTS

ACKNOWLEDGMENTS

I am grateful to W. W. Norton for approaching me at the 2008 annual meeting of the American Psychiatric Association and asking me to write this book. Without their appreciation that most American families are dealing with mental illness in one way or another and that most doctors do not feel comfortable talking to those families about their mentally ill loved ones, this book would never have been written.

Writing this book gave me the opportunity to put on paper many, though by no means all, aspects of my 20 years of clinical experience as an inpatient and outpatient psychiatrist. The names and identifiers of individual patients and their family members have been changed to protect their privacy. I remember all of them and I am deeply grateful for their trust in my skill and judgment.

This book would not have been completed without the help of volunteers in the Family Center for Bipolar Disorder (FCBD). I would like to thank Leo Bierman, Winter Halmi, Gillian Jennings, Lauren Klayman, and Elizabeth Menaker for reading chapters of this book and giving me their editorial feedback. I would also like to thank my coauthors on Chapters 1, 4, and 10—Annie Steele, Janine Samuel, and Michelle Foster, respectively.

This book would not have been possible without my work in the FCBD. The center's mission—"Care for the Patient, Care for the Family"—reflects my conviction that mental illness should be treated openly without stigma and with family members' active participation in the therapeutic process.

I am deeply grateful to Lucy Lamphere: without her dedication, hard work and enthusiasm, the Center would have never been created. I would like to thank all the center funders for their financial support. I would also like to thank all the FCBD's patients and their families for their courage, grace, generosity, and openness in the face of a very tough illness.

I am indebted to my chairman and mentor, Dr. Arnold Winston, for his unwavering support of my many initiatives over nearly 20 years at the Beth Israel Medical Center, including that of the FCBD. Finally I would like to thank my own family, who were early believers in my writing abilities: my mother, Raya; my son, Ben; my daughter, Natalia; and my love, Asya, as well as Ester, Sonia, Riva, Babulya, and Manya the devil-dog.

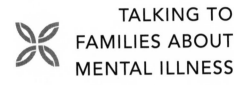

TALKING TO
FAMILIES ABOUT
MENTAL ILLNESS

INTRODUCTION

Why did I decide to write this book?

Three years ago a distraught woman walked into my outpatient office. She handed me a short manuscript she had written that described her experiences following her former husband's diagnosis of bipolar disorder. The pressures of navigating the mental health care system had left her feeling frustrated, disappointed, devastated—they had ultimately, she felt, led to her divorce. I asked her to sit down.

She spoke with me for 2 hours, often on the verge of tears. She felt that her husband's psychiatrist and therapist had completely shut her out of his treatment, suggesting she find her own therapist to deal with her problems. She had many children, three of whom saw their own therapists. None of the clinicians were talking with one another. We agreed that this was absurd, and likely counterproductive.

Since meeting that woman, I have devoted my career to the creation of the Family Center for Bipolar Disorder, where doctors aim to function as family psychiatrists, with one psychiatrist per family, just as you would have one family doctor per family. Through my work in the center, I have seen clearly how mental illness affects the loved ones and family members of those with bipolar disorder—patient crises can lead to depression, anxiety, and panic in the people around them. Just as importantly, I have seen how distressed family members can affect the patient, leading to an increase in symptoms or a decrease in treatment participation.

It is because of my experiences with families at the Family Center for Bipolar Disorder that I decided to write this book. Clinicians at every level—doctors, nurses, therapists, counselors, administrators—have the opportunity to make huge differences in the lives of patients and their loved ones every day. Although it may seem a small thing, it is through clear, compassionate communication that we can provide superior support to families in crisis, leading to a transformation in how patients and their families feel about and respond to mental health treatment.

WHY IS IT IMPORTANT FOR CLINICIANS TO KNOW HOW TO TALK TO FAMILIES ABOUT MENTAL ILLNESS?

The incidence of psychiatric diagnoses in the United States continues to rise. In 2005, 26.5% of Americans were diagnosed with a psychiatric disorder—the highest percentage of any country in the world (Kessler, Chiu, Demler, & Walters, 2005). Between 1957 and 1996, the number of Americans who indicated they would seek informal support to deal with an anticipated nervous breakdown increased by more than 400% (Pescosolido, Martin, Link, Kikuzawa, Burgos, & Swindle, 2000). This number is likely to increase in the near future for a number of reasons, among them increased access to psychiatric care, new diagnostic labels for troublesome behaviors, improved treatment efficacy, and greater cultural acceptance of mental health care. As more clinicians begin to provide treatments that improve lives, more people, not only those with acute or debilitating mental illnesses, are recognizing the possibilities available to them through treatment with a mental health care practitioner.

Thus, it is likely that over half of all Americans will receive some form of psychiatric diagnosis in the near future. Because most of these individuals have at least one family member or loved one who cares about their well-being, this means that fundamentally all Americans will deal with mental health care as a regular part of their lives. When a person is diagnosed with a mental illness, the life of that person changes, in some instances for the rest of the life course, and so do the lives of those closest to him or her. How a patient's loved ones respond to the pressures of caring about someone who is chronically ill and sometimes difficult to be with can even have an impact on the patient's health (Miklowitz, 2004).

As a doctor who has worked for over 20 years on an acute inpatient psychiatric unit, and more recently with the Family Center for Bipolar Disorder in New York City, I have developed a great appreciation for the importance of creating a supportive alliance with patients' loved ones. Meeting time and again with families in crisis, I learned to speak with family members in a way that allowed me not only to convey treatment information but to relieve their anxieties. Loving, caring, often frustrated and at times depressed, family members have plenty of questions: "Is this for life?" "Will she ever get better?" "Are you telling me my wife is crazy?" "Will he always need medication?" "Will she ever get married?" "What should I tell the children?" "What should I say when I see him?" "How should I behave?" "Will he ever speak to me again now that I have put him in the hospital?" The answers are never quite the same, and finding the best approach often is not easy.

Your ability to manage these questions and concerns effectively can have a huge impact on how the family relates to you, to other specialists, and, most importantly, to the patient. Confident, straightforward, and plain language delivered in a supportive manner helps ground families in reality and guides them toward making the best decisions for their unique circumstances. Finding the balance between the sometimes conflicting needs of the patient and his or her loved ones lays the foundation for a lifelong partnership in health—the most effective treatment of all.

Patient care is always the clinician's first priority; however, because research shows that the experiences of loved ones can have an impact on patient health (Miklowitz, 2007), family support necessarily becomes a priority as well. Those close to someone who is struggling with any form of mental illness can greatly benefit from professional support for a number of reasons. A sudden increase in caretaking responsibilities can result in loved ones feeling burdened and overwhelmed, which can lead them to experience anxiety or depression (Perlick et al., 2008). Psychoeducation promotes understanding, which results not only in improved interpersonal relationships but also in improved treatment participation. Lastly, blood relatives of patients may also be genetically vulnerable to developing a number of mental illnesses (Cross-Disorder Phenotype Group of the Psychiatric GWAS Consortium, 2009). Establishing open lines of communication with family members allows you to provide support, treatment, or referrals if necessary, ultimately resulting in improved patient treatment.

WHO IS THIS BOOK FOR? WHAT SPECIAL SKILLS DO I NEED TO USE THIS BOOK?

This book is mainly intended for general practitioners and medical specialists, who often not only identify but also treat psychiatric problems when treating patients in their medical practices. They currently prescribe a staggering 62% of antidepressants, 52% of stimulants (mainly drugs to treat attention-deficit/hyperactivity disorder), 37% of antipsychotics, and 22% of anti-mania medications (Mark, Levit, & Buck, 2009). Besides general practitioners, hospital administrators, who often meet with family members of patients, may also find this book helpful.

While this book is written for health care professionals, no special knowledge is required to understand what is written here. In language and terminology that is easy to understand, this book provides a resource for mental health professionals—psychiatrists, psychologists, social workers, nurses, and counselors—that will help them provide support to families in a way that is realistic, hopeful, caring, therapeutic, and truthful.

Finally, this book is written for the caregivers of those who suffer from mental illness and find themselves searching for words when talking with other relatives, with friends, and with strangers. My greatest desire is that the book will be helpful to them. If it makes discussing a loved one's mental illness with others a little easier, I will consider this book's mission accomplished.

Part I

GENERAL RULES
AND APPROACHES

CHAPTER 1

Key Skills

Written with Annie Steele

Talking with the families of patients with mental illness requires a different mind-set from that used when one is talking to families of patients who are considered mentally healthy. These differences are more pronounced when the mentally ill relative is severely ill and possibly lacks the ability to make his or her own decisions, as may be the case with schizophrenia. One of these differences is that most of these conversations happen in the absence of the patient. When the mental illness is less serious, for example, generalized anxiety disorder, conversation with families of psychiatric patients may be similar to those with the families of patients without mental illness and often include the patient. In the first seven chapters I describe a set of skills that you can use when talking with families, regardless of diagnosis. Later chapters are devoted to issues specific to each of the common psychiatric disorders.

This chapter is devoted to general listening and interacting skills that can be of help when one is dealing with all families. The next three chapters describe how to interact with different types of families and different family members or caregivers, and how to foster communication among family members.

BEFORE YOU TALK WITH FAMILIES

Listen

A discussion with a family is a blend of a confidential doctor-patient conversation and a business meeting. Because of its business-like quality, it requires more planning and more listening than a one-on-one conversation. Regardless of what family you are talking to, you should always start by listening to what the family has to say. Listening before expressing an opinion is so critical that you should do it even if you have a crystal ball and know beforehand everything the family has to say. In general, people, and that includes the families you will be dealing with, want to be heard before being offered advice, counseling, and solutions. Otherwise, even the most brilliant advice might be mistakenly perceived either as an attempt to cut the conversation short by somebody who is in a hurry or as a generic handout from somebody who is indifferent or even callous.

In addition, even if you are a very experienced physician, if you advise before listening by relying on your experience and knowledge or on your intuition, in some cases you will miss the target. Your chances of making a mistake are highest when you encounter a clinical situation that you have never encountered before or that is an exception to the rule. When coming across one of these, if you misjudge by a little, even if you know you erred and the family does not, you will not be the most effective clinician or patient advocate. Some perceptive families will recognize your mistake, and in these cases you may lose treatment alliance with the patient and the family, who will leave dissatisfied and will look for another clinician. Occasionally, you will run the risk of looking ridiculous. Finally, on very rare occasions, you may do significant harm by making a decision based on an incorrect assumption.

Sometimes when you are tired or rushed, it is hard to listen. You can make a habit of cuing yourself in by starting each encounter with "Talk to me," "I am all ears," or a similar statement. At other times, you may be in such a hurry that you simply do not have time to listen before you speak. On those occasions, it is good to apologize in the following way: "I need to apologize for not having enough time to sit down and listen to you today, as I do usually. I can still make a couple of suggestions, but I may miss the mark. So please take what I am about to say with a grain of salt."

Make Sure You Heard and Understood What Was Said

An essential skill in any communication is active listening, which means paying attention to what is being said, asking clarifying questions, and repeating what was said in your own words. Generally you can tell that you understand something when you are able to both visualize the described situation in your head and paraphrase it. After you do the latter, you should ask the family if you understood them correctly. If the family does not endorse your version of what they told you, you need to ask follow-up questions until they do. Having several members of the family speak will help you quickly understand the family landscape: the language and the labels they use with regard to mental illness, the history of their relationship with the medical and psychiatric system, and the family history, family roles, and family beliefs. Observing the family in this way will also enable you to understand their internal alliances and conflicts. Here is an example of paraphrasing:

> The wife of a bipolar patient says, "He is always sitting at the desk in his own world, typing. He rarely eats with me and my daughter. I do not know what is in his head anymore. The only things that are important for him are his video games."
> The clinician paraphrases: "Are you saying that you feel alone raising your daughter and get no support from your husband?"

WHEN YOU TALK WITH FAMILIES

Be Mindful of and Deliberate About Your Emotions and Feelings

Emotions are raw mental experiences that are neither identified nor processed through reason before they are expressed. In contrast, feelings are emotions that are perceived, cognitively processed, registered, and understood. Turning emotions into feelings takes effort and sometimes is not possible in your life outside the office. However, in the office all emotions must be processed. When you reason through your emotions and turn them into feelings, you put thinking ahead of acting your emotions out. This process gives you a chance to keep your negative emotions to yourself and to express them through a related positive feeling. Expressing your *negative* feelings should be a conscious decision that you make with a clear purpose in mind. In a clinical setting with families, such instances are very rare.

> Anger and frustration (negative emotions): "I am the doctor and I know what I am talking about!"
> Regret and sympathy (related positive feeling): "You have come to see me and are paying for this consultation. Would you like to hear what you are paying for?"

Be Confident

Families and patients know that the future is uncertain and that medical knowledge is limited. Facing this uncertainty, they want to be reassured that you are using the best, most current, and most widely accepted treatments available. Doctors should be able to deliver this statement to patients with a true sense of confidence. Opinions and recommendations given with confidence are reassuring to families and are more likely to be followed. A confident statement such as "You are in good hands" brings a measure of comfort even when somebody is facing a grim prognosis. Lack of confidence, on the other hand, fosters anxiety, uneasiness, and distrust. A hesitant "At some point you should get better" is an example of one such discouraging pronouncement. Confidence is gained from and is a reflection of training, knowledge, and experience. Part of this experience is learning how to be and sound confident when one is facing uncertainty. One way of gaining confidence on the spot is reasoning out a complex problem in front of the family. This exercise forces you to think clearly and to translate your reasoning into layman's terms the family can understand. If your thinking is correct, this will increase your confidence in your own judgment in the future. Being confident in admitting your lack of knowledge is preferable to being uncertain about your knowledge. It sounds like wordplay, but it is important to understand the limits of your knowledge. Admitting to a deficit in an area of your knowledge could in fact inspire confidence among your patients because they know that you would never intentionally misinform them. Finally, for some people, projecting confidence requires a little acting, which can be taught and learned.

Confidence and admission of limited knowledge: "I have to tell you that smoking pot is very harmful to your daughter: You have bipolar disorder in your family and recent studies show that smoking pot can actually cause bipolar illness in some people. I do not know if your daughter will get ill, but the chances are not zero."

Lack of confidence: "I'm not sure if pot is harmful or not—I can't predict the future. A lot of people smoke it and are fine, and some get sick; it is probably genetic. It is still better not to smoke."

Be Direct

One of the most common complaints about doctors from families is "They are not telling me anything." In truth, it is often the case that families have been given the information they asked for, but it was done indirectly. Most of the time, being direct is the best approach if it is done supportively. The opposite approach of trying to spare the family's feelings by being indirect and offering no support leaves families frustrated. It is best to start with the most important message, after which you should provide an explanation for your opinion, extending it if necessary, until the family can repeat it in their own words. This is another time when paraphrasing is extremely useful. The more acute the situation is, the more families appreciate directness in communication. Such is the case with acute exacerbation of serious illness—bipolar disorder, schizophrenia, and the like. Even when one is talking about less serious outpatient issues, families appreciate directness. If you cannot or do not want to give a direct answer, it is better to say, "I don't want to answer that," and to explain why.

Direct delivery of good news and bad news: "Good news: Your daughter most likely does not have manic depressive illness. The bad news is that she has been doing a lot of drugs that are affecting her brain and giving her these bizarre ideas. This is bad news because substance abuse can be difficult to treat, and we do not know to what extent it can cause permanent damage to the brain. I cannot say right now whether the damage is permanent in your daughter."

Indirect, conveying neither good news nor bad news, just uncertainty: "It is too early to tell, we need to wait several days. I don't know what will happen—it depends on the person. Substance-induced mood disorder can present like bipolar disorder. Chances are that she does not have bipolar disorder, but she may. We'll see."

Be Clear and Explain Your Reasoning

Being clear is difficult and requires a conscious effort as well as an understanding of how much information the listener can register and process in a short time. In my experience, most people cannot remember instructions for even two medications the first time they hear them and need to go over them several times. The biggest impediment to clarity is excessive use of psychiatric terminology. This pertains to the overuse of both psychiatric terms (such as "delusions") and psychological terms (such as "self-esteem"). The latter has been so overused in the media that it and other such terms have earned the nickname "psychobabble." When you are dealing with the family as a whole, it is crucial to tailor your delivery to the person with the least experience in the mental health field. Not doing so may disrupt family hierarchies, as would be the case with immigrant parents who are unfamiliar with English psychiatric terms and their Americanized children who are much more knowledgeable. It pays to be very deliberate about using medical and psychiatric terms and is best done only with explicit explanation. Finally, it is good to remember that you cannot be too clear.

Clear: "She has schizophrenia and one of the symptoms is delusions, which are unusual beliefs you cannot reason with or talk the person out of. Risperidone clearly is not working. I suggest that we should try ziprasidone because it is the drug least likely to cause weight gain and diabetes. You told me that she is concerned about her weight."

Unclear: "She has schizophrenia and low self-esteem, she doesn't feel good about herself, and she also has delusions. She is not responding well to risperidone, so we may need to try another atypical neuroleptic. Let us try ziprasidone. It is a good drug."

Take Responsibility for Your Judgment and Actions

Most families who come to a doctor's office want that doctor to act like a doctor—that is, to make the best possible decisions based on state-of-the art medical science, exercise their judgment, and take responsibility for their decisions and actions. Sometimes families who either have been confused by direct-to-consumer advertising into thinking that they are experts in a mental illness or just have strong opinions about psychiatric issues do not make their wishes clear. In fact, sometimes they act as if they are in charge of making medical decisions and tell doctors how to treat them or their loved ones. When encountering such families, doctors often get angry, resentful, and frustrated and say, "You know, you decide." The response to this pronouncement is typically "What do you mean? *You* decide—you're the doctor!" Ultimately, even the families who have seen it all and have strong opinions want you to carry the burden of decision making. When you put the responsibility on them by presenting treatment choices impartially and equally, families often get irritated and throw the decision back to you. Indeed, making decisions is what we were trained to do and what we should do. With oppositional families, a good strategy is to present your decision to them and give them control by giving them the opportunity to agree or disagree with you. In this way, such a family will think and feel that they have made the decision but will not feel the burden of actually making it.

Try: "There are many antidepressants on the market. For your wife I would recommend Bupropion because it has no sexual side effects and is unlikely to cause weight gain. We can discuss the alternative if you would like, but this would be my first choice."

Avoid: "There are many antidepressants on the market. We can try Fluoxetine, which is the oldest, or we can try Wellbutrin, which has no sexual side effects. Many people like Escitalopram. Which one do you want to try?"

Tell the Truth, But Be Positive

Being truthful is easy when the message is positive: "Depression is treatable!" Telling the truth is much more difficult when the message is negative: "Bipolar illness is incurable and progressive." Thus, this discussion is really devoted to saying difficult things in a way that is palatable and even optimistic. In communicating difficult information to a patient and his family, it is important to always be truthful. One way to accomplish this while making the news less discouraging is to convey a positive message. Even with the hopelessly and terminally ill, there are ways to be both truthful and positive: "You are in good hands" or "We are not going to leave you alone." Before you make such statements, you need to find out what each particular family is prepared to hear through active listening. Very few families, especially in the early phases of an illness, want or are able to hear that their child's illness is incurable, that he or she will never work, and that his or her future life is that of a persistently and severely mentally ill individual. However, most families can be receptive to the message that their child has a chronic but treatable illness of the brain that makes it difficult for him or her to tell imaginary events from real ones. They can accept that the illness makes it hard for their child to think, concentrate, and understand the subtleties of relationships. Most families are grateful to be told how they can help compensate for their child's deficits.

Schizophrenia is a tough illness, both for your son and for you. As you have seen, he and others with schizophrenia can hallucinate and have really strange thoughts. It is also hard for him to think clearly and to be with people. He will need your support and help in learning how to live with these deficits. We could talk more about it if you would like.

Keep Hope Alive

Mental illness can be very tough. Whether progressive or relapsing and remitting, it is often chronic, and families of mentally ill patients sometimes become discouraged and hopeless about the possibility that things will ever get better. When family members become hopeless, patients sense it and become hopeless themselves. Hopelessness is a risk factor for suicide, and 10% of persons who are seriously mentally ill kill themselves. Thus helping the families of mentally ill individuals maintain hope may help save lives.

Families of even the sickest patients can be given some kind of hope. Hope for a cure is often remote, although you can mention that some very ill patients have been known to recover dramatically with new medications like clozapine. You can offer more concrete hope that both the patient and the family can be at peace, content, and even happy. In order to do that, you need to keep reminding families that the world in which their ill relatives live is different from theirs and can be full of pretty scary hallucinations, delusions, and terrible moods. You can offer the hope of inner comfort for the patient, with the absence of painful hallucinations or delusions. It is good to remind families about new medications, about reduction of symptom intensity with age, and about the alleviation of suffering in general that will occur as their loved ones learn how to live with their chronic symptoms.

The fact that your son has a mental illness does not mean that he cannot be happy. It is just that his happiness is not like yours or mine. For him happiness is days without voices, walking around the city listening to his iPod, and doing the same familiar things again and again. It may not be what you would want for yourself, but it works for him. Of course even with schizophrenia, people may get better with time. There may also be better medications with fewer side effects. Also, the symptoms sometimes either weaken with age or become less bothersome. With treatment and support, he will be OK.

Be Supportive

Being supportive to families, which is not to be confused with being helpful, means supporting the family's strengths. It means validating and refining families' own conclusions, plans, and methods of dealing with the illness. Offering support implies that the family is competent to handle a situation. Families are often insecure about their behaviors and choices, and about whether they are helping their ill relatives or making matters worse. Being unsure about what to do, they will ask you again and again, "Am I doing the right thing?" Support means giving reassurance that their ways of dealing with mental illness are basically OK or may even be wonderful. Even the most "dysfunctional" families have their strengths. For instance, overinvolved families have closeness; distant and aloof families have love. For each individual, try to find something to approve of, support, and even applaud.

> *You have been very good at not blaming her for her illness and staying calm during the episodes. Continue to do what you are doing, and remember as you do that when she does not behave rationally, it is not her, but the illness. You are very good at not taking what she says personally.*

Being critical is the opposite of being supportive. When one is talking with demanding families, it is sometimes difficult not to be critical. When feeling an urge to criticize, try to recognize your negative emotions behind the criticism and process them into a more appropriate feeling. Otherwise you can find yourself saying something like: "You should not have pushed her so hard and used your connections to get her into a high-pressure competitive college when she barely got C's in high school. This is a setup for a psychotic break."

Be Helpful

Generally speaking, being helpful means aiding somebody in doing what he or she either cannot or would not do alone. When one is dealing with families, this means shoring up their weaknesses, improving on their flaws, filling gaps in knowledge, and identifying and improving maladaptive or harmful behaviors. Typically, help without prior invitation is often perceived as an unwelcome intrusion and an implicit suggestion of incompetence. While uninvited but helpful suggestions can be welcome in emergencies, help and advice in the outpatient setting are received well only when families ask for it. Expressing support to the family of a particular mentally ill individual often prompts a request for help, which you may then respond to appropriately.

You are not as strong as you think. Let me help you figure out how to deal with your daughter when she is this sick. She needs decreased stimulation, so arguing with her is not a good idea. You may want to call her psychiatrist—maybe he will increase the dose of her antipsychotic until the episode is over. You can always call me, you know where I am.

Do Not Start Important Discussions When You Are Running out of Time

This is an important technical point, particularly when you are pressed for time. It may seem self-evident and ridiculously obvious, but it is not a good idea to end family discussions with anxiety-provoking and highly charged statements such as "He could become suicidal" or "He may develop tardive dyskinesia." If such a situation arises, it is better to say, "There are a number of other important things to talk about, but we are running out of time. Let's start with those next time."

No discussion of guidelines for conversations with families can possibly cover all the necessary topics. I have tried to cover the most important ones. Following the suggestions in this chapter should make your talks with the families of mentally ill patients productive and rewarding.

CHAPTER 2

Every Family Is Different

Although this is self-evident, the starting point of your communication with families is the family member who is your patient. For that reason, the most important rule for determining how to deal with different families is to remember that every family member might be a caregiver for your patient, either now or in the future. By "caregiver," I mean not only a person who is intensely involved in caring for a severely mentally ill relative but a person to whom the individual with mental illness turns for support when there is a crisis. It may or may not be a close relative, but it is the person who will take the ill person to the emergency room and whose name the patient would give as the preferred contact when he or she is being evaluated in the ER or being treated in a hospital. Debra Perlick and colleagues (2004) offer a more expanded definition that is used in research but is beyond the scope of this book.

Families and caregivers differ from each other in a multitude of ways. Leo Tolstoy, a great Russian writer and an extraordinary observer of human psychology, started *Anna Karenina* with the following (now textbook) observation: "Happy families are all alike; every unhappy family is unhappy in its own way." Following this truly universal observation, each family of a mentally ill person carries his or her unhappiness or caregiver burden and deals with it using his or her own caregiving style. Although caregiving styles are unique to each family, they can be categorized according to their differences in the following critical domains: the caregiver's degree of involvement with the patient, knowledge of the illness, material and spiritual resources, and resilience. Understanding these parameters is an important part of planning your interaction with the family. Not the least of them is the family member's attitude toward you—the health care provider and representative of the medical profession.

FAMILY INVOLVEMENT

To a large degree, your interactions with family members will depend on the extent to which they are willing to be involved in the care of their mentally ill relative. With regard to their involvement, caregivers generally fall into three categories: willing and involved, reluctant, and overinvolved. The following pages describe possible strategies for talking with each of these groups.

Willing and Involved Families

Willing and involved caregivers are usually unproblematic to talk (and work) with because their goals generally coincide with those of their mentally ill relatives and clinicians. One can take the most straightforward approach with them because no preliminary steps need to be taken to engage them in a caregiver role. In contrast, reluctant caregivers may require quite a bit of encouragement, whereas overinvolved caregivers may need a lot of reassurance and limit setting. With willing and involved families you can be open, supportive, friendly, and often relaxed and informal. The aim is almost always to validate their commitment and their special role in your patient's life as you welcome them as a partner in caring for their ill relative. The following vignette is an example of how this can be done.

I am so glad you were able to come! Martha looks much less anxious. She is actually smiling! She has not had any

panic attacks since her last visit. I asked you to come to my
office with your sister today because Martha told me that the
two of you are very close and that you are willing to be in-
volved in her care. Your involvement will help her stay well.
As a rule, I ask family members to get involved because they
are in the best position to observe and help patients on a
daily basis. Sometimes patients, including Martha, have a
hard time monitoring their own behaviors and symptoms.
Maybe we could all agree that you will become a helper and
an early warning system of change, good or bad. I would
like to offer you a partnership agreement. In other words, if
Martha agrees—and she does—we could empower you to
monitor her symptoms. Would that be OK with both of you?"

Reluctant Caregivers

Talking with reluctant caregivers is somewhat more effortful than talking with willing caregivers, because you may need to spend some time encouraging them or even convincing them to take on the caregiver role. Reluctant caregivers are frequently either friends or distant rather than close relatives. However, even close relatives can be reluctant to get involved in patients' care, especially if they lead busy lives or have had conflicted feelings about the patient. Ex-spouses, although technically not relatives, often appear more willing to get involved in the care of mentally ill individuals than some spouses. Thus, at times, an ex-spouse can be the closest person who cares about a mentally ill individual. Individuals who divorced their mentally ill partners so that the latter would be able to get better public assistance and associated benefits often belong in this category.

One of the strategies I find useful when conversing with reluctant caregivers is briefly mentioning all the positive aspects of being involved in caring for the patient, thus giving family members an opportunity to "choose" the one that resonates with them best. I often underscore the importance and uniqueness of their involvement in terms of family unity. Other times I implore relatives to think about their involvement from a moral, spiritual, or ethical point of view. Some reluctant families become more willing to get involved for altruistic reasons; others are more willing to get involved if they are financially compensated. If you have a good relationship with the family, your personal appreciation and gratitude for their help (as in the first of the two following examples) may mean more than you think. Finally, a little harmless flattery (otherwise known as an appeal to narcissism) can also go a long way (as in the second example).

Dr. Aronoff, you are clearly the closest person to your wife, and also the one who knows her best. This is the time to put all your knowledge to good use. You helped many people before you retired, but not her, because she was always proud and independent. Well, there is time in life to help others, there is time to accept help yourself, and there is also time to help your sick wife who always refused your help. I would appreciate it, and so will she. You are with her all the time and will be able to help me catch her depressive episodes early on, before she gets really sick, so that she will not need to be hospitalized as she was last time.

Mr. Brunswick, I am so glad that with your work schedule you were able to come and I can see you with my own eyes! I cannot tell you enough how important this is for your son. Your wife has come here several times, but with your participation, his future will be much brighter. You are the head of the family, and as head of the family, you should have firsthand knowledge of your son's treatment plan. Given your own success as a business owner, I think you will be able to assist your son with the difficulties he is having at work and help him to be more productive. Perhaps you can create a position for him within your company or secure a job for him through your business connections. He will be happier, and you will always know that you did the best for your son. This may bring you some peace concerning his future. You see, it may be that he will not be able to hold a fully competitive job, but working in a somewhat sheltered environment like a family business could make a real difference in his life.

Even after agreeing to play a caregiver role, many reluctant caregivers may still have some resentment toward the patient for the burdens that come with their new role. Some of this resentment can be directed at you as the messenger who brought difficult choices to their attention. It may take skill, time, and resilience to withstand and defuse such resentment. The best technique for turning the reluctant caregiver into a willing one is placing an emphasis on the rewarding aspects of being a caregiver and pledging your support and appreciation for his or her involvement.

Overinvolved Single Caregivers

"Overinvolvement" is a clinical term used to describe a particular pattern of emotional interactions within families (Allen & Farmer, 1996). Hostility, criticism, and overinvolvement make up the three components of a clinical term Expressed Emotion (EE), a pattern of emotional exchanges within families that is associated with adverse outcomes for all, particularly the mentally ill patient (Brown & Rutter, 1966; Vaughn & Leff, 1976). Overinvolvement frequently takes two forms. The first is an unjustified conviction that the person being cared for is incapable of independent behavior or decision making even in the smallest matters. The second is a belief on the part of the caregiver that he or she can deduce hidden motives for patients' behaviors. Although mentally ill people may have limited judgment and cognitive capacity, overinvolvement is a harmful response.

Caregivers usually get overinvolved with the best of intentions and out of a sincere desire to help their ill relatives navigate the world. Often they are also motivated by a wish to protect them from the possible disastrous consequences of their behavior. Some devote so much time and emotional and financial resources to this that it becomes the sole purpose in their lives. I have known many children, spouses, and parents who gave up not only their free time and hobbies but also their personal lives and careers for their mentally ill relatives. The damage of such behavior to their own lives is usually obvious within families and to outsiders. Less obvious are the ways overinvolvement can harm the patient.

Overinvolved family members who are mistrustful of an ill rela-tive's independent behavior or decision making tend to have simi-lar mistrust of the patient's friends, other relatives, and doctors, including psychiatrists. They give the patient the feeling that he or she is constantly under a microscope as they look for real or im-aginary symptoms of the illness. Such families tend to be very controlling of their ill relatives' behavior, and their thinking, even with the best of intentions, tends to follow the "blame the patient" rather than the "blame the illness" pattern (Barrowclough & Hoo-ley, 2003). Caregivers who tend to overinterpret their loved ones' behaviors and motives also tend to interpret symptoms of the ill-ness as volitional behavior.

Blaming the doctor is also common among overinvolved car-egivers, resulting in constant doctor shopping, frequent care pro-vider changes, conflicting advice, and unnecessary procedures. These caregivers not infrequently want to know the details of psy-chotherapy sessions, second-guess doctors' decisions, and occa-sionally encourage medication noncompliance. They have diffi-culty stepping back and accepting that some manic, depressive, or psychotic symptoms are just a manifestation of the illness and can-not stop anxiously interpreting the patient's actions as well as the doctor's. This anxiety may lead them to intrude on the clinician's time with frequent and often inappropriate phone calls and, on some occasions, to negatively interpret your thoughts and motives.

Needless to say, interactions with such families require a lot of attention, significant emotional effort, and intellectual multitask-ing. The goal of all this mental activity is to support the family in caring for the patient, educate family members about the appro-priate level of involvement, and set limits on harmful and inappro-priate intrusions into the patient's and your life. It is also important to monitor your own negative feeling that such intrusions may en-gender.

Support for the overinvolved caregiver's care can be shown in a number of ways. I find it useful to directly acknowledge and even admire the caregiver's commitment to his or her mentally ill relative. After all, some family members not only do not become

overinvolved but are completely uninvolved. I also explicitly acknowledge, appreciate, and attempt to relieve their emotional
stress. This interchange places you and the family on the same
side—that of caring for the patient. Communicating in this way
will also help you distance yourself from any possible negative
feelings caused by previous intrusions and diminishes the risk of
confrontation. The next step is to assure the family of your availability and to clearly establish the limits of that availability. Once
you and the caregiver agree on how often and how you will communicate about the patient, stick to this structure and be aware
that it may have to be re-enforced, perhaps more than once.

*Mrs. Prince. I know how much you love your son and that,
now that you know that he is sick, in your head, you keep
going back to when he was a child and asking yourself what
you did wrong and whether his illness is your fault. I want to
tell you very clearly (and please remember what I am saying): It is not. Most of it is biological and genetic and needs
to be treated with medications and therapy. The fears that
he has about his colleagues at work are psychosis, which is
provoked by anxiety about his performance and future career. He has high expectations for his future, and that comes
from the family values you instilled in him. He did get those
from you when you did not know that he was sick. Now that
you know, those need to be adjusted and we need to figure
out how to do it.*

*In order to do that, we need to establish clear lines of
communication. You know that I am available for emergencies all the time and I answer my cell phone when you call.
However, if you or others call me with routine matters that
can wait until the next meeting, I will not able to deal with
those emergencies. I can promise you that I will be speaking
with you once a week and I will schedule a meeting with you
separately or with your son when you feel that is necessary.
This arrangement should work well, as it has in the past with
others in your situation. If it does not, I am sure you will let
me know!*

Overinvolved Caregivers in Conflict

Some families of mentally ill patients share caregiving duties and are able to do so harmoniously, whereas the relationships between others are tension ridden. Nevertheless, instances of tension reaching the level of open or veiled hostility are relatively rare. However, when such circumstances do arise, they may involve a very diverse group of people, such as family members, friends, business partners, or paid help. Managing a group of feuding caregivers is a daunting task and may bring about the most challenging, emotionally draining, and memorable family meetings you will ever facilitate.

Conflicted and competitive caregiving almost exclusively arises under two sets of circumstances. The first is when working with several siblings who either have a mentally ill sibling or parent, and compete for either the love and attention of the parent (in the case of siblings caring for a sibling) or for the love and attention of the parent who is well (in the case of siblings caring for a parent). In these cases caregivers play out family dynamics that have developed over the years and are normal for them, except that they are magnified by the stress of the illness. Financial considerations, such us inheritance, are generally either nonexistent or secondary.

When dealing with such families, I have found that the best first step is to conduct a family meeting without the patient. The initial goal of this crucial meeting is to establish everybody's relationship and proximity to the patient, and to bring into the open their willingness (or lack thereof) to take on the role of caregiver. Once the caregiving hierarchy within the family becomes clear, the next step is to ask the family to choose one spokesperson for the family. Explain that it is not humanly possible for you to communicate with all of them consistently, and thus one person should be designated the spokesperson. The last step for such a meeting is to help the family establish and clarify the lines of communication among themselves.

If this first meeting is successful, the spokesperson will be contacting you at regular intervals. If other family members call, you should refer to the ground rules established at the family meeting and ask the caller to speak to the family spokesperson. If lines of communication break down over time, another family meeting may be necessary to reestablish them. The main challenge here is to be able to resist either implicit or explicit invitations to take sides in family conflicts.

> I opened the meeting: "Welcome all. It is great when a patient has such a large and involved family. Before we start, please help me understand who is who and what everybody's relationship is to Jared." One of the sisters answered: "Here are Mom and Dad. I am Jill, one of Jared's sisters—I am actually the one who called you. Helen is his other sister." I asked Jill: "How close do you live to Jared and how often do you see him?" Jill responded: "He lives with Mom and Dad in Vermont, and we live in New York and see him over the holidays . . . I felt I needed to get involved because the situation at my parents' house has become unmanageable. I talk to them almost every day." I said: "Great. Since you all talk to each other, it should be easy to select one person whom I will communicate with and who will speak for and communicate with the rest of you. This will be the person, for example, I should be able to reach in an emergency." The family members talked among themselves and decided it should be the mother. I continued: "Mom—so let it be Mom. This means that if you, the sisters, feel that something is not right, you should call Mom and have her call me. Will that be a problem? No? Great!"

The second situation in which conflicted and competitive caregiving can arise is when various extended family members—current and former spouses, children from several marriages, and even household help, who have either straightforward or less obvious financial interests in the patient's well-being—compete for his or her attention and good graces. These cases are even more complicated than the previous type because they almost inevitably lead to frustration, anger, and hostility on the part of some or all members of the caregiving conglomerate. Unfortunately, at times the rage gets distilled and channeled into legal action against physicians.

With divorce rates as high as they are, complex extended families are at least as common as traditional nuclear families. When one is working with them, it is still useful to have a meeting to select the family spokesperson and to define lines of communication. However, before such a meeting, it is necessary to lay some groundwork by establishing which family faction was chosen by the patient to be a caregiver, which one has power of attorney, or who the health care proxy is. Sometimes preliminary meetings are necessary to determine who is who and what each person is empowered to do. After family members either chosen by the patient or legally empowered to be caregivers have been identified, it may be necessary to limit the first family meeting to those family members. After that is done, the meeting can be conducted along the same lines as the meeting described previously.

KNOWLEDGE

It is patently obvious that families differ widely in their level of education and intelligence and their knowledge of mental illness. Generally speaking, it is prudent to tailor your interactions with families to their educational level. This is usually possible, but with some caveats, because talking with some families will often challenge you to step beyond your level of comfort. At one end of the spectrum, some families are as (or more) knowledgeable about mental illness as most nonspecialists, and even some psychiatrists. These families are often quite demanding and not likely to tolerate even minor gaps in knowledge on the part of physicians and, at the first sign of perceived incompetence, will start looking for a physician elsewhere. In order to successfully work with such families, you may find yourself scrambling to read up on the latest advances, experimental treatments, and even fringe treatments.

At the other end other spectrum are families who know very little about mental illness and are either not able or not willing to fully understand its broad meaning and implications. This may happen either for cultural reasons or because they themselves are not in good health either mentally or physically. These families may require more than what a single doctor can provide, and they may get better care in outpatient clinics, social service agencies, and private nonprofit treatment centers staffed by social workers, therapists, and case workers.

Consumer Expert Families

As I just mentioned, some "consumer expert" families know more about their "favorite" mental illness than all but a very few experts in the field. Arthur, the father of a bipolar college student, put it to me as follows: "I am a depression and mania junkie." Knowing about everything bipolar was his hobby. He read all the lay literature, both in print and online; he participated in chatrooms and forums; and he went to consumer and professional meetings. He knew more about the illness than all but a few psychiatrists. This father knew the latest findings from the STEP-BD studies (Thase, 2007) and ongoing clinical trials, and about obscure patents for ultrasound and electrical devices for treating bipolar mood disorder. He took his daughter to the best hospitals and the best doctors, and she was being treated by a private psychiatrist at one of the best teaching hospitals in the country.

Depending on their means, such families often take their loved ones to the best private specialists or the best clinics in the world. If you are not an international expert on their illness, you may come into contact with them at a party or some other social setting or they may come to you once they have become disillusioned with the unfulfilled promises of "the best" institutions. Another common reason for turning to a "regular" physician is the lack of personal attention that patients and their families receive from experts and the absence of improvement on the part of the patient commensurate with the family's expectations and the expert's clout. In Arthur's words, at some point he realized that "there was no 'there' there."

When one is talking to Arthur and others like him, it is essential, although sometimes not easy, to acknowledge that in some respects, between the two of you, he is indeed the expert. By talking with these families, you can actually learn a lot that you otherwise would not have known about what is happening in the trenches of the war against the illness. For instance, I have learned about families paying large sums of money for their mentally ill relatives to have diagnostic brain scans. Although they have no scientific basis, they made the families feel like they were doing "everything possible." From talking to such families, I have also learned of the popularity of herbal and meditation treatments that can only be paid for in cash.

I found that the best approach with such families is to be sympathetic to their burden, respectful of their choices, and skeptical of the outcome of unfounded or questionable but not harmful "treatments." This type of approach brings you down from the pedestal and prevents you from becoming competitive and defensive. It allows you to develop a rapport with the patient so that later you can be authoritative when necessary. It is essential both to feel and to demonstrate respect for such families' knowledge of the illness and their efforts to help their ill relatives.

Because knowledgeable families are what they are, you can only be successful with them if you take extra time and effort to discuss and explain both your simple and sophisticated or complex decisions with regards to treatment. With knowledgeable families, you may spend more time discussing diagnostic uncertainties, possible conflictual trends in the field, and even research data including original publications in peer-reviewed journals. Such an approach will earn you respect, and sometimes admiration. In contrast, intentional use of complicated psychiatric terminology as a means of keeping your distance and escaping detailed discussions is likely to provoke frustration and anger. For the educated illness experts these families have become, it is only fair if you treat them as colleagues and partners in decision making. The following excerpt is an example of one such conversation.

> You see, Curren, clinical trials are designed to serve the interests of pharmaceutical companies, and the medication your son is on may never have been appropriately researched. It may be effective for some patients, but not in your son's case. I do agree with the diagnosis of bipolar depression. Now that I have heard his story (and yours), let us talk about bipolar for a few minutes, and then we'll come

back to what we are going to do. See, at present the bipolar field is in flux. In the past, only the classical bipolar disorder with alternating depressive and manic episodes and a couple of others were considered bipolar, and now some experts in the field feel that any treatment-resistant depression is bipolar depression; the person just has not had a manic episode yet. In my opinion, although there may be cases like that, such a position may be a little extreme. However, at present there are about 10 different diagnostic labels that describe various subtypes of bipolar disorder. Some may be redundant, but others are legitimate and in fact are close to what one of the early great German psychiatrists described 100 years ago.

"Typical" Families

Most families of psychiatric patients have some knowledge about the mental illness that afflicts their relatives and about other similar illnesses that at some point were considered in their differential diagnosis. The degree and the depth of their knowledge vary, of course, but you should be able to speak the illness "language" (i.e., use clinical terms for symptoms, syndromes, and medications). In terms of knowledge base, talking with these families is similar to talking to medical students doing a psychiatry rotation: You will mainly need to do some supportive education and guidance and be mindful of not overwhelming them with your knowledge.

Most of the time, a typical family in your office will be under some degree of stress. If it were otherwise, you probably would not be talking with them about mental illness. Some typical families just want additional information by way of an informal second opinion and are fairly open about it. In this case, you would consider supporting them and helping them expand their knowledge.

Other families are more guarded about their goals. Some may feel stigmatized by the mental illness in their family and will pretend that they are talking not about their own families but about their friends'. Others, without admitting it, may be mistrustful of their current psychiatrists and will use the knowledge they obtain from you to undermine them.

Understanding the latter families' true goals may require time and effort beyond what you typically have to spare. However, just being sensitive to the possibility of these different scenarios should help you decide whether to be open or restrained.

> I started by asking: "Luke, how is your wife doing?" Luke said: "She has been feeling really good. We have started going back to the gym together. It is just her lips are moving all the time. Her psychiatrist has been good to her so far, but now I am not sure he knows what he is doing" I then tried to support his alliance with her psychiatrist: "She is on a new medication that seems to be working much better for her but is giving her tardive dyskinesia. She has been going out and working. This is a big difference. You know, agreeing to take medication that works for you but has some side effects can sometimes be a difficult decision. I can tell you what *I* think but this is just another opinion. You have been happy with her psychiatrist up until now—why change?"

Families With Very Little Knowledge About Mental Illness

Despite the fact that close to one third of Americans are at some point given a psychiatric diagnosis, and that TV programs and the Internet are populated with professional and amateur therapists and their clients, amazingly, there still are some families who know very little about mental illness. As always, listening to them and understanding the reasons for their ignorance will help you talk with them subsequently and will inform your actions.

For the majority of families with little knowledge of mental illness, it is very likely that you are the very first health professional they have spoken with about psychiatric issues. Indeed, when people know nothing about mental illness and psychiatry, the main reason is that they have not needed to—that is, until now. Talking with such families puts you in the enviable position of being able to put your stamp on their knowledge of mental illness and their future relationships with mental health professionals. Even if in the future they talk with many psychiatrists of various professional statures, their encounter with you could be very memorable.

It is worth emphasizing that your own attitude will affect whether they will have respect for psychiatry, be willing to help their loved ones enter psychiatric treatment, take psychotropic medications over psychotherapy, and be compliant with either treatment. Quite a bit of pressure, isn't it? However, whether or not you realize it, the first serious discussion about mental health for the family facing a crisis *is* going to affect them. Thus it is most ethical for the physician to direct the discussion knowingly.

> I said: "Matt, thank you for bringing your mom here—you brought her to the right place. Before we start, I need to understand how much you know about depression, particularly depression in the elderly, which is a somewhat different illness. Is this your first time at a psychiatrist's office?" Matt answered hesitantly: "More or less . . . " I continued with a sense of optimism: "Then I am really privileged, because I can educate you both about depression in the elderly and about psychiatry."

Another group of people know very little about mental illness for cultural reasons. Some families come from regions of the world and countries where even the notion of mental illness may not be acceptable. Most of these are the elderly immigrant parents and grandparents of assimilated or somewhat assimilated individuals. In most non-Western cultures, mental illness is perceived as a family disgrace. Psychiatric problems are often discussed in terms of a person's character or intelligence, or a medical illness. For example, the family of the mentally ill Virginia Tech shooter for a long time thought of him as stupid rather than as someone who was mentally ill.

In an open society such as ours, hundreds of cultures intermingle in the workplace. However, they tend to socialize separately and maintain their cultural attitudes. A detailed discussion of cultural adaptation to the concept of mental illness is worth a book of its own. For now, I will just mention one example. Others are discussed in more detail elsewhere in the book. In the Russian culture, depression and anxiety are discussed in terms of blood pressure and chest pains. Depressed patients can spend months being treated in the hospital without ever acknowledging they have a psychiatric problem. Talking with such families may require a transitional step of discussing a "brain disease" before the illness is ever addressed by name. A similar approach can be taken with assimilated families who do not understand or accept mental illness because of a lack of education.

Lena, the reason your husband has been so different lately is because he has really severe depression. Lying in bed, not washing or dressing, constantly complaining—these are all symptoms of depression. It seems that he is a different person, but he is not; the old person is still inside him and will come back after the depression is treated. He will stop being weak and will become strong again. When he gets better, both of you need to know that he has this brain disease and that he will need to take medications to treat it. He should start now.

Families of those who become ill with devastating mental illness with a poor prognosis sometimes stay in denial and refuse to accept both medication and treatment. It is tough to face a diagnosis of chronic schizophrenia in a college-age person in the prime of life. Comprehending and dealing with dementia in a 40- or 50-year-old is equally devastating. Denial allows families to avoid facing the realities of catastrophic illnesses that befall their loved ones. Talking with them can be very frustrating because they clearly have the intellectual and cultural capacity to understand and to assist in the treatment of their ill relatives. However, they often seem to refuse to hear what the clinician is saying so they can maintain hope, or so they can blame the medical profession, or both.

In the case of schizophrenia, the results can be disastrous because of high suicide rates in those with untreated psychosis. Families tend to blame medications for their loved ones' symptoms and discontinue treatment when patients are discharged from the hospital. Several years ago a young man who had been treated on my inpatient unit killed himself after his parents stopped the neuroleptic he was taking 2 weeks after his discharge. (I cover most of the issues surrounding denial in Chapter 4.) It is important to remember that giving these families hope for some relief in the future, whether in the form of medical advances or a remote (or sometimes not so remote) possibility of a remission, generally makes it easier for them to accept the inevitability of the illness and form a trusting relationship with their ill relatives' physicians.

> *Lucy, there is bad news and there is good news. The bad news is that your daughter does have an illness, and it is a serious mental illness. The good news is that she will finally get the right treatment and should improve. It is hard to say at this stage whether this is schizophrenia, but even if it is, there are different kinds. I treat patients with schizophrenia who work and have families. You may want read up on this illness, and then we can talk more when you know more.*

Finally, some families are not eager or not able to learn about mental illness because, for various emotional, financial, or logistical reasons, they find it difficult to take responsibility for their mentally ill relatives. These families either openly demand that care for their ill relatives be provided exclusively by medical professionals and social service agencies or, in a somewhat passive-aggressive manner, come up with obstacles that prevent them from becoming actively involved in their care, which in the end is still left to medical professionals and social service agencies. Such families can be aggressive in their demands and do not wait long before complaining to the hospital or agency administration.

Some of these families are dispersed and overworked and live out of town. They rarely come in for family meetings yet can be very demanding when they do or in conversations on the phone. Others are families of substantial means who pay for the best care possible and are accustomed to getting "only the best." For such families an invitation from a doctor to get more involved may suggest that the doctor is not doing his or her job and that they need to find a "celebrity" specialist who provides comprehensive services, including exclusive hotel-style accommodations at a private facility. The Sierra Tucson Treatment Center and its copyrighted Sierra Model of treatment (www.sierratuscon.com) are the best examples of such comprehensive treatment. The staff has perfected a holistic approach that involves elements of Alcoholics

Anonymous/Narcotics Anonymous and a structured family week aimed, among other things, at optimizing family involvement in the patient's care. When dealing with such a family, the physician needs to be honest with him- or herself about his or her ability to provide such "total service" and, if it does not seem feasible, refer them to Sierra Tucson or a similar enterprise.

Brittany, I have to be frank with you: You are underestimating the seriousness of Olaf's illness. His illness is a new experience for you and there is a lot to learn. You may want to read about cannabis and psychosis. Doing a Google search is a good place to start. For now, however, I am just asking you to trust me. He attempted suicide twice while psychotic when smoking weed, and he is likely to do it again unless he stops. There is only so much I can do without you getting more involved in his care. If, as you are saying, you do not have time because you are caring for your other three children and for your estate, I can give you a referral to an excellent inpatient institution on the West Coast. They have a wonderful holistic program that will take care of all his needs. They have worked with young people like him and their families and would rely less on family involvement than I would. We can talk again about future care when he is stabilized and discharged.

ATTITUDE

Patients and families' views on the medical field are shaped by a combination of their own health care experiences, their experiences taking care of their relatives and friends, what they hear from the media, and their own professional interests and experiences. Most people have reasonably realistic ideas about what doctors do and how much to expect from them—most, but not all. For some families, any doctor is a potential savior, upon whom are placed extraordinarily high expectations. However, as almost always, there exists the opposite extreme. For some people, a doctor is a callous representative of a heartless and greedy health care machine and, worse, the enemy from whom proper care needs to be extracted with military force.

In discussions with families with realistic views of doctors and doctoring, professionalism and common sense are usually sufficient to achieve success in building rapport and communication. The only caveat here is not to appear mechanical, indifferent, or short because of burnout or fatigue. If that is the case, you may find the chapter on stress helpful for both yourself and your patients (see Chapter 14).

On the other hand, families who see you as the savior or the enemy may require special attention and care. Between these two extremes, being a savior is not necessarily the easiest one to deal with. First of all, when people let you know that they see you as their savior, the statement itself is not usually straightforward. Some may indeed feel that way because you came highly recommended by a grateful family friend or because this is the opinion they have of most doctors. Others just want to put you on notice that they have very high expectations and they are counting on you to meet them.

High expectations are hard to meet, particularly if you came recommended as a miracle worker. As the saying goes, "the harder they come, the harder they fall," and you are in danger of falling hard if miracles are not delivered as anticipated. When you are meeting with such families, it is often beneficial to make sure that they (and you!) know that you are not God and that miracles happen only occasionally, and not with any regularity. While favorably predisposed families are unlikely to believe you if you try to convince them that you are just a regular MD, they may be able to alter their initial view of you from that of a savior to that of somebody who is exceptionally good but still limited by his or her humanity. On these occasions, humor can be particularly helpful.

Simone, I appreciate Dr. Rogers's referral and also your trust. I would love to help your son. We perform miracles occasionally, and I hope your son will be one of them. Your friend's daughter fortunately was. My mother, who was also a doctor, used to say that you have to be a truly terrible doc-

*tor not to save at least one person during your career. If you
are a competent doctor, you save several. If you are very
good, you may help many. Yet when miracles become routine, they stop being miracles. We'll do our best to help your
son, and let us hope that we will use medical science crea-
tively enough that it will look like a miracle.*

On the other hand, families may at times consider you, if not an
outright enemy, definitely not an ally. They may have had bitter
experiences with doctors in the past. They may not have been
ready to accept the devastating news that a child or a spouse has a
mental illness, their mentally ill relatives may have been misdiagnosed, treatments may have been ineffective, treatments may have
resulted in severe side effects, and so on. Last but not least, family
members may also be mentally ill—they may be paranoid, or depressed and irritable, or have severe personality disorders. Particularly tense meetings are often held in the hospital when patients
either are committed against family wishes for fear of the danger
they may pose to themselves or others or become restrained either
for agitation or violence.

When you are facing a hostile family, listening carefully to understand their concerns becomes even more important than usual.
In a hospital setting, you are often required to talk with families
you do not know well and there may be many unknowns you just
cannot anticipate or make assumptions about. One unusual example that comes to mind involves two priests who were concerned
about the health of a woman who was admitted to the hospital
after a suicidal gesture. The woman had three children, and her
husband was about to be released from prison after a 2-year sentence for fraud. On the surface, the priests behaved similarly. They
were very active in her care, visiting her frequently in the hospital
and calling her treatment team. In reality, only one of them was
the priest from the family parish; the other was her lover. This example is given to illustrate that in such cases, deciphering the family terrain can be difficult but is essential before you engage in any
substantial discussions. In fact, this was one of the few cases when
adherence to HIPAA laws and the use of HIPAA forms to identify

legitimate family members and other caregivers proved most helpful in promoting appropriate discussions.

Cultural issues are also important. Immigrants from totalitarian societies can be very aggressive and hostile toward anybody they perceive to be a part of "the system." To some of them, doctors appear to be part of the powerful medical machine poised to take advantage of them. Therefore, they believe the medical system needs to be resisted, fought, and taken advantage of in return and, for some, preemptively.

When you are talking with hostile family members, it is important to stay calm and in control of your own anger at and frustration with their unreasonable expectations, excessive demands, lack of respect and gratitude, and lack of social graces. When you feel overwhelmed and begin to feel that you have had enough, try to employ the communication skills of active listening (Fassaert, van Dulmen, Schellevis, & Bensing, 2007). Separating the content from the delivery and responding only to the content is one element of active listening that is a particularly useful skill under these circumstances.

With hostile families it is nearly always useful to help them understand your place in the hospital hierarchy. If they see you as a part of the medical–industrial complex, you may point out to them that you are not necessarily responsible for the transgressions of other doctors. If they are angry with you as the bearer of bad news, then do just the opposite: It is helpful to remind them that you must follow the rules of ethical practice and hospital policies. This may help them either defuse their anger or refocus their hostility on a more appropriate target.

In tense discussions with a distressed and suspicious family, it is helpful to be extremely clear in describing the patient's symptoms and their meaning and consequences for the patient and the family, as well as the reasons for your recommendations and actions. Although I know at least one doctor who is able to make jokes even when facing mistrustful families, most, including me, do not. Joking with suspicious families—as well as paranoid patients— usually confuses them and makes them even more suspicious and paranoid.

Finally, even the most professional, experienced, and patient doctors have their limits. It is important to understand and know your own and be able to monitor your emotional state when you are getting close to losing your sense of control and, with it, your composure. "Losing it" is a good way of ruining your chances of winning the suspicious family over and giving them the help they need, as well as losing the mentally ill patient you are treating. When you have difficulties controlling your emotions when talking to suspicious families, keep in mind that it is the angry family who becomes litigious and sues. In short, know when you are about to lose control and take a break before that happens. Excuse yourself, walk out, and get help.

> Question: "What are you doing to my wife? What are you giving her? She is staring at me and not talking. I am going to take her to another hospital."
>
> Answer: "Mr. Yasuda, I understand why you are upset. She is not doing well at the moment. But she will get better soon—let us talk in my office. Your wife cannot talk because she is experiencing what is called catatonia. It is scary but fairly easily treatable with medications, and the symptoms should resolve by tomorrow. Her depression will also get better, but it will take longer. She is getting the treatment recommended by our professional organizations and medical literature and she will get similar treatment from another physician here or at another hospital. Let's take a break now—I have somebody waiting for me—and talk tonight. I will ask one of your wife's nurses to join us then."

To repeat Tolstoy's sentiment: "Happy families are all alike; every unhappy family is unhappy in its own way." Families of mentally ill individuals can be different in countless ways, and in this chapter I did not even come close to covering all of them. However, the differences I did discuss play an essential role in defining how families interact with doctors and, in most cases, should be sufficient to guide interactions with different families to a successful outcome.

CHAPTER 3

Communication Strategies

 HOW TO TALK TO DIFFERENT FAMILY MEMBERS

Although different family members of different generations can have a variety of attitudes toward their mentally ill relatives, some generalizations can be made. Family roles and expectations with regard to mentally ill individuals obviously differ among parents, children of various ages, siblings, and more distant relatives. Although parents are the most common caregivers for mentally ill individuals, sometimes, when they are ill themselves or are not willing to take on the burden, siblings and more distant relatives step in and take on the caregiver role.

Family members' roles and attitudes vary substantially from culture to culture. Families of Western European background tend to live in nuclear families, whereas those of Eastern European, Latin American, and Asian ancestry function to various degrees as extended families. There are also substantial class differences: In my experience, wealthier Americans tend to rely less on family members and more on paid treatment and care specialists. Not unexpectedly, in most general terms, the higher the family income and more industrialized the country of origin, the less reliance there is on the extended family.

Despite these differences, common themes and concerns become evident in discussions with family members of all cultures. Those mentioned here by no means constitute an exhaustive list but should be helpful in guiding interactions in most encounters.

Parents

Parents of individuals with mental illness are typically extremely dedicated to their care and are reluctant to leave their care to outpatient organizations and inpatient institutions. This applies to both biological and adopted children. The latter have much higher frequency of mental illness, particularly when they were adopted from countries where abandoned children live in poor orphanages rather than with foster families (van der Vegt, van der Ende, Ferdinand, Verhulst, & Tiemeier, 2009). Moreover, some Eastern European countries only allow adoptions of children with birth defects and psychological problems. In many cases adoption agencies assure the adoptive parents "off the record" that the diagnoses were only given in order to make adoptions possible and that the children are actually healthy. They provide DVDs and pediatricians' notes as supporting evidence. Nevertheless, upon leaving the country after adopting, and sometimes even on the way to the airport, the parents find that their adopted children have begun behaving very differently and may have been medicated for the recording.

Whether the children are biological or adopted, parents often blame themselves for their children's illness, most often feeling that they caused it by making the wrong decisions such as sending them away to a boarding school, changing residences because of demanding careers, not spending enough time with them, or not paying them sufficient attention. When there is no major mishap to blame, many parents blame themselves for not being supportive enough, for not pushing their children hard enough to achieve, for pushing them too hard to achieve, for loving and spoiling them too much, or for not paying enough attention to them. While these are the general themes one encounters among parents, there are as many specific reasons for parents to blame themselves as there are parents.

Even if the parents' guilt is justified, unless there are suspicions of child abuse, there is nothing to gain from being judgmental and confirming the parents' feelings of guilt when you converse with them. In fact, by blaming the family or agreeing with the family that they are at fault, you are likely to lose the family's trust and the therapeutic alliance. A much better approach is to affirm the family's attempts to cope with their children's mental illness and to buttress their efforts to find care and support in the community. A referral to a mental health support group such as the Depression and Bipolar Support Alliance or the Mood Disorders Support Group of New York City can help families focus their caregiving efforts and give a reference point for what is and is not appropriate or sensible.

Adult Children

As I discuss in Chapter 16, many women with mental disorders—even those with the most severe mental illnesses—have children and families. By their early 20s, when the onset of illness usually occurs, the majority of women are sexually active, and even schizophrenia does not substantially change their ability to reproduce. Consequently, many children grow up with mothers who have a mental illness. Young men with serious mental disorders are much less likely to father children. As a result, you are less likely to encounter adult children of men with schizophrenia or early onset severe bipolar disorder.

For both genetic and environmental reasons, children with a mentally ill parent or mentally ill parents grow up with a considerably high risk of developing psychiatric problems. For example, preschool children with one bipolar parent have an eightfold risk of having ADHD (Birmaher et al., 2010; Hirshfeld-Becker et al., 2006). Therefore the family members with whom you will be talking are much more likely to have ADHD, anxiety, mood disorder, or conduct disorder than an average family. Adult children of individuals who became ill at a young age may have painful memories of growing up with a mentally ill parent. The Broadway musical *Next to Normal* vividly and accurately portrayed what it is like for a young woman at risk of becoming bipolar to grow up living with a bipolar and psychotic mother.

When you are talking to adults with mentally ill parents, it is useful to keep all these issues in mind. You have to be aware that they themselves may have psychiatric problems, including bipolar mood disorder. Even if they are not ill, they may have had difficult childhoods in moody, erratic households full of tensions and high expressed emotion (see Chapter 14 for more on this) and may be feeling or exhibiting prodromal symptoms of a major psychiatric illness (Brown & Rutter, 1966). Whether or not they are ill, they may have concerns about their own children becoming ill or they may be conflicted about whether to have children at all.

Adult children of individuals with serious mental illness have often seen it all and may need little in terms of psychoeducation but can still use help navigating the maze of the American mental health care system—finding the right psychiatrists within their insurance network, getting entitlements and disability, optimally using family resources. They may need encouragement to look for second opinions, to find better specialists, to admit that the medications are not working as they had hoped and may need to be radically changed. Families in which there are many siblings often need help organizing the care for the ill parent and stepping back from competing to be the "top" child.

Schizophrenia, bipolar mood disorder, and most frequently major depressive disorder may have a late onset, when people are in their 50s, 60s, 70s, and 80s. With current life expectancies, even people with late-onset illness can live with their illness for decades. Children of patients with late-onset psychiatric disorders experienced their parents as completely different people during their childhoods and have childhood memories of healthy, capable, and loving parents. Such families need help either bringing their "old" parents back or reconciling their memories of their capable parent with the new mentally ill parent, who is likely to be less functional and more dependent on them.

Like any other illness, late-onset mental illness can be unpredictable. Major depressive disorder, treatable in theory, can turn into a chronic, severe, and unremitting illness, whereas typically more debilitating late-onset schizophrenia (paraphrenia) can have a relatively benign course. When talking with these families, even in the most difficult cases, you should discuss both the possibility that patients may never regain their old pre-illness selves and the possibility that, with proper treatment, it may be possible to achieve substantial resolution of symptoms such that the core identity and level of functioning of the person with mental illness remain intact. Anticipatory grief at the potential loss of a parent—in this case, of a mentally healthy parent—is typically expressed as "She is not herself" or "This is not him" or "Will she ever be herself again?" When one is facing such grief, it is helpful to emphasize that the old healthy self may still be there and may just be hidden by the illness. The patient's "old self" may either be glimpsed or re-emerge with successful treatment.

Issues of heritability are raised less frequently in these cases because the children are often in their 30s and 40s and have already had children of their own. Caregiver children of adult parents with late-onset mental illness often do not have the inner resources to focus on both their parents and their children and rarely discuss what may happen to them or their own children when they get old. We know relatively little about the heritability of late-onset mental illness, which should be readily acknowledged if such questions do arise.

Adolescents

For an adolescent, taking care of a seriously mentally ill parent or sibling is often a life-changing or even life-defining experience. The extent of this influence depends on the person's own resilience, the seriousness and duration of the relative's illness, and the extent to which the adolescent assumed (or was forced by circumstances to assume) the role of the caregiver. Incidentally, this applies not only to mental illness but to any prolonged serious illness, such as cancer. Having a severely depressed brother who eventually kills himself or being the main caregiver of a mother with schizophrenia or taking care of a father who is dying of cancer is an experience that can scar an adolescent for life.

When talking with adolescents about their mentally ill relatives, you should find out whether they have been unwillingly thrust into the main caregiver role and, if so, what family resources may help alleviate that burden. In some families, adolescents assume parental roles that a timely intervention might relieve them of. Families may or may not be aware of this role reversal, and sometimes just identifying family roles may help parents reassume the adult roles and relieve the burden on their adolescent children. If the family resources needed to relieve an adolescent from the excessive stress of caring for a mentally ill relative are either absent or insufficient, you may be able to ease that burden with supportive talk. First, in order to reduce the stress and potential trauma of caring for a severely ill relative, you need to be aware of the adolescent's understanding of the illness and of his or her role. Just as you would do with patients, first listen and say very little until you have a coherent mental picture of the adolescent's predicament. Once you have achieved this, use the adolescent's vocabulary and terminology to support his or her character strength and coping style as well as relieve him or her from excessive guilt. Feeling personally responsible for the course and the outcome of the illness and having thoughts such as "Will I be like that?" are predictive of future psychiatric disorders related to traumatic caregiving such as PTSD.

Adolescent siblings of mentally ill individuals may have particularly difficult and traumatic experiences. It is likely that before he or she became ill, the mentally ill sibling experienced long prodromal states, during which he or she engaged in behaviors that were misinterpreted as odd or defiant: excessive shyness in schizophrenia, irritability and aggressiveness in bipolar mood disorder, and social withdrawal and isolation in major depressive disorder. The ill sibling often receives the lion's share of parents' attention and preferential treatment, igniting fierce sibling rivalries and resentment. Whether adolescent or adult, the caregivers may perceive their ill brother or sister as manipulative or selfish, an opinion fueled by the latter's many instances of either neediness or inappropriate behavior. The parents, on the other hand, may have long ago adjusted their expectations for their mentally ill child and created a double standard that would be considered unfair and arbitrary if he or she were healthy.

When helping adolescents cope with or care for their mentally ill parents, brothers, or sisters, I suggest that they try to imagine themselves as wearing two hats: one of a close relative and the other of an almost professional caregiver, say, a nurse. I often ask which one they feel like most: a doctor, a nurse, a home attendant, or a social worker. After they decide what type of caregiver they feel like, I propose that they practice putting these "hats" on and taking them off at will. I advise them to be caring but "professional," that is, to assume the stance of a somewhat detached observer when wearing the "nurse hat," and to be themselves when wearing the "relative hat." I then suggest switching into the caregiver mode when the personal mode gets tough and vice versa, and leaving, if possible, when both modes are difficult.

> *Deirdre, let me make a suggestion about how to deal with Allison without losing your temper. She has a pretty serious mental illness, and you have to be aware of her symptoms as if you are a psychiatrist. You need to observe her in a detached way, wearing your "psychiatrist hat" first. If she is having symptoms, continue in the same mode as long as you want to or until you start getting tired or angry and then excuse yourself and leave. If you determine that Allison is herself, then you can put on your "sister hat" and relax.*

Spouses, Partners, and Significant Others

When talking with spouses and other partners about a mentally ill loved one, the most important thing to remember is that regardless of how committed they are to the well-being of the mentally ill individual, at any time they could decide to leave. Surprisingly, the divorce rate in bipolar families is about 50%—about the same as in the general population. I suspect that breakups between mentally ill individuals and their partners are more frequent than they are in the general population. Nevertheless, comparison with the average American family notwithstanding, the likelihood of the relationship of a person with mental illness ending is higher than 50%; divorces and abandonments are very common.

As I discuss in Chapter 16, young people considering marrying individuals with a history of mood disorders can be astonishingly unwilling to research the illness and get information that might help them understand the difficulties of living with a mentally ill person. Instead they decide whether to start the relationship or get married based on their own experience interacting with the person with a psychiatric disorder. As a result, when the illness is in remission, the healthy partner tends to think that the relationship is stable and that the ill person has been cured. Living through the partner's acute episodes, however, makes such denial difficult.

When talking with mentally ill persons and their partners who act as healthy caregivers, whether you want to or not, to some extent you play the role of a couples therapist and face the ethical dilemma of whether to be concerned with the well-being of the couple as a whole or of the healthy partner. You may find that you ask yourself questions like, What is the right thing to say when a woman married to a bipolar man for 15 years and the mother of three tells you that she cannot take it anymore and is getting out of this marriage? Should you be brutally honest with the boyfriend of a woman with severe borderline personality disorder and depression who experiences panic attacks? Unless the healthy partner is abusive, the relationship is clearly beneficial to the patient, insofar as the stress of a breakup or divorce can have catastrophic affects. On the other hand, for the healthy partner, staying together may mean the ongoing lifelong strain of being a caregiver for the mentally ill person.

In conversations with the healthy spouse or partner of a person with psychiatric illness, my first suggestion is *not to take any drastic actions* in terms of making a decision to stay or leave at the time of an acute episode. Leaving somebody who is acutely ill deprives him or her of critically needed support, makes him or her feel betrayed and abandoned, and increases suicide risk. For the healthy person, abandoning an acutely ill partner plants the seeds of prolonged guilt and remorse. On the other hand, I encourage families to note and analyze their experiences with acutely ill persons and try to make rational decisions about their future with a clear understanding of what the future may hold. Staying with a mentally ill husband or wife blindly, without such understanding, may cause an intolerable level of stress for the individual caregiver, leading to anger, hostility, constant criticism, and high EE in general, which is associated with a poor prognosis for both partners and may be better avoided for the sake of both partners.

Asking caregiving partners to remember their experiences during acute episodes helps them gauge the cost of staying in the relationship and helps them take action regarding the future of the relationship when the patient is in remission. Paradoxically (or understandably), when the ill spouse is more stable and more resilient and can withstand the stress of the breakup better, partners who were stretched to the limit and felt they could not take it anymore during acute episodes tend to stay when the stress in the family diminishes with remission. Although there is probably a relationship between mental illness severity and divorce rates, whether couples stay together depends equally on their mutual affection and resilience. Some couples break up when there is no mental illness; others stay together despite grave disability.

In any case, given the emotional cost of divorce (second only to the death of a spouse in the amount of stress caused; see Chapter 14), I consider it my ethical and moral responsibility to support the couple's relationship and advocate staying together, except in cases of clear abuse or exploitation on the part of either the ill or healthy partner. In doing so, I emphasize the positive and rewarding aspects of caregiving—altruism, gratification, moral satisfaction, love. I also remind them that with time and treatment, mood and anxiety improve and psychosis lessens or resolves, and that none of us can see the future and know for sure what will happen. This approach validates the caregiving partner's devotion and helps keep hope alive until symptoms improve.

Friends

Some psychiatric patients identify friends as their confidants and caregivers. This may happen when family is unreachable, when the patient is estranged from his or her family, or when the patient's relationship with close relatives is problematic. For example, I recently treated a woman who came to our ER because she was having urges to jump in front of a subway train. When I told her I needed to call her husband and ask him to come to the ER, she was scared to disturb him at work and opted to call her girlfriend instead. Although some patients' friends become more involved than their close relatives, most will do so only in cases of an emergency and for a short period of time.

Whereas the intervention of some friends may be supportive, the inclusion of others during acute periods, though well-meaning, can have negative influences on the patient. In extreme cases, they may be using and encouraging the use of drugs or creating a truly stressful and erratic environment, or they may be exploitative or abusive. Some may have a tumultuous relationship with the patient and therefore be unreliable. Often friends are well intentioned but have very little experience with mental illness and lose their resolve once they understand it better. Other friends, while altruistic and helpful in the truest sense of the words, may want to help but lack the maturity, resources, or time to deliver on their commitment. One does not choose one's relatives but one does choose one's friends, and when friends are contributing to the patient's illness, you may in some cases need to suggest that they cease having any contact. When talking to friends, you may need to be even more mindful than usual about HIPAA laws and make sure that a willing and available caregiver friend is welcome and that his or her name is on the HIPAA form.

HOW TO FOSTER BETTER COMMUNICATION AMONG FAMILY MEMBERS

Communication is such a basic element of the human experience that even the notion that many people lack basic communication skills and need to be taught how to talk with each other is often surprising. Communication has been explained in books and taught in specialty courses and yet most people, including health care professionals, remain unaware of basic communication skills

(Blanchard, Hawkins, Baldwin, & Fawcett, 2009; Schaefer & Block, 2009). Of course, some families are communication masters, but in many families, members feel that they speak different languages and need an interpreter to understand each other.

The inability to communicate engenders frustration, anger, anxiety, and depression. Families who cannot communicate effectively around a member who is mentally ill may not survive the stress of coping with the burden of the illness. When people do not know how to talk with each other, it is difficult to discuss and delegate caregiver tasks, to support each other at times of exhaustion, and to maintain mutual affection and respect. Marriages often disintegrate in response to escalating acrimony.

When you are talking to families in an office setting, there is rarely time for detailed discussions on communication skills. However, you may have time for just one key suggestion that, if followed even occasionally, can help families understand each other better, reduce tension and expressed emotion, and function more as a team and less as individual players. What follows are several suggestions for how to improve communication that families frequently find not only useful but enlightening.

Pay Attention to the Content, Not the Form

This suggestion is particularly useful for the parents of ill young adults. Young adults are particularly sensitive to what they perceive as lack of respect, belittling, and infantilizing on the part of their parents. On the other hand, because mental illness interferes with the ability to face life's challenges and the personal growth that comes with life's successes, adult children with mental illness are almost invariably less mature and less independent than they should be at this stage in life. This creates a situation in which parents treat their adult children as if they are adolescents or younger than they are and the children regress and respond in kind with anger, resentment, and rebelliousness. Alerting the family to this dynamic and asking them to focus on the content, not on the often irritating form, of communication can help them negotiate some of the touchier issues of dependency involved in caregiving.

Michelle, Robyn really knows how to get under your skin. In that she is truly being a rebellious teenager. When you feel that you can no longer control your irritation, try to disregard her voice and her posturing and just listen to the content of what she is saying. Not looking at her directly might make it easier.

Paraphrase to Make Sure You Understand What the Other Person Is Saying

Paraphrasing (i.e., repeating what you thought the other person was saying in your own words) is one of the three essential components of successful communication. This skill is particularly useful for spouses of mentally ill individuals. After suggesting that families paraphrase what they are hearing from each other, you will need to explain what paraphrasing is and even demonstrate how it works in a real conversation. Depending on the family's cultural background and educational levels, you may avoid the term "paraphrasing" and just instruct them to make sure they understand what the other person is saying by repeating it in their own words. At this stage you should also tell family members to keep asking follow-up questions until they both agree on what is being said.

Let me make a simple suggestion that should help the two of you communicate: To make sure you understand each other, repeat what you think the other person said to each other in your own words. Keep repeating until you agree on the meaning.

Make Sure That Positive Statements Outweigh Negative Statements (the 5:1 Rule)

The 5:1 rule originates from the concept of the "emotional bank," the idea that each family has an emotional bank into which members make deposits—positive emotional statements—and from which they also make withdrawals—negative emotional statements (see Chapter 14). How you explain this concept will depend on how much time you have and on how much interest you anticipate each particular family has in psychological concepts. If the interest is minimal, you may simply say that in order to keep family interactions pleasant and productive, family members need to make sure that positive statements outweigh negative statements by a 5:1 ratio. The best way to accomplish that is to say all the nice things that people often think about each other but never bother to say because "It goes without saying" or "I do not say things, I do things" or "He is not the touchy-feely type." For families who are psychologically minded and are consumer experts, you can briefly describe the emotional bank concept as something that was invented by researchers in the field of mental health. Just saying that each family has an emotional bank, and that to keep the positive balance you need to make five deposits for every withdrawal, is usually sufficient for families to understand.

Have you heard about the 5:1 rule? No? OK, for any relationship to be happy, positive statements need to outnumber negative ones by at least a 5:1 ratio. Therefore when you say, "I love you. You are not spending enough time with your daughter," you are putting yourself at a serious 4-point deficit. What do you think your ratio is? One to ten? Well then, you have your work cut out for you.

There are other ways to improve communication between family members that I use less frequently. One is explaining the concept of expressed emotion as a way of interacting that involves a combination of hostility, overinvolvement, and criticism and is harmful to both the patient and the rest of the family. Another is delineating differences between help and support. Support means helping a person do something by him- or herself and implies that he or she is competent to do so. In contrast, helping is doing something for the person, which implies at least to some degree that the person is incompetent. Offering help to mentally ill individuals (and to everybody else) without being asked is often perceived as demeaning and results in anger and hostility.

Finally, suggesting waiting a day before reacting to anything that makes one angry to give oneself a chance to calm down and think rationally is also a simple piece of advice that families can use and appreciate. All these communication skills are addressed in greater detail elsewhere in this book.

Part II

DIAGNOSIS AND
TREATMENT

CHAPTER 4

Diagnosis and Prognosis

Written with Janine Samuel

The discussion with the family of a person with serious mental illness when it is first diagnosed may well be the most important conversation they will ever have. It sets the tone for what kind of relationship they will have with their sick relative, how they will interact with the world regarding his or her illness, what opinion they will have of mental health professionals, and to what extent they will be at peace with the role they believe they played in causing the illness or not doing enough to recognize and prevent it.

At this time the family's world has changed, probably forever. Whatever dreams and aspirations they had for the patient will have to be adjusted, and often drastically downgraded. Instead of anticipating the patient's future as a successful lawyer, they may need to think about whether he or she will be able to hold a job or be self-sufficient. The hopes and dreams of the family may have been threatened, possibly even shattered, by the diagnosis. With all this to digest, family members may approach the treating clinician with very mixed feelings, which often include hopefulness for a cure, anxiety about the future, and sometimes anger toward the clinician for being the bearer of bad news.

These circumstances necessitate a special kind of warmth, support, and positive regard. When you are speaking to the families of newly diagnosed mentally ill people, it is important to help them create new emotional and linguistic frameworks that will enable them to effectively navigate the world of mental illness. In this scary, traumatic, stressful, and most likely permanent new world, they will need a lot of reassurance, support, and help. The most important points to cover in your first conversation with the family are their feelings of guilt, hope or lack thereof, stigma, and uncertainty, and the issue of differentiating symptoms of the illness from the patient's personality. When doing this, you may need to deal with the family's denial or resistance. This chapter presents a series of questions family members may ask or be wondering about when a relative is first diagnosed with a mental illness. Some of these questions may not actually be articulated because of stress or a lack of familiarity with the pertinent issues.

Furthermore, when the illness is first diagnosed, families are often not able to articulate all the questions and concerns they will have later on. They certainly cannot be expected to understand the scope of the issues they will face over the long term. Part of your responsibility as a clinician during these early conversations is to preemptively speak to those questions that have not yet arisen. Other families, in contrast, may ask an array of questions relating to various aspects of the illness. This level of detailed probing is often seen in cases of patients with a more extensive family history of mental illness. At this stage, the best strategy is to give fairly short answers that cover a range of possibilities. I cover some typical topics here. Some of them will be covered in greater detail elsewhere in this book.

WHY?

Is This My Fault? What Did I Do Wrong?

When someone—particularly an adolescent or a young adult—develops a mental illness, family members generally feel some degree of guilt. They go over past conflicts in their minds, second-guessing and blaming themselves, often paradoxically, and simultaneously citing conflicting kinds of past misdeeds. They may lament not paying enough attention and being too overinvolved, spoiling their children or not being generous enough, having a particular fight, being particularly critical of that one school performance, and so forth. In fact, in identical twins raised together, the concordance rate for schizophrenia is only 50% (Tsuang, 2000). That means that only 50% of factors that determine who will get ill are environmental; the other 50% are simply genetic. At present we cannot definitively say what causes mental illness. Even if you feel that the family contributed to the illness, to say so would be presumptuous and counterproductive at this phase in treatment. In my experience, it is best to emphasize the genetic component of the illness and to support the family structure. Here is a suggestion for how to engage in this type of dialogue:

> *All psychiatric illnesses have a genetic component. There are many genes involved and we still know very little about which ones contribute to this illness and in what ways. Your son happened to inherit a vulnerability to it. You could not have predicted that, nor did you do anything wrong. This is his first serious episode; most likely he was symptomatic in ways that were not immediately obvious for many weeks or years. He was always shy and needed more attention than his brothers? When children are becoming sick, parents often sense that something is not quite right and in response treat them differently than others. So did you, and it probably helped. You seem like a close, caring family. At this time, the last thing you would want to do is blame yourself and each other for things that most certainly could not have caused his illness. Try to be supportive of him, as before, and help him with his medications and doctor's appointments.*

Could This Be From Drug Use?

The question of the role of substance abuse in the onset of psychiatric symptomatology frequently emerges in discussions with family members. In my opinion one cannot be too emphatic when communicating about the likely relationship between the use of

illicit drugs, particularly cannabis, and the first episode of a psychiatric illness. For many years I observed in my own clinical work,
at about the rate of once every 3 months, youngsters who abused
marijuana on a daily basis being admitted, psychotic and often
manic, to our inpatient unit. Recently, research has confirmed my
clinical experience, particularly in young adults who started using
illicit substances before age 14 (Hall & Degenhardt, 2008). New
studies have shown a correlative link between cannabis use and
schizophrenia and a causative relationship between the abuse of
cannabis and bipolar disorder. These findings do not prevent le-
galized medicinal use of cannabis for pain control in cancer patients, nor do they mean that all people who smoke marijuana will
become psychotic. However, a not insignificant minority with vulnerability to developing major psychoses, will. Families are best
served by straight talk when this discussion arises.

>   *Your daughter became psychotic while smoking mari-
>   juana daily. Cannabis is associated with bipolar disorder and
>   causes schizophrenia in some people, who may be geneti-
>   cally vulnerable. For your daughter pot is poison. Let us
>   hope that with medication and time her symptoms resolve.
>   But if she starts smoking again, she will become psychotic
>   again, and there is a good chance that next time her symp-
>   toms may not improve.*

Is Stress the Cause?

Mood and anxiety disorders are often brought on by stress. The
most common stressful events that trigger mental illness in young
people are the first year of college and a new and demanding job.
Other obvious stressors are a promotion and, alternatively, a professional failure. Betrayal and abandonment in a relationship are
also high-risk situations. In elderly patients, an abrupt retirement
or the death of a spouse or close friend can cause substantial psychological stress. I find it useful to discuss these stressors with the
family and suggest strategies for their management.

>   *You see, a large investment bank is not the friendliest or
>   psychologically healthiest environment to work in. When
>   Sara's boss left, she was asked to basically do the jobs of two*

people. Being the conscientious person that she is, she could not say no. She began working more and more and sleeping less and less. Her excessive work schedule is what eventually pushed her over the edge, given her genetic vulnerability. She will get better, but now that she has the illness, she will need to really watch her mental hygiene in the future. Regular sleep, regular work hours, and relaxing rather than adventurous vacations will help her to manage her illness.

Is This a Boyfriend or Girlfriend's Fault?

Indeed, some relationships are stressful enough to precipitate a psychotic or mood episode. People often begin seeing a psychiatrist for the first time when they are in an abusive or masochistic relationship they cannot break out of or after a painful breakup. When speaking with families who are faced with such relationship crises, I try to clarify their nature by being emphatic and serious:

It depends on their relationship. Some relationships can be lethal. You read the tabloids—you know that in extreme cases people kill themselves or get killed for love. More frequently, the stress of being in an unstable and abusive relationship can be a trigger for the first episode of psychiatric illness. If this is the case in your son's situation, continuing such a relationship may trigger more episodes in the future.

Wouldn't Anyone Be Depressed in His Place?

Since depression is often precipitated by stress—serious illness, divorce, death, loss of a job—family members may consider depression a natural response to these events. I hear this question most frequently from children of elderly physically ill patients. When asking this question, healthy family members are often responding to feelings of sadness and despair at the sight of their ill mothers or fathers. The answer to this question is an emphatic no. People react very differently to even the most traumatic and difficult situations. Nobody feels happy, and almost everybody has a lot of painful feelings—sadness, anger, resentment, frustration, and so forth. But not everybody gets depressed even when facing the most dire circumstances. Only some people develop major depressive disorder, which is a treatable illness. The same people who are incapacitated by paralyzing depression and hopelessness may feel well and deal with their condition forcefully and even happily once it has been treated. I often remind families that depression is not a natural condition but a treatable illness.

> *When did your mother get depressed? When her best friend of 50 years died? No, not everybody gets depressed. Only some people who are vulnerable to developing depressive illness get depressed. Your mother is having a clear episode of major depression in reaction to the very identifiable stress of her recent loss. Depression is treatable and should be treated.*

THE FUTURE

Is This Illness Curable?

Often mental illness is not curable but the symptoms might be treatable. This is not very different from other branches of medicine, with the exception of surgery and infectious disease, for which antibiotics can be used to cure the infection. This is an important point to articulate very early on. Families need to understand that medications may eliminate the symptoms of bipolar disorder, but not the illness itself. This means that the symptoms will return when medications are stopped.

> *No, it is not curable, but it is treatable. There are medications that can remove or improve the symptoms to a point where your sister can lead a happy life, which may include holding a job and having a family, depending on how adherent she is with her medications.*

Will She Get Better?

If this question is asked in the course of the very first acute episode, the answer depends mostly on the patient's response to medications. It is important to be clear and direct when addressing this reality. For example, one might reply: "It is hard to say at this moment. With psychiatric illness, a lot depends on how you respond to medications. Generally the faster you respond, the better."

Clinicians should also bear in mind that relatives benefit significantly from being kept informed on how the patient is responding to medications. Thus, it is worthwhile to spend time during family sessions addressing the patient's responsiveness to the medication regimen.

If the patient is responding well to the medications, one might say:

> It has only been 48 hours and your daughter is much calmer. She is responding really well—this is a good sign for the future. We'll continue with the same regimen. In psychiatry, medications often need several days or weeks to reach their full potential.

If there has been minimal or no response to the medications, one way of addressing this is:

> It is often the case—in as many as 30% of cases—that the illness does not improve with the first set of medications. This may be the case here. So we'll change his medications and watch for a response. Although often it takes several weeks to achieve a full response, you can often tell sooner than that. We'll change medications pretty frequently, every few days or so, until he feels better—and he should.

If the question is asked after the first acute episode has been treated, the answer is usually a tentative yes. There are many medical reasons for this answer. The most important ones are that mood disorders are cyclical and can improve unpredictably; schizophrenia eventually assumes a chronic course, which can be more predictable and less traumatic for the patient, and occasionally symptoms improve spontaneously; and more effective new medications and other treatments may be developed. Initial misdiagnosis resulting in less-than-optimal treatment is another reason for possible future improvement. For mood and anxiety disorders especially, changes in lifestyle may reduce stress drastically (for example, moving back in with supportive family members or moving away from ones with high EE), resulting in improvement. However, a non-medical reason for the tentatively affirmative answer is that none of us can see the future, and acting as though we can is unethical, whereas depriving people of hope is inhumane. An example of a short answer that takes all this into consideration is:

> Most likely yes. It is a tough illness, but patients do get better. Mood disorders are cyclical; schizophrenia evens out and occasionally improves; and new, more effective medications are being worked on as we speak. Lifestyle changes to reduce stress can contribute to your daughter's improvement.

Will She Ever Have a Normal Life?

Every family has dreams about the future. Families have distinct ideas (some articulated and some not) about what constitutes a normal life, a successful life, or a failed life. Those expectations may include having and supporting a family, obtaining a specific career goal, fulfilling the potential and the promise shown earlier in life, and achieving financial success. When families ask questions about their loved one having a "normal" life, these questions are often informed by idealistic hopes and expectations. Patients with serious mental illness such as schizophrenia or bipolar disorder generally will not be able to fulfill those often lofty dreams; others with less severe disorders may. In either case, I find it useful to begin reframing the relatives' expectations from that of "typical" achievements that would make the family proud to instead emphasize the patient's personal happiness.

> It depends on what you mean by "normal." He has a pretty serious illness that affects his thinking and his feeling. It is more difficult for him to concentrate and relate to people. You cannot measure his success with the same yardstick with which you measure everyone else's. People with this illness are capable of working and having relationships. They are certainly capable of feeling happy. With support from you, he could be happy. You may need to adjust your expectations a little bit so as not to put unnecessary pressure on

him. Please remember, though: Even the most chronic pa-
tients sometimes improve with time. New treatments may
also be developed that may change things for the better.

Does This Mean That She Will Never Be Independent? Will I Have to Take Care of Him for the Rest of My Life?

These questions arise with severely mentally ill individuals regardless of diagnosis. Frequently, the answer will have a substantial effect on whether spouses stay together or not. Some partners
opt for divorce either because the burden of being a lifetime caregiver seems unbearable or for practical reasons. Under certain
circumstances, a single person with mental illness gets better benefits than he or she would if married. It is important to keep all
these factors in mind. In my experience, the best answer is the one
that is both informative and supportive.

There are various possibilities. If his condition does not
improve—although I think there is a good chance it will—he
will not be able to provide for himself. He will probably need
either financial support or practical guidance in finding low-
stress but steady work. Also, the state provides numerous
services for the mentally ill, which include psychiatric care,
subsidies, and housing assistance. What is available to you
varies by state, and the differences may be substantial. In
some states, disability payments are sufficient to pay for
housing and psychiatric care, with some spending money
left over. Residences differ widely and some are quite nice. I
can refer you to the National Alliance on Mental Illness or
the Mood Disorders Support Group of New York City for
more information. It pays to be an educated consumer.

Will He Always Need to Take Medication?

Families of even the most severely mentally ill, particularly the
parents of young adults, worry about the need for lifetime treatment with medications. Sometimes this worry appears to super-
sede concerns about the effects of the illness. Most of the concern
betrays the family's unease with the stigma of mental illness. Some

concern arises from fears of medication side effects. I find that this question presents a good opportunity for hopeful psychoeducation on the differences between treatable and curable illnesses.

> *Like many medical illnesses such as hypertension and high cholesterol, this illness is not curable but is quite treatable. Millions of people take antihypertensives or allergy pills for decades and have very few symptoms. Similarly, if your husband takes medications, there is a good chance his symptoms will either improve or disappear. However, just as with hypertension and high cholesterol, if he stops medications, the chance that his symptoms will return within one year is over 90%. Now, all medications, including psychotropic drugs, have side effects. We'll try to find a drug or a combination of drugs that is effective and to your husband's liking.*

Will He Get Married? Can She Have Children?

This is a truly emotional question, the answer to which carries life-defining implications both for the patient and for the family. As with other questions in this text, the answer depends very much on the illness. When responding, keep in mind that amid these queries lie the hopes and dreams of families for the future of their loved ones. Your answers should speak to their underlying concerns, some of which may not be voiced—for example, will the patient's parents have grandchildren, and if so, who will eventually care for them? Will the patient's fiancé break off the engagement? What are the risks of having children both for the patient, and for his or her offspring? Will the patient be able to have children while on medications, and if not, will her illness worsen while she is off them? My typical response to these questions is:

> *Of course she can get married, just like any other woman, as long as she takes her medications! She can also get pregnant and have children, but this needs to be planned carefully so she is able to get off all medications that can harm the developing fetus. If she does not take any psychiatric medications she is likely to get ill during her pregnancy. We*

will need to develop a medication regimen during that time that does not harm the baby, but we will cross that bridge when we get there.

Will He Be Able to Finish School?

The answer to this question is generally "Only after a leave of absence" or, unfortunately, "No." Many patients with schizophrenia, bipolar illness, or severe depression experience the first episodes of their illness in their early 20s, while in college. In those who are genetically vulnerable, the illness is often brought on by the much greater demands of college compared to high school, by distance from a supportive (though at times overly demanding) home environment, by romantic disappointments, or by illicit drug use. Even under the best of circumstances, it takes up to 6 months (i.e., one or two semesters) to fully recover from a manic or depressive episode. It takes even longer to reach a newly reduced level of functioning after the first episode of schizophrenia. This disheartening news needs to be delivered gently. I find that it works best to discuss these issues in terms of stress and rest.

Your daughter has had a vulnerability to bipolar illness, given your family history. Now, the illness itself, in its manic form, was brought on by the stress of freshman year. Her school is notoriously tough, and she took a lot of challenging courses. On top of that, she is in a big city, living in a dorm full of strangers. This was a big change from living at home in a small town with loving parents. It was all just too much. Now she will need to rest for several months, take her medications, and recover. After she gets better she will need to make some decisions about which school to return to—this one may just be too demanding.

Could He Kill Himself?

The truth is that about 10% of patients with schizophrenia, bipolar disorder, major depressive disorder, and borderline personality disorder do commit suicide. Many patients become suicidal either during or following their first episode. With schizophrenia, in particular, patients' knowledge of their diagnoses and the nature of their delusions increase suicidal risk (Bourgeois et al., 2004). For this reason, the risk for suicidality needs to be discussed with the families of all schizophrenic patients and the families of suicidal mood-disordered patients. The former should be instructed not to reveal a diagnosis of schizophrenia to their loved ones, while the latter should be prepared to take their loved ones' suicidal ideations and threats seriously. The subject of possible patient suicide may be the single most terrifying aspect of mental illness for the family and needs to be addressed with the utmost support, sympathy, and hope. As always, you need to emphasize the need for medication treatment and psychiatric follow-up in general. What follows is an example of how to talk about the possibility of suicide with the parents of a young man who was just diagnosed with schizophrenia.

> *Unfortunately, he could. The suicide rates for untreated— and I must emphasize,* untreated—*schizophrenia can be as high as 10%. However, there are several things we can do to decrease his risk of a suicide attempt. One is to make sure that he is being treated! If he is on medications, his chances of hurting himself are much lower. Another precaution we will take is to make sure that he is not immediately labeled with a diagnosis of schizophrenia. Doing so actually increases suicide rates, probably because of the stigma of being "crazy." There are other ways to prevent even the possibility of a suicide, but these are the two to remember for now.*

COEXISTING DIAGNOSES

Can You Have Two Diagnoses at the Same Time?

Most patients with psychiatric disorders have more than one diagnosis. This can be due to a true diagnostic uncertainty when more than one diagnosis is being considered. Sometimes patients have been misdiagnosed in the past, whereas others have been given several diagnoses for reimbursement reasons. Finally, many actually do meet diagnostic criteria for more than one diagnosis. In general the most common secondary diagnosis is drug or alcohol dependence. When this is the case, it is important to distinguish whether a patient's psychiatric symptoms were present before the patient started abusing drugs or alcohol or whether they are the result of substance abuse, as in our next case example. Otherwise, the real concern for most families is whether more diagnoses means a more severe illness and a bleaker future. To address this concern, most of the time you can reassure them that this is not always the case and then discuss the specifics. In answering questions about multiple diagnoses, you might respond: "Yes, you can have more than one diagnosis. There are many reasons for this; let us see what those reasons are in your case. However, having two diagnoses is not necessarily worse than having one."

Is He Suffering From Alcoholism or Is He Drinking Because He Is Depressed?

This is a very common question among families of patients with a relatively newly developed drinking problem who are having a difficult time acknowledging that their loved one is an alcoholic. The answer is that one does not preclude the other. Alcoholism is a disease with a strong genetic component. Some patients were depressed or, more likely, anxious before they started drinking and began using alcohol as a way to self-medicate. Many became depressed because of professional or personal difficulties. However, a developing drinking habit results in substantial neurochemical changes, particularly in the areas of reward circuitry, exacerbating or even causing alcohol dependence. Similarly, alcohol is a depressant that, while transiently reducing anxiety, may cause profound depression that supersedes any premorbid depressed mood. This dysregulation in mood often lifts about 2 weeks after cessation of alcohol use. So the answer to the family is that while he may have started drinking because he was depressed, he is now suffering primarily from alcoholism, and his current depression should be considered a secondary effect of this. This answer can be given more or less as stated here, followed by an appeal for alcohol rehabilitation:

> He may have started drinking because he was depressed, but now he is suffering from alcoholism and is depressed because he is drinking. His depression is likely to improve in as little as 2 weeks after he stops drinking. But I am unsure he will be able to stop on his own. Will you be able to convince him to go into inpatient rehabilitation? How about him joining AA?

DIAGNOSTIC UNCERTAINTY

The discussion of diagnostic uncertainty is a difficult one, wrought with anxiety for both doctors and family. Admitting that you do not know the diagnosis while clearly explaining various options and possibilities builds trust between you and the family and leaves hope for a favorable outcome.

Why Can't You Tell Me What He Has?

Both apprehension about a possible devastating psychiatric diagnosis and a mistrust of doctors, perhaps psychiatrists in particular, often underlie this question. When you respond, it is important to be levelheaded, explicit, and reassuring. Admitting uncertainty does not signify personal incompetence but points to current limitations in the art of medicine. One such diagnostic limitation is the need to observe the course an illness takes. A balanced and honest response might sound something like:

> I would love to, but sometimes it is just not possible this early on. In psychiatry, various illnesses may look the same over a short period of time. Schizophrenia can look like depression, bipolar disorder may resemble schizophrenia, and cannabis-induced mood symptoms or psychosis can look like bipolar disorder. Only by evaluating a patient's symptoms over a protracted period of time and assessing his response to medications can we find the correct diagnosis. Consist-

ently our only recourse is to treat the patient the best way
we know and to wait.

Nobody Is Telling Me What It Is, and She Is Getting Worse and Worse. What Is Going On?

This line of questioning conveys not only uncertainty about the diagnosis and frustration with the poor response to treatment but also a sense of unsatisfactory communication with the doctor. No verbal response will fully satisfy a family who feels ill at ease with what is happening to their mentally ill relative. However, an appropriate response might involve calling a family meeting. This will facilitate a clear exchange between all parties, and a frank discussion of explicit and underlying anxieties will defuse the tension. Thus, I often give the following diplomatic answer: "I will be very happy to tell you as much as I can, but this will take time. Let us make an appointment for a meeting, and I will answer all your questions."

Which Is a Worse Diagnosis to Have?

When asking this question, some people genuinely do not know the answer. Others seem to have some knowledge of a diagnostic hierarchy of severity and understand that schizophrenia carries the bleakest prognosis, followed by schizoaffective disorder and bipolar disorder, and then depression. Regardless, relatives are best served by an answer that is reassuring and gives them hope. I generally respond by confirming this hierarchy while also acknowledging a significant overlap in terms of prognosis, functioning, and happiness. For example, some patients with typically more severe illness like schizophrenia, particularly women, develop a benign form of the illness and are able to have families and work. On the other hand, some patients with typically less severe disorders such as major depression experience severe and unrelenting depressive episodes that are altogether debilitating and preclude work or family life. In this way, it is important to communicate that there are no hard-and-fast rules linking a definitive prognosis to each disorder.

In general, schizophrenia is a most serious chronic psychiatric illness. However, I have treated patients with schizophrenia who, when properly medicated, had families and were quite happy. I have also treated patients with less severe disorders that did not respond to medications and remained quite ill. So there is a lot of variation.

Is It Better to Have a Personality Disorder than Bipolar, Schizophrenia, or Schizoaffective Disorder?

This question is usually asked by the families of individuals diagnosed with borderline personality disorder, which can at times symptomatically resemble schizophrenia and mood disorders. Personality disorders are different from major Axis I disorders but not as different as was once believed. Historically, personality disorders were coded on Axis II because in contrast to mood and anxiety, personality was perceived as an innate quality that did not change with time. In contrast to schizophrenia and mood and anxiety disorders, personality disorders were believed to be fixed entities and therefore not responsive to medication treatment. Now we know the distinction is not so cut and dry. Personalities do change with time, and personality disorders do respond to medications and psychotherapy.

The historic tendency in the field to regard personality disorders as less serious than Axis I disorders such as MDD or schizophrenia has also contributed to the perception that a personality disorder diagnosis might be "better." In fact, insurance companies often still do not reimburse for treatment of personality disorders. In reality, some personality disorders, specifically borderline personality disorder, can be as severe as any Axis I disorder and can carry the same level of disability and risk. When answering this question, I separate the clinical and insurance realities and essentially give two answers:

I wish I could tell you in two sentences, but the answer is really complicated. Suffice it to say that, clinically, it depends on what personality disorder we are talking about and

*how severe the depression is. Some personality disorders
cause more impairment and suffering than an episode of
major depression. Other personality disorders can be fairly
mild. I also have to mention the insurance point of view,
which affects how your psychiatric care gets reimbursed.
From that point of view, any Axis I illness such as major depressive disorder is better reimbursed than even the most
severe personality disorder. However, this is a different subject for discussion.*

He Was Diagnosed With Schizophrenia, Bipolar, and Schizoaffective Disorder—Which One Is it?

It is often impossible to diagnose a psychiatric illness after seeing a patient for just a short period of time. Nevertheless, psychiatrists are often forced to do so prematurely for insurance and billing
reasons and also because families want an answer. These pressures can result in several different diagnoses from different hospitals and different psychiatrists. In answering this question, just
admit it: "After seeing your son once, I can give you what I think is
the most probable diagnosis. At this time, a diagnosis is necessary
for billing purposes, but it is by no means certain."

She Has Depression, But Can She Still Be Bipolar?

This question stems from the ambiguity in *DSM-IV-TR*, which
describes two depressions—unipolar and bipolar. This distinction
is confusing for both patients and families. It is also an important
distinction because treatments and prognosis are different for unipolar and bipolar depressions. In answering this question, you
need to make it clear that when a bipolar patient becomes depressed, her diagnosis does not change to depression and she is
still bipolar.

*Yes. Patients with bipolar disorder get depressed, and
they are much more often depressed than they are manic. It
is different from cases of major depression—or a "regular"
depression—where patients never become manic. Bipolar*

depressions are unfortunately more difficult to treat than unipolar depressions. We can discuss this in more detail if you would like.

If He Stops Drinking and Using Drugs Will the Symptoms Go Away?

This is a very common question from families of dual-diagnosis patients. It most often comes up either in the context of cannabis abuse and psychosis or in cases of alcohol abuse and depression. The short answer is: "Only time and her response to treatment will tell." A longer answer is that for patients with inherited genetic vulnerabilities, drug and alcohol abuse can cause schizophrenia, bipolar disorder, and depression. Once precipitated, these illnesses can be treated but cannot always be reversed. In less severe cases, drugs and alcohol can lead to drug-induced psychosis and drug-induced mood disorder. Patients in such drug-induced states as these sometimes spontaneously recover, but typically drug-induced symptoms last long after the drug is out of the system. How long they persist may depend on the age at which onset occurs for the addictive disorder, family history of psychiatric illness, and duration and severity of substance abuse. They may signify a vulnerability to developing schizophrenia or bipolar disorder in the future. In the acute stage, you cannot distinguish a drug-induced syndrome from a new-onset permanent psychiatric illness. So a thorough answer to the question should take into consideration the aforementioned deliberations: "It depends on how many times this happened before, how the symptoms responded to treatment before, how old he was when he started smoking pot, and your family history. We can discuss this in more detail if you would like."

CHAPTER 5

Psychiatric Symptoms

Families of newly-diagnosed mentally ill patients often have no prior experience with mental illness, psychiatry, or psychiatric terminology. They may be unaware of the most common psychiatric symptoms and unfamiliar with the proper terms for describing them. For that reason, they appreciate you taking the time to explain basic signs and symptoms of mental illness as well as key psychiatric concepts. I will not be able to cover all of them in this chapter because there are too many. Nevertheless, this chapter discusses several representative questions I have had to answer in the past and examples of the answers I gave, which families generally found helpful.

When explaining psychiatric concepts to families, you want to be mindful of the level of stress they are under as they deal with the new reality of having a mentally ill relative. If possible, try not to alarm them. This is why, whenever I can, I try to start by saying something to normalize the symptom at hand and indicate that it is not uncommon and not unique to the ill relative. In most cases it's wise to begin by introducing families to the full spectrum of diagnostic possibilities, starting with the most benign. Furthermore, I try to conclude my answer with a positive comment about treatment.

About a recently hospitalized daughter just diagnosed with schizophrenia: "She has been staring into space, why is she doing that?"

It is hard to know exactly what is going on at this early phase, and the vacant stare you're describing could mean many things. It could simply be a reaction to stress, but we'll need to rule out more severe causes. One possibility is that she could be catatonic. Catatonia is a syndrome that occurs when the brain has a problem connecting thinking and movement. People with catatonia have racing thoughts but do not move very much and can have a hard time talking. It can be present in many illnesses and is easily treatable. Alternatively, she may be lost in some troubling thoughts or she may be seeing something or hearing something that we do not. In other words, she may be hallucinating. Hallucinations are also treatable.

About a recently diagnosed relative with mania: "He has been using words and saying things that I do not understand."

At times, when you cannot understand what someone is saying, the problem is not with the person's speech but with his or her thinking. Sometimes people with mental illness have difficulty reasoning. When they have trouble thinking coherently, they cannot articulate their thoughts in coherent sentences and sometimes even words. In psychiatric terms, this is called thought disorder, and it should improve as she responds to treatment.

About a recent conversation with an emergency room psychiatrist: "What does the word 'psychotic' mean?"

When you hear it for the first time, and only then, "psychotic" can be a really scary term. This word describes a group of symptoms most often seen in schizophrenia, but also in other illnesses, like depression, or even severe anxiety. Psychosis involves hallucinations, delusions, and thought disorder. Hallucinations occur when you see, hear, smell, or feel something that is not there. When a person has a delusion, he or she believes something that is clearly false, and it is impossible to talk the person out of it, regardless of how absurd the belief may be. Thought disorder is an inability to think coherently. So when people say psychotic, *they can be referring to hallucinations, delusions, or thought disorders, or all three. Often, the scariest psychotic symptoms— like really strange ideas or visions—can be the easiest to treat.*

About a depressed relative: "She is lying in bed all day, not doing anything!"

If you have never been depressed yourself, it is hard to understand how awful it can feel. Severe depression feels as bad as having a 104-degree fever: Everything hurts, different parts of your body ache all at once, you have no energy, no appetite, no interest in anything. This is probably how she feels right now—ask her. Unfortunately, feeling like that prevents her from doing what she needs to be doing to feel better: seeing friends, going to work, and exercising. It will be easier for her to start doing these things once the antidepressants I have prescribed start working.

About a young man who has a not let his parents into his room for several months: "You should see his room. He has so much stuff on the floor, I can't open the door."

People collect stuff more often than you would think. The name for that is hoarding. Your son has obsessive-compulsive disorder with hoarding. He cannot throw out useless stuff—junk mail, newspapers, old boxes, even his homework from 15 years back, when he was in high school. For him and others like him, the stuff in the room feels almost like an essential body part, like a part of him. For Roger, throwing out old boxes is like having his fingers amputated. Let us hope that one of the medications for obsessive-compulsive disorder helps him. They can be quite effective.

DISTINGUISHING THE ILLNESS FROM THE PERSON

The manner in which individuals understand or react to the behaviors of an ill relative plays an important part in shaping their relationship with that loved one post-diagnosis. Viewing the problematic behaviors of an ill person as intentional and originating in free will generally leads to a toxic family atmosphere and worsens outcomes for both the patient and the family. On the other hand, appropriately attributing odd or questionable behaviors to the illness reduces negative emotions, reduces stress in the family, and improves the prognosis of all involved.

Thus for families of mentally ill persons, it is very important to differentiate symptoms of mental illness from personality. This is not an easy task even for a clinician. The most typical problem is figuring out how to judge oppositional behavior and lack of cooperation. When a mentally ill person refuses to talk, refuses to clean up after him- or herself, or refuses to do what he or she needs to do, the natural reaction is to think that the person's behavior is volitional and part of his or her personality. While this may be the case, more often the mentally ill individual is catatonic, delusional, or severely depressed—and these behaviors are a manifestation of the illness. When families ask a general question about differences between illness and personality, I usually give a stock brief description of what behaviors may result from the illness under what circumstances:

> Sometimes it is hard to tell the difference. Some symptoms, such as hallucinations, delusions, and severe mood swings, are always due to the illness. Other symptoms like isolation, aggression, and verbal or physical abuse can be the result of an illness or alternatively may be due to the person's personality. When these behaviors come and go with time and change with medication, they are part of the illness. For example, a depressed person can spend weeks doing nothing and not taking care of him- or herself and this behavior disappears with the resolution of the depressive episode. Likewise, the nicest people can be verbally abusive during psychosis and mania and, after the episode is over,

return to their usual selves. However, when aggression, abuse, or isolation is always present, it is likely to be a feature of personality.

There are two special clinical situations in which families of individuals with slow personality changes require more specific answers: bipolar mood disorder and early Alzheimer's disease. Changes in behavior that occur during the initial phases of bipolar mood disorder are often experienced as a change in personality. In adolescents and young adults, parents often initially interpret these changes as phases or as resulting from social and academic pressures at school. Progressively uncharacteristic behaviors that develop in adults are usually a sign of the slow onset of unrecognized and untreated bipolar mood disorder or, much less often, of severe unipolar depression. Thus, the new and alien features of the person with mental illness are often the symptoms of his or her mood disorder, whereas when the family speaks of the "old" person, they are referring to the pre-illness personality.

In cases of bipolar mania, the pre-manic personality may have already manifested in the illness prodrome. Before the first manic break, patients with bipolar disorder can be exceptionally charming and charismatic. Often their spouses fell in love with them and got married just because of their prodromal charm and charisma. The realization that those features are symptoms of bipolar illness can be sobering and difficult to process. When talking with a spouse about his or her "old" and "new" partners, I try to gently balance the realities of having a mood disorder with the hope of getting the old personality back with treatment.

About a husband who just had his first manic episode: "This is not the person I married. What had happened?"

The person you married may still be in there somewhere. Your husband has bipolar illness and probably had some symptoms when the two of you met. From what you have told me, his energy, charm, and vigor were probably part of what we call productive hypomania. His recent behavior that initially was just difficult to take and then became destructive was the result of irritable mania. I am hoping that with

mood stabilizers we can get back some or most of his vigor
without him becoming manic.

Personality changes are an intrinsic part of Alzheimer's disease, and they often manifest themselves several months or years before an individual's memory changes. In some people, these changes continue throughout the disease process. Unfortunately, apathy and indifference are the two most common symptoms of the illness, and callousness and aggressiveness are not uncommon. Some elderly patients with Alzheimer's disease can insidiously change from pleasant, loving spouses to habitually abusive ones. Personality changes can be so subtle that patients' partners may not even connect them with the illness. Not infrequently, families of elderly patients with Alzheimer's disease think the abuse is a reflection of the patients' "real" personalities, which were previously contained by social conventions. When talking with the spouse of a patient with dementia, you should make it emphatically clear that all changes are part of the illness and that what he or she is seeing is an Alzheimer's disease personality, not a reflection of the loved one's true inner self.

"Is that what he *really* thinks about me and, now that he can't control it, it's coming out?"

> *Not really. Alzheimer's disease is a very tough illness, and it is often tougher on the family than it is on the patient. Regrettably, parts of the brain that make our personality are also diseased by Alzheimer's, often in a way that makes people cold, indifferent, and sometimes cruel. All the changes that you see in your wife are due to that process and have little to do with what she was like before she got ill. We'll try to reverse some of these symptoms with treatment.*

STIGMA AND WHAT TO TELL OUTSIDERS

Mental illness has been known to humans since ancient times. In fact, the ancient Greeks invented the words "melancholia," "hysteria," and "phobia" to describe psychiatric phenomena. Since ancient times, mental illness has been treated with a combination of apprehension, scorn, fear, and pity. "Madness" or "craziness" has always been a mark of shame, and societies' reactions to the mentally ill have generally ranged from neglect and banishment to outright persecution, as in witch hunts. Although this may vary from society to society, families often conceal their mentally ill members out of fear of ridicule, ostracism, and discrimination. One hundred fifty years ago Dostoyevsky wrote: "The degree of civilization in a society can be judged by entering its prisons." One might say that the degree of civilization in a society can be judged by how the mentally ill are treated.

In recent times in the United States, mental illness has become less stigmatized. The terms "depression," "bipolar," "obsessive compulsive," and "phobia" have entered the popular lexicon, and some American celebrities have even disclosed their own psychiatric diagnoses, taking on mental illness awareness as a cause. Well-known examples are William Styron, Kitty Dukakis, Brooke Shields, Tipper Gore, Jane Pauley, Buzz Aldrin, and Carrie Fisher. Recent passage by Congress of a bill for parity in mental health coverage has guaranteed equal insurance coverage for mental and psychiatric illness. This legislation is a milestone in the effort to destigmatize mental illness.

Nevertheless, people with mental illness still face discrimination and stigma. They are frequently viewed as damaged and incomplete. They have limited opportunities for employment and housing and often have trouble getting and maintaining a driver's license and obtaining custody of their children. Often they need advice in practical matters such as where to seek appropriate employment or how to apply for disability and housing. The families of mentally ill individuals are also likely to ask your advice about how, when, to what extent, and with whom they should discuss the mental illness in their family. There is no single answer for this and other similar, very difficult questions. Your answer to each individual family should take into account the acuity and severity of the illness, the family's willingness to be open with the outside world about mental illness in their midst, and patient and family stress. In the following pages I address some of the typical questions asked by families and a few of the issues to consider before giving an answer.

What Should We Tell His Friends?

This question is usually asked by parents of young adults and adolescents in the context of a recent hospitalization. When this topic arises and the child in question is returning to his or her previous social milieu, encourage family members to be truthful and to acknowledge that the patient is ill. Adolescents today are very familiar with terms like "bipolar" and "depression" from the Internet and other media. Given that bipolar disorder is greatly overdiagnosed, most adolescents have at least one peer with bipolar disorder and will not be shocked to learn that a friend has been diagnosed with this disorder. Advise parents to describe possible changes in the child's behavior and affect that his or her close friends might observe. Parents might also consider suggesting new behavioral guidelines for friends, which mainly include being supportive and suppressing surprised reactions to possible changes in the patient's behavior and appearance. When discussing this topic, the clinician should emphasize the importance of maintaining supportive friendships to the patient's prognosis.

What Should I Tell Her School?

This question is most frequently asked by parents of young college students during or after a hospitalization for an acute mood disorder episode. If mental illness is severe enough to require hospitalization for more than a week, the patient almost certainly will not be able to return to school and complete the semester. Abruptly shifting gears from focusing on getting the best grade to concentrating on rest and getting healthy is difficult for both patients and families. Your goal is to help them accept the reality of their child's illness and to help minimize its impact on the child's schooling and future. I usually tell the parents that it is always better to take a semester off than to return to school facing even more pressure to get a good grade because of missed classes. I then offer to write a note to their child's school, initially without specifying the diagnosis.

What Should We Tell His Fiancée?

This question typically emerges among families from more traditional cultural backgrounds where premarital relationships can be formal and even distant. While a sudden diagnosis of mental illness can make young people change or cancel their wedding plans even in the most liberal societies, in more traditional arrangements, it is often the parents who decide what to tell the fiancé and what to hide. Nearly always, it is better to tell the truth, leaving enough room for the uncertainties associated with possible diagnostic mistakes and a benign course of illness. In my experience, fiancés and fiancées are more tolerant of the illness than patients' parents may expect. In my own practice I have seen several patients with diagnoses of major depression and bipolar disorder get married to partners undeterred by their diagnoses. However, because weddings are invariably stressful, if the illness is acute or post-acute, imminent wedding plans will need to be postponed.

What Should We Tell Her Employer?

Employers should be told as little as possible beyond the fact that the patient is ill. A note from a psychiatrist on neutral stationary stating that the patient will be out for awhile because of an unspecified illness should suffice, unless the patient works in a very small business where relationships are typically more personal. In the latter circumstance, it is better to disclose the illness using relatively benign terms such as "bipolar" and "depression" without going into treatment specifics.

Can He Go to the Wedding Next Week?
He Was So Looking Forward to It.

The answer here is definitely no. Weddings and parties are truly stressful and often precipitate crises and worsen the illness. Positive stress is still stress. The best thing to do is to come up with an excuse and politely back out of the obligation.

I Don't Want the Diagnosis on the Record, and I Don't Want Her Insurance Company to Know About It. Can This Be Avoided?

Navigating this question is complicated. Medical insurance records are supposed to be kept confidential and never to be used as grounds for employment discrimination or termination. Nevertheless, as discussed previously, there is a stigma attached to mental illness, and one cannot pretend that this is not the case. Many patients prefer for their psychiatric records to remain completely private, paying out of pocket if they can to avoid the release of diagnostic information to insurance providers. Many psychiatrists bill with less stigmatizing diagnoses such as generalized anxiety disorder, dysthymia (mild depression), or major depression. As a clinician, you need to have a frank discussion with the family about the risks, benefits, and moral and ethical implications of involving or not involving insurance.

PATIENT/FAMILY DENIAL

Family denial is near universal and, depending on the context, can be harmful or helpful. You will need to address the denial on the basis of its potential harm to the patient. When the family believes that the patient is not ill and sabotages the treatment, the discussion in response to the denial must be very forceful. When the family supports the treatment, hopes for the best outcome, and believes that their loved one may fare better than an average patient with his or her diagnosis, such "denial," better termed "hope," must be encouraged.

Similarly, a patient's denial can have advantages and drawbacks. For young patients with schizophrenia, awareness of the illness is associated with higher suicide rates. Thus with schizophrenia, some degree of denial can be protective and is associated with better prognosis. On the other hand, complete denial of the illness, which is most common in patients with bipolar disorder, can result in chronic noncompliance with treatment, broken families, revolving-door hospitalizations, and a malignant course for the illness.

Here are some statements families might make and questions they might ask where the key issue is their denial of the illness.

She isn't crazy.

This is probably one of the most alarming and unambiguous statements loved ones can make when the patient is first diagnosed. The clinician needs to explore what "crazy" means to different family members. Most often, "She is not crazy" means that the family is not yet ready to accept the reality of their loved one being diagnosed with a serious and often lifelong mental illness. Frequently, after getting over the initial shock of the diagnosis and adjusting expectations, one or several family members will accept the role of caregiver and will become your partner or partners in treatment. In these cases, it is best to demonstrate your own acceptance of psychiatric illness in your response as a legitimate medical problem and to encourage the family to do the same.

Of course she isn't crazy! The word "crazy" was used in the Middle Ages, when people did not know very much about psychiatry. Now we know a lot more about different psychiatric disorders and we have medications to treat them. What is it that you were told about her psychiatric problem? I may be able to help you understand the diagnosis and possibly some general treatment options.

Another form of such denial has to do with stigma. Frequently, relatives may be embarrassed about having a mentally ill person in the family. They will take care of their ill loved one and agree to participate in the treatment as long as the mental illness is not labeled as such. In this case it is prudent to use euphemisms such as "mood changes," "chemical imbalance," and "thinking problem." It is often easier for both the family and the patient to accept this terminology than clinical vocabulary like "psychosis," "hallucinations," or "mania."

On rare occasions, "He is not crazy" can take on a meaning dangerous for the patient. In these cases, some or all family members believe that the newly diagnosed patient does not need treatment. Often relatives believe the patient is being his or her usual self or is going through a temporary phase and will "snap out of it." Such attitudes may result in patients' deterioration, which can be very rapid. In extreme cases, suicides may occur.

Since even a minor possibility of suicide is risky, such complete denial needs to be confronted. If the family is not receptive to reasonable persuasion, you are faced with one of those infrequent and difficult situations where you cannot be too emphatic about making your point. Under these exceptional circumstances, the family denial needs to be addressed with the strongest wording possible. You may need to tell them directly that their behavior is dangerous to the patient and they will feel or be responsible if the patient commits suicide. Here is a hypothetical example of such a conversation:

> *Your son most likely has had his first schizophrenic break. Knowing how much it hurts you to witness this, imagine how hard it must be for him to experience it firsthand. Young people suffering as he is right now may feel so much pain that they can have a very strong and sudden urge to end it all and commit suicide. I must tell you that if your son is not treated, his chances of killing himself are far from zero. He needs to be in treatment and you need to be there for him. Imagine how you'll feel if you do not support him entering treatment now and then he kills himself. Who would be to blame?*

Why are the medications you have her on making her like *that*?

Families of recently diagnosed mentally ill people sometimes are too stressed to fully articulate their thoughts. Therefore, at times you may face a question, like this one, that can have multiple meanings. In instances like this, it is important not to assume that you understand their meaning. Instead, gently prod for more descriptive words. In time, it may become clear that they are referring to the medication's side effects. A common complaint is that the patient is "looking like a zombie." Whenever there is a possibility of such a drug reaction (which is nearly always the case in proper treatment of acute psychosis or mania), I prepare the family by discussing potential side effects in advance and emphasizing that they are temporary and may even be useful in assessing treatment progress.

> *In order for your daughter to get the best treatment for acute mania and to minimize any long-term damage this episode may cause, we will have to do everything possible to shorten its duration. This means that I will have to give her enough medication so that she sleeps about 10–12 hours per day. It may not be easy initially, but we should be able to achieve this in 2–3 days. This also means that she may be very groggy during the day, but this is exactly what we need to achieve; it's a good thing. Her sedation will go away within 24 hours after we start reducing the medications and will not have lasting harmful effects.*

Occasionally this same question might not refer to medication side effects but may be the product of a family's anger at their loved one's illness, which is directed at you. In such cases, this question implies that the ill family member is in reality healthy and his or her mental illness is caused by the medications you prescribed. This can occur in rare instances—most often in cases of antidepressant- or stimulant-induced mania. However, in the vast majority of circumstances, this is not the case. Although your initial reaction might be to become defensive in the face of what could be perceived as an accusation of poor treatment, it is important to temper that impulse with a measured response. Instead, recognize that at the core of this question is denial. In actuality, what the relative is saying is "She is not crazy." Thus this exchange provides a perfect opportunity for education on the symptoms of the illness, its treatments, and the expected side effects of medications. Lastly, conclude by assuring them that virtually all studies of major psychiatric disorders in adults show that, once diagnosed, patients do better when they are in treatment and on medications.

Doesn't everybody get depressed once in awhile?

"Depression" is clinical shorthand for major depressive disorder but also a colloquial expression used to describe feeling down.

Many confuse these two meanings of the word "depression" and think that clinical depression and short periods of relatively low moods are the same.

People who have had transient low moods but are unfamiliar with major depressive disorder underestimate its seriousness and normalize its symptoms. In your clinical practice you would often have to correct this misconception.

Major depressive disorder is an illness of the whole body, not just the brain, and carries as much risk for heart attack as does high cholesterol (see Kendler, Gardner, Fiske, & Gatz, 2009, in case the family wants to know more). In the following example I gently prod the family to accept that major depressive disorder is a true illness.

> *Everybody feels down once in a while, including you and me. Clinical depression though is a real illness and it feels quite different. It may be hard to appreciate this difference, if you have never been depressed. Clinical depression is really an illness of the whole body. It affects your brain, your gastrointestinal system, and your heart. Wouldn't you want to reduce your husband's risk of having a heart attack, among other things?*

He doesn't think he has a problem—what should we do?

This is one of the most difficult questions to answer because there may be no good solution. Some patients with mental illness, most often those with bipolar disorder and with addictions, are not aware of their own illness. By far, the main reason patients need to accept that they have a problem is because, without this understanding, they will not accept treatment. Being in treatment improves their prognosis and quality of life. Of those who do not think there is a problem, some can be taught and, with time and the experience of repeated hospitalizations, learn to comply with treatment. For others, their inability to understand their illness is part of the illness itself, and they may never accept that they are ill. There are no magical solutions. Sometimes you advise the family to be conciliatory; other times loved ones will need to give the ill relative an ultimatum.

Here are some of the approaches, listed from most lenient to most severe, that may be discussed with families when the illness is first diagnosed:

- Use less stigmatizing and less clinical language to make it easier for the ill person to accept the problem. Examples are "help" instead of "treatment," "nerves" or "chemical imbalance" rather than "mental illness," "depression" instead of "bipolar," and "thinking problem" instead of "psychosis."
- Present the idea of a visit to a psychiatrist as a one-time consultation. A good psychiatrist should be able to forge treatment alliance in one session.
- Take them to a "celebrity" psychiatrist.
- Suggest that seeing a psychiatrist and even taking medications may be very common, and even a cool thing to do; give examples of celebrities with mental illnesses (e.g., Ted Turner, Jane Pauley, Carrie Fisher).
- Offer a tangible reward.
- Bring the patient to a multidisciplinary office to see an internist and then also see a psychiatrist.
- Be ready to withdraw financial support if the ill young adult or adolescent refuses to comply with treatment.
- Threaten divorce or separation if a spouse or partner refuses to seek help.
- Threaten admission to the hospital and bargain down to an office visit.
- Call 911 for an ambulance in case of dangerous behavior (threats to harm oneself or aggression).

When the "carrot" does not work, the family needs to practice tough love. It is important to remind relatives to mean what they say. Bluffing usually does not work. A patient's decision to call the family's bluff will seriously affect all future attempts to help him or her accept the illness and treatment.

CHAPTER SIX

Treatment

Because of the general stigma of mental illness, attempts to talk with somebody who has never been in psychiatric treatment about seeing a psychiatrist may be met with embarrassment and an indignant response, such as "I'm not crazy." This type of reaction would be unheard of if you were advising a patient to see any other specialist. As discussed in Chapter 5, stigma is the source of much unhappiness in the lives of patients with mental illness and their families. Because of stigma, many of those suffering from depression, anxiety, and other mental illnesses either refuse to see a psychiatrist or postpone treatment until the illness has wreaked havoc on many aspects of their lives. The families of mentally ill people often remain in denial with regard to the illness. As a result, it is not uncommon for mentally ill persons to be at risk for suicide—all because families are hesitant to refer them to a psychiatrist. Finally, partially because of stigma, patients with mental illness often prematurely stop taking their medications, equating not taking medications with mental health.

REFERRING A LOVED ONE TO A PSYCHIATRIST

When you are seeing a patient who needs psychiatric help along with his or her family, you have the choice of directly addressing the problem or doing nothing and hoping that the problem goes away. On some occasions, such as in situations involving grief after the loss of a loved one or a panic attack after an isolated stressful event, it will. However, even then you should acknowledge the problem with a supportive statement and offer treatment. Otherwise, families will perceive you as uncaring and even callous. In all other cases, the only ethical choices are either to refer the patient to a psychiatrist or to treat the patient yourself. In either case the family is your ally.

> *I am very sorry about your father's passing. It is a terrible loss for you and a very hard thing to go through when you are so young . . . or, as a matter of fact, when you are not so young. Would you like me to give you a prescription for a medication that should help you with your sleep?*

I am a believer that psychotropic medications should be prescribed by psychiatrists only. My personal opinion is that a little knowledge is a dangerous thing, and non-psychiatrists simply do not have the training necessary to know when psychotropic medications will do more harm than good. If prescribing by PCPs is absolutely necessary because of a high patient volume, or because psychiatrists are not available, preferably it should be done in a collaborative treatment team that includes a psychiatrist, or after a consultation with one over the phone.

A little knowledge is dangerous even in the hands of professionals, and it can be catastrophic when it is given to the lay public, as happened after the Food and Drug Administration caved in to the pressure from the pharmaceutical industry and allowed direct-to-consumer advertising. The advertising of psychotropic medications directly to consumers has resulted in patients asking general practitioners to prescribe psychotropic drugs. For some people, this is a way to avoid seeing a psychiatrist altogether and avoid being stigmatized as a psychiatric patient. However, this turn of events contributed to the much more widespread and often inappropriate use of psychotropics and to less-than-ideal treatment of psychiatric disorders.

At this point, you will not be surprised to learn that I believe that when a family is discussing a relative's psychiatric issues, you should give them a referral to a psychiatrist or a therapist. It helps your practice if you can refer the family to either one, depending on the family's preference. Both patients and their families often have surprisingly strong and unpredictable opinions on which psychiatric treatment—talk therapy or medication treatment—is more appropriate or less stigmatizing. Some families believe that counseling or talking to somebody, since it may not involve medical doctors, is more acceptable. Others feel that psychotherapists are crazier than those they are trying to treat and would rather take a pill prescribed by a medical doctor.

For these reasons, often the best place to start is to ask the family what they think about psychiatric treatment. Most psychiatrists work closely with one or several therapists, and almost all therapists refer their patients to psychopharmacologists. Psychopharmacologists are psychiatrists who do not practice psychotherapy and limit their practice to prescription medications. They often get their referrals for therapists who cannot prescribe medications—mostly psychologists and social workers. Since all psychiatrists are skilled in prescribing psychotropic drugs, psychopharmacologists should be consulted when referred to by a non-prescribing therapist mostly for a second opinion in complex cases.

After you help the family make the first contact with a well-trained mental health professional, at the end of the evaluation, he or she should be able to determine what the appropriate treatment is and make further referrals if necessary. To help the family overcome their ambivalence, you can emphasize that a psychiatrist is a specialist, like any other, and indicate that you would refer a patient to a psychiatrist just as you would to an ophthalmologist. You should explain that this is the proper way to practice medicine, and doing otherwise would be unethical. Adding that the psychiatrist you are referring to them is a really nice person, that you have seen positive results from previous referrals, and that you would refer your own daughter to them are all helpful points of encouragement. In the following vignette, an internist speaks with a woman who is worried that her husband is becoming depressed after the breakup of his business partnership.

The internist said: "What do you think about him getting an evaluation for his depression? You know, depression is treatable." The wife replied: "Would you treat him?" The internist responded: "I don't treat psychiatric problems myself because I don't think it is the right way to practice medicine." She responded: "He will never go, because he thinks all psychiatrists are crazy." The internist's response was: "Who does he think is crazier, psychiatrists or psychologists? The difference is that psychiatrists prescribe medications and psychologists offer talk therapy." The wife said hopelessly: "He hates talking." The internist replied: "OK, then let me give you a referral to my favorite psychiatrist. He has helped many of my patients and they love him. Yes, I would send my daughter to him . . . And if your husband is an exception and doesn't love him, I know of another one."

If such an emphatic referral still fails to convince the family or the patient to see a mental health professional, and you feel that he or she might be harmed by not getting psychiatric treatment, you may try treating the person yourself. However, you must still keep in mind that a future referral to a specialist is necessary. When starting such treatment, you should be explicit that you are doing so reluctantly and only as a stop-gap measure while you help the family become more comfortable with the idea of psychiatric treatment. You should also indicate that the family is choosing inferior treatment by not seeing a specialist.

> Aviva, I think you are making a mistake. According to what you've said, your husband is depressed. Depression is a medical illness just like any other. Having depression increases your risk for a heart attack more than having high cholesterol. I am willing to prescribe an antidepressant for your husband, but you and he should be aware that I am not nearly as skilled in treating depression as a psychiatrist because I have not been extensively trained, because I am not as experienced, and because I am ethically opposed to doing so. In this case, however, the alternative is that your husband will get no treatment, and I think that is worse than receiving mediocre treatment from me. Bring your husband to your next appointment, and I will start him on an antide-

pressant and will try to convince him to continue treatment
with a psychiatrist.

MENTAL ILLNESS AS MEDICAL ILLNESS

Drawing an analogy between mental illness and medical illness
is useful, because the boundaries of mental illness are confusing to
families. Some questions that arise are: Where is the boundary between illness and normalcy? What is the difference between having the illness and having a vulnerability to that illness? When is
the right time to seek treatment? What is treatable, and what is
curable, and what is the difference? Having a ready medical illness analogy helps make discussion of these complicated issues
clearer. The best "fit-all" analogy is that any serious mental illness
(though particularly bipolar disorder) is a lifelong illness like diabetes. To stay healthy, diabetics need to take their medications
and maintain a healthy lifestyle that includes a healthy diet and
exercise. Seriously mentally ill people also need to take medications and lead a healthy lifestyle that includes low stress and regular sleep and exercise. In each case, family support has a positive
impact on the course of the illness.

Beyond diabetes, also useful are analogies between individual
psychiatric disorders and medical illnesses with similar degrees of
disability. For example, schizophrenia is an incurable but treatable
serious mental illness. Even with the best treatment, patients suffer from substantial residual symptoms such as lack of initiative,
poor socialization, poor hygiene, and social isolation. A good medical analogy for schizophrenia would be a serious lifelong illness
such as congestive heart failure, rheumatoid arthritis, or systemic
lupus erythematosus. Even at their best, people who suffer from
these medical illnesses have a lot of deficits and limitations in their
functioning. Just as with those with schizophrenia, their facial ex-
pressions, posture, and movement may look different, so they tend
to stick out.

Mood disorders such as bipolar mood disorder and recurrent
major depressive disorder are also lifelong illnesses that are typically less severe. The major difference from schizophrenia is that

patients with mood disorders in remission can be completely asymptomatic and can function at the level of a healthy person. In fact, when asymptomatic, they may be indistinguishable from healthy people. However, when they stop taking medications, or when they are under stress, they quickly become symptomatic again. The best analogy for bipolar mood disorder and major depressive disorder is actually with diabetes. Bipolar mood disorder is like type 1 diabetes: Once you have it, it will never go away and one must control one's diet and take medications for life. Major depressive disorder is more like type 2 diabetes: In the early stages, the illness can be cured with reduced stress, improved sleep regulation, and, say, getting out of an unhealthy relationship.

Steve, Emma does have bipolar disorder. She did not have it when you got married; she was in what is called a prodromal stage of the illness. She was "pre-bipolar" for several years until her first break, and now she has it. It is like adult-onset diabetes: You do not have it, then you are a pre-diabetic, and then you've got it. No, it will not go away. As you have seen, it is not a fun illness to have for her, or for you or for the children. However, if she takes her medications, gets the right amount of sleep, and has a predictable low-stress lifestyle, you and she should be able to lead a fairly normal life.

In the case of generalized anxiety disorder, patients appear physically and emotionally well most of the time. Even when they are very anxious inside, they may appear completely healthy. A good analogy for generalized anxiety disorder is hypertension: People with very high blood pressure may look completely well on the outside. The two illnesses are connected: Anxious people have high blood pressure. Both anxiolytics and antihypertension pills like propranolol and diuretics can work very quickly to relieve the symptoms. Asthma provides a good analogy for panic disorder: Both involve quick dramatic episodes when the patient is under stress, and both panic and asthma attacks improve quickly with treatment. (In addition, patients in both cases develop shortness of breath.)

Phobias are highly similar to allergies because they are idiosyncratic and very specific. Arachnophobia (fear of insects) can be likened to an allergy to strawberries or oranges. Finally, when talking
to families, you can conceptualize personality disorders as limitations in patients' ability to learn necessary life skills such as regulating their moods or reading social situations. Viewed within this
framework, personality disorders are most similar to limitations in
our intellectual and physical abilities. Some people are very talented athletes; others are uncoordinated. Some people have perfect pitch; others are tone deaf. Psychotherapy then can be likened
to ether physical training or ear training.

MEDICATION VERSUS TALK THERAPY

Families often have strong preferences for psychotherapy over
psychopharmacology or the other way around. Discussions about
choosing medications versus psychotherapy used to happen mostly
in the offices of mental health professionals. However, with many
general practitioners prescribing psychotropic drugs, it can also
happen elsewhere. Regardless of where the topic is discussed,
these preferences should be given the utmost consideration for
two reasons. First, if you do not acknowledge the families' per-
spectives, you will create an atmosphere of poor rapport and resistance to the treatments you suggest. Ultimately families may
decide to find a more receptive, though not necessarily more competent, psychiatrist. Second, in similar clinical situations, treatments are more effective when families and patients believe in
them because of powerful placebo effects. The well-known joke
"How many psychiatrists does it take to change a lightbulb? Just
one, but the lightbulb really needs to want to change" has more
than a grain of truth to it. Both psychotherapy and psychopharmacology work much better when families and patients believe in the
treatment. For some disorders, such as dysthymia, several anxiety
disorders, and phobias, the results of medications and psychotherapy are similar enough that the choice may lie with the family. The
following vignette is an example of a discussion with the parents
of an anxious 18-year-old girl going off to college.

I began: "I am not even sure that she needs to be taking her antidepressant. She has been taking the drug for anxiety since she was 12, and it may have helped her. However, at the same time she also started seeing a therapist she really liked. Psychotherapy is both a potent antidepressant and an excellent anxiolytic. For all you know, it may have been the psychotherapy, not the medication, that made her feel better." Her mother asked: "Do you know that for sure?" I responded: "No, I can't tell for sure, but it's always best not to take medications unless they are absolutely necessary. But if you and she think that it is the antidepressant and not the therapy that has helped, I'm not going to argue with you, at least at this time. Perhaps we'll discuss this again in the future, after she settles into college, if you do not mind."

In other instances the most effective treatment is unequivocally medication. To give just a few examples, pharmacotherapy alone is indicated for schizophrenia, psychotherapy alone is often the only therapy indicated for personality disorders, and a combination of psychotherapy and psychopharmacology is clearly the most effective treatment for bipolar mood disorder and major depressive disorder. When you are talking to families about treatment options, this may be a good place to start your psychoeducation. Because you will be dealing with ossified prejudices, be prepared for families not to be as receptive of your efforts as you would want them to be.

As I have mentioned elsewhere in this book, families' and patients' intuitive preferences for a particular treatment are most often expressed in two hostile clichés. "I don't want to put any chemicals in my body" is a veiled pro-psychotherapy statement. Alternatively, "He's not the talking type, give him a pill" is a not-so-veiled vote of confidence for medications. Fortunately, families' preferences are often in accordance with the most effective treatment approaches. In some cases, however, families want treatments that are either unrealistic or ineffective. Two such examples are a request to use talk therapy for a loved one with schizophrenia and asking for, or even demanding, a magic pill to cure disagreeable character traits (i.e., a personality disorder).

As with most issues in the field of psychiatry, it is best to make families' decisions easier by presenting the options in black and white terms rather than in shades of gray. For instance, delaying pharmacotherapy is harmful, as an acute episode of schizophrenia may occur or mania may escalate. In these cases it is best to be firmly hopeful but realistic about the outcome of medication treatment and at the same to convey your pessimism at the probable outcome without such treatment in fairly stark terms. Alternatively, if you feel that medication treatment is premature and would be harmful because of the side effects, you need to be equally emphatic and clear. When you are doing so, it is always important to show respect for the family's point of view. Here is an example of an argument in favor of medications for a 20-year-old Ivy League student who just had her first psychotic break:

> I understand your reluctance to accept Heather's need for medications. Believe me, I would not have suggested that she take them and insisted that she be treated immediately and aggressively if I saw any other options. Although I appreciate your preference for meditation and holistic psychotherapy, at this time, for your daughter, this treatment would be a disaster. If she were having panic attacks, then yes, even an enthusiastic yes, but not for psychosis. This is time for medications and only medications.

After discussing the pros and cons of psychopharmacology versus psychotherapy, you will often be asked for a referral to a good therapist. Finding and recognizing the right therapist is not a trivial matter and deserves a separate discussion.

FINDING THE RIGHT THERAPIST

Finding the right therapist is one of the most important decisions you or your patients or their families will make in their lives. An untoward number of people spend years being treated by therapists who are either not useful or, not infrequently, harmful. You can recognize them either by their outright anger at the mental health field or by statements such as "She has been seeing this therapist for years and all he did was just sit there . . . What a waste." Here is another characteristic statement: "The therapist came highly recommended, he charged an arm and a leg, we spent all that money, and she is as crazy as she has always been."

Finding a good therapist is harder than finding a good internist. With the latter, the issue of an individual's qualifications is objective: If he or she is well trained and experienced and has reasonable bedside manners, you will be well taken care of. With therapists, the most important factor in therapeutic success is personal. In addition to having appropriate and preferably good credentials, the therapist has to be right for *you*. The most important predictor of success is the relationship between the patient and the therapist (Botella et al., 2008; Rozmarin, Muran, Safran, Gorman, Nagy, & Winston, 2008). The specific aspects of this relationship that are important for success are not well understood. Nevertheless, the commonsense rules of how to find the right therapist are very simple and if you, your patients, and their families follow them, everybody will receive the best possible psychotherapy:

1. Spend at least as much time and effort finding a therapist as you would finding a contractor. You should interview at least two (preferably three) back to back.
2. Beyond legitimate training versus quackery, neither pedigree nor the type of psychotherapy makes a significant difference with regard to the treatment outcome. The only important predictor of how you will do in psychotherapy with a particular therapist is how you feel after the first session, which is an indication of what kind of therapeutic alliance you can form with that therapist.
3. If you like the therapist, if you felt good leaving the office and the feeling didn't go away, if you felt that the therapist was smart, that he or she got you and what you had to say, if you felt that during the session you heard something new, fresh, useful, or, even better, revelatory, then you are with the right therapist. Make another appointment and give him or her a chance, which means staying with the therapist for at least a year, regardless of occasional feelings of anger and disappointment that you may feel. Those feelings are an inevitable part of any relationship, including the one with the therapist.

4. If you did not like the therapist, if you left the office angry or upset or if you had a delayed reaction of anger or disappointment, if he or she looked weird, rubbed you the wrong way, or said things that seemed trivial, stupid, or irrelevant, then he or she is not the right therapist for you. Do not make a second appointment, regardless of recommendations or degrees; it will only get worse. Many people stay with such therapists and suffer because they either did not improve from the treatment or were actually harmed by a treatment that was wrong for them.

5. If you are not sure whether or not you feel good about the therapist, make a second appointment and by the end of the second session, you should be able to say confidently whether it is one or the other.

I would like to give you two examples of what staying with the wrong therapist may feel like. One of my 60-something patients, a father of four and a grandfather of 11, spent 20 years in analysis working on his childhood conflicts with his mother. His therapy did not even address the issue that whatever these conflicts may have been early in his life, by 60 he had become the highly successful patriarch of a large family and a partner in a large law firm. My patient had mixed feelings about his analyst from the very beginning and for years ignored pleas from his wife to stop seeing him because she felt that the therapist was just making her husband anxious. He finally was referred to me after experiencing a serious episode of major depression after his mother got gravely ill. I refocused his therapy on coming to terms with the success that he was able to achieve despite certain imperfections in his character. Within several months, he had learned to see his life in a different light and to appreciate it as a success. His mood improved and his anxiety lessened. He successfully tapered off and terminated his therapy after 18 months.

The other example is Alice, a very anxious and distressed woman who was having a difficult time dealing with her suicidal teenage daughter, Olivia. Alice's therapist did not recognize that Olivia's suicidal behavior was an attempt to develop a closer relationship with her mother, who had a very active social life and was frequently absent from her family. Alice persisted with this therapist even as Olivia became increasingly suicidal and she herself became more and more anxious and depressed. Alice continued her therapy because the therapist was "highly recommended" and because she was intimidated by the therapist's celebrity status and sophistication. As Olivia's suicidality worsened, Alice was wrongly advised by her therapist to encourage her daughter's independence, which only made the suicide attempts more serious and resulted in Olivia's hospitalization. In the wake of this event, Alice was informed by her daughter's doctor that Olivia felt abandoned and that her therapist was actively harming both of them. As a result, Alice changed therapists. During the first session, her new therapist was able to convince her how much she was needed by her daughter, which felt to the patient like a revelation. She improved rapidly, and so did her daughter.

In both of these cases, the patients felt increasingly unhappy with their therapists but continued to see them because their therapists came highly recommended and were popular in their respective social circles. Only near-catastrophic events in their lives allowed them to become disloyal to their therapists, to finally leave the treatment, and, after finding the therapist who was right for them, to improve.

PROACTIVE VERSUS REACTIVE TREATMENTS

When you are talking with families about proactive versus reactive treatments, an analogy between those with heart disease and with bipolar illness is a good place to start. In this chapter, "proactive" is used to refer to treatment designed to avert the onset of the illness or of an acute episode, whereas the word "reactive" is used to describe treatment after the onset of the illness or after the acute episode has begun. Even with heart disease, being proactive in treatment is hard. Let us imagine a 35-year-old man with a strong family history of heart disease, his father and his grandfather having had massive heart attacks in their late 40s. Being proactive in preventing a heart attack at an early age would mean first of all not smoking, limiting his alcohol consumption, watching his weight and waistline, and exercising regularly starting at an early age, preferably in adolescence or in his 20s. Additional proactive measures would include being on a fairly strict low-fat diet, not eating red meat, watching his cholesterol and triglycerides, and doing regular stress tests.

This sort of lifestyle is difficult to lead because the patient has to limit his spontaneity and possibly endure ridicule from friends and potential girlfriends, with no hope for an immediate reward or gratification, as well as dubious rewards in the distant future. Consequently, most people live in denial of the possibility that they may have a heart attack in the not-so-distant future and get treatment reactively, after they have suffered one, if they survive. After the first heart attack, some of them (though not all) will quit smoking, limit their drinking, and possibly start a regimen of diet and exercise. Out of fear of having another even more serious heart attack, they may also start taking medications. However, even if they do, they would have already lost quite a bit of their myocardium and acquired lower ejection fraction and exercise tolerance.

A close psychiatric analogy would be somebody with a strong family history of mood disorders whose mother suffered from recurrent depression and committed suicide at age 40, and whose uncle on his father's side is bipolar and has been hospitalized repeatedly with manic episodes. This hypothetical person has about a 30% chance of developing a serious mood disorder and about a 70% chance of having any Axis I disorder such as generalized anxiety disorder, panic disorder, phobic disorder, OCD, major depressive disorder, or bipolar disorder. If he were to be treated proactively, he would start treatment as a teenager under the care of a psychiatrist, who would encourage a healthy lifestyle and watch for early warning signs of a mood disorder. He would need to stay away from both illicit and licit stimulants and cannabis and limit his drinking to one or at most two drinks per day. He would need to maintain rigorous sleep hygiene and avoid stressful careers that require unpredictable travel and working through the night to meet deadlines.

Even more so than with heart disease, this proactive treatment would feel like an unnecessary restriction that does not bring tangible benefits. Unlike the lifestyle recommended to prevent heart disease, this lifestyle may also stigmatize the person either as mentally ill or as someone who will be mentally ill in the future. Consequently, proactive treatments in psychiatry are almost nonexistent. Instead, treatments are administered reactively after the first serious episode of major depression or after the first manic break. Even then, patients and families are reluctant to be proactive with regard to the next episode! Families must know that each successive episode of mood disorder worsens the prognosis, and they must understand that proactive treatment improves it substantially. This information, however, needs to be presented with a sense of humility and the understanding that we cannot really know how the illness will proceed in the future. This uncertainty will allow families to feel hopeful that their children may fare better than most with the same illness. For all we know, this actually may be the case.

The following vignette is an example of a discussion with the father of a young man from Central Asia who does not want further treatment for his son after the resolution of his first depressive episode:

> Mr. Kim, Gene did have a pretty severe episode of depression. It was severe not only because he felt depressed, but because his thinking was altered and he had to stop working for several weeks. He needs to continue to take his medications on a regular basis to prevent other such episodes in the future for two reasons. First, they are painful to him, to you, and to the rest of the family. Second, each episode like this leaves its memory in his brain which can make the next episode more severe and easier to happen. Now, nobody can see the future and under the right circumstances it may be possible to stop his medications completely, but for now he needs to continue and take his pills religiously.

The issue of having an illness, or vulnerability to developing one, most often arises after successful treatment of an early depressive episode in an individual who has recurrent major depression. Both the family and the patient will ask what the chances are that the patient will get depressed again. The probability of somebody experiencing a second episode of major depressive disorder after stopping medications is 50% (Perahia et al., 2006). Thus at this stage of the illness, the patient has demonstrated a vulnerability to developing depression and has a 50% chance of never having depression again. In this example, the illness is treatable for 100% of patients and curable for 50%.

Because bipolar illness and schizophrenia are less prevalent than depression in the general population, you will encounter fewer families with these disorders. When you do, a similar discussion regarding one's chances of developing the disorder must take place. Both illnesses are not curable but are readily treatable with medications. It may surprise you to learn that psychotropic drugs are as or more effective in treating symptoms of the illness as, say, drugs for common medical illnesses such as diabetes, heart failure, or renal insufficiency that alleviate but not eliminate the symptoms completely. Most patients would be pleased with 90% improvement in their glucose control because such improvement would allow them to continue their lives as if they were healthy. On the other hand, very few psychiatric patients and their family members would be content for patients to feel only 90% of their usual selves, because incomplete remission does not allow for a return to full functioning. When patients regain only 90% of their usual intellectual or emotional ability, both their families and their coworkers can tell that they are not quite back to their usual selves. Ironically, quite a few patients entering psychiatric treatment hope to feel 150% of their usual selves and function even better than they did when they were healthy. Because of these unrealistically high expectations, the effectiveness of psychotropic drugs is often underestimated.

CHANGING DOCTORS AND SECOND OPINIONS

When a patient's condition deteriorates or does not change for the better for a long time, even the most compliant and trusting patients and their families can start losing faith in their doctor's treatment strategy. As a result, they might think about changing doctors or getting a second opinion. Indeed, even the best doctors can make mistakes or, after treating a particular patient for a long time in a particular way, may lose perspective on other treatments. In this context, seeing another psychiatrist for a second opinion and changing doctors is only rational and even necessary.

Most of the time this is indeed the case, and second opinions and, at times, changing psychiatrists should be encouraged. Families most often return to the first doctor either with confirmation of the current treatment plan and renewed faith or with a suggestion from a consultant that can be discussed with the family at the next meeting. The consultant's suggestion can be either accepted and tried or rejected with an explanation that the family can accept.

Many families will be reluctant to seek a second opinion out of fear of offending the treating psychiatrist, with whom they have a pleasant personal relationship, and fear that this conflict would undermine the future treatment of the patient. These families need to be reassured of their doctor's professionalism. If you are that doctor, your best course of action is to refer them to a consultant, to speak to that consultant personally, and to reach an understanding on that consultant's treatment recommendation. You will then be in a good position to discuss new options with the family and agree on future treatment, altered or not.

The following example concerns the family of a psychotherapy patient who is apprehensive about getting a second opinion for their daughter, who is not improving.

I have to agree with you that her progress has stalled. She feels much better, she is no longer depressed, she has not had any panic attacks, and she is doing well in school. However, she feels lonely because her relationships are very short lived and she is not sure about her sexual orientation. I have an idea how to deal with her confusion but I am not a specialist on issues of sexual orientation. I know that you like me and that you trust me as a doctor. However, I know my professional limitations and this is one of them. Let me refer her to specialist for a consultation. He is an excellent doctor and I have known him for many years. I will give him all the

important information before her appointment, then the two
of us will talk after the appointment and then we'll all meet
to discuss the plan.

Other families will do the opposite and will constantly second-
guess their doctor's actions and seek second opinions from multiple "highly recommended" specialists. These families are often,
though not always, affluent and have access to the best physicians
and hospitals. However, paradoxically, their loved ones not infrequently get inferior care because of frequent treatment changes in
response to the often contradictory opinions of multiple consultants. Additionally, such families tend to take control of treatment
and effectively tell treating physicians how to treat based on their
consultants' opinions. Under these circumstances, functionally, the
physician is like a surgeon doing a procedure with the family
standing behind his or her back, telling him or her where to cut.

I find that in these cases, the best strategy is to determine one's
own professional comfort zone and communicate these boundaries
to the family. If they cannot respect them, you may need to ask
them to seek treatment elsewhere, or you may end up doing them
harm. Both you and the family need to remember that your first
responsibility is to do no harm. Hearing the words "Do no harm"
may help the family understand that your thinking and decisions
are not personal but professional. Ideally, in your comfort zone you
should be able to complete a treatment plan without interference
and then reassess the patient's condition.

Mrs. Cohen, it has been 4 weeks since I started treating
your husband, and we have not made any progress because
each time we begin a treatment plan, you go to see another
highly esteemed specialist who had a different opinion and
so our original plan is not carried out. I understand that you
want your husband to get the best treatment from the best
doctor. For me, this means one doctor whom you trust and
do not second-guess on a weekly basis. I may or may not be
that doctor for you and your husband. I have a suggestion as
to how to determine that. Please go to several specialists and

choose the one who, in your opinion, is the best and whose treatment plan you understand and respect. All the specialists you have consulted over the last month are fine specialists. After you find the right person, which may or may not be me, I recommend that you stay with that doctor and let him or her treat your husband until he gets better or treatment fails. In the latter case you can design another treatment plan or seek a second opinion or even change doctors. I recommend that you do not see other doctors while your trusted doctor's treatment plan is in progress because this could cause harm.

But not treating your husband over the last month, as I effectively have done, when he could have been getting treatment means that I have been causing him harm, at least in my book. The first thing you learn in medical school is to "Do no harm." For that reason I cannot continue treating him as I have been; it would be unprofessional. I would like to ask you to continue looking for a doctor you trust until you find one and then follow his or her recommendations. And if you decide that you trust me, I would be happy to treat your husband . . . but then please follow my recommendations!

MEDICATION SIDE EFFECTS AND ADHERENCE

For the families of mentally ill individuals, medication side effects and medication adherence are the most pertinent issues on a daily basis. Medication non-adherence in general is a very serious problem, and barriers to medication adherence in all fields of medicine, including psychiatry, are being actively researched. Some degree of non-adherence is universal and, for instance, only 50% of patients with hypertentsion who do not have mental illness are able to be not fully adherent to their medication regimens one year after the treatment has been instituted (Lau et al, 2010). For the mentally ill, even sporadic non-adherence can often result in relapse.

Even psychiatric patients with adequate access to psychiatric care and adequate drug insurance plans are non-adherent with medications because of their side effects. Families are often painfully familiar with some of the side effects that are manifested externally: weight gain, tremors, stiffness, decreased range of affect. Other side effects that families have to deal with are medical, for example, diabetes, hepatotoxicity, and renal toxicity. Some side effects, though felt by patients, are not noticeable to others. Examples of these are decreased sex drive and not feeling like oneself—an altered range of emotion and reactivity to emotion. Yet others are initially noticeable only to doctors, such as treatment-emergent mania, anxiety, and akathisia—a medication side effect that makes people experience feelings resembling severe anxiety and also makes them physically restless (Poyurovsky, 2010).

Most families understand that psychotropic medications have side effects, some of them serious. Some families might also understand intuitively that patients could be reluctant to take medications because of these side effects. Some families read package inserts, and more and more of them read equivalent materials on the Internet. Some read various mental health–related blogs, and a growing number are bloggers themselves. This group of caregivers mostly needs help sorting out common side effects from those that are listed in package inserts. In the case of inserts, side effects might be listed because they occurred in one person in a clinical trial and were subsequently reported because of FDA regulations. On the other end of the spectrum, some families either are not concerned with side effects or are unaware of their existence. This group requires psychoeducation and a reality check.

The prescription drug labels required by the FDA for all approved drugs are very complicated multilevel documents (Lal & Kremzner, 2007). They are products of a very lengthy, complicated, and expensive process that starts with a series of clinical trials conducted by a pharmaceutical company and guided by FDA regulations. At the conclusion of the pivotal trial, the company applies for drug approval for a particular clinical indication, which in psychiatry is a *DSM* psychiatric diagnosis. The contents of the informational package for the consumer are the result of the often painful reconciliation of several contradictory needs and interests. The main conflict is between the FDA requirement for the information to accurately reflect the risks and benefits of the drug and pharmaceutical companies' wish to emphasize the efficacy of the drug and minimize the associated risks and side effects. The pharmaceutical companies' motivation in doing this is to increase sales and profits.

The side effects sections of prescribing information are organized, in order of importance, into contraindications, black box warnings, warnings and precautions, and adverse reactions. The last two sections are very long, are written in small print, and contain tables with side effect frequencies, which are invariably confusing and contradictory because they come from different sources. For example, a table under warnings and precautions might prominently show the risk of weight gain for drug Y as 5%, compared to the risk of 1% in placebo. These risks seem minor and rare (1 in 20) compared to 44% risk of developing dry mouth (1 in 2), a minor side effect of many drugs. In fine print, the adverse reactions section states that in two trials the frequency of significant weight gain was 23% and 21%, which is clearly higher than 5%.

Both numbers are correct in that 5% of subjects reported significant weight gain and investigators found significant weight gain in 23% of subjects. However, such subtle differences are not immediately obvious even to a professional, let alone a patient or his or her family.

Weight gain is of concern to every single patient taking medication for mental illness. Weight gain is also the side effect that most frequently leads to non-adherence with treatment. However, in the warnings section for the same drug, weight gain is given similar or even less prominence than priapism, which is exceedingly uncommon. Cases of priapism with several drugs have been published as rarities in case reports. However, in 20 years I have never seen one in clinical practice.

Involved family members read prescription information in detail and need help distinguishing near-certain side effects—such as weight gain or sexual dysfunction—that will affect medication adherence from possible but rare clinical oddities. It is important to consider each patient individually and to tailor your discussion specifically to each case. Changes in weight and libido mean different things to different people and occasionally can be therapeutic. It is, however, always important to offer alternative treatments with different side effect profiles and to discuss how the issues related to adherence and side effects may affect the family as a whole and the therapeutic alliance with the doctor.

Judy, I have asked you to come here because I wanted to talk to you and Esther about some of the her medications' side effects. She has not been taking her antidepressant regularly. She has been complaining to me about her increased appetite and also about the decrease in her sex drive. I will talk about these in a minute, but before that, let us talk a little about her depression and panic attacks. We all agree that side effects notwithstanding, Esther is feeling much better: Her mood has improved, she has had no panic attacks for 6 months, she is keeping up with school, and she has been dating!

If there were no side effects, she would continue taking her pills and we would call her treatment a success. Now, on to the side effects. Let us talk about her weight gain and loss of libido separately. She did gain 5 pounds and, unless you are below minimal body weight, any weight gain is contraindicated. Esther is more concerned with her looks, but gaining weight also carries an increased risk of diabetes and cardiovascular disease. Therefore, we need to do something about the weight. I am much less concerned with libido. Yes, it is more subdued, but she has never stopped feeling sexual attraction and she has become much more selective in whom she dates. Some of this new wisdom is the result of psychotherapy, and being in better control of her emotions, as well as her libido, certainly has helped.

So the way I see it, we have come to a fork in the road: Either we continue current treatment and try to control her appetite, or we change the antidepressant. There are antidepressants that cause less weight gain but each antidepressant is only effective in about two out of three people . . . So let us decide which road we are going to take and stick with

it, because not adhering to the treatment plan will get us
right back to where we started.

If educated consumer parents are at one end of the spectrum, then at the other end are families who have a "fix him" or "fix her" attitude (sometimes in combination with "do whatever it takes") and little understanding that all medications have side effects and may or may not work. These families want a magic pill and need education and support.

Mahmud, I also wish your son weren't gaining weight. In
fact, I wish I knew of a miracle drug I could give him so he
would wake up a new man tomorrow morning. Unfortu-
nately, neither I nor anybody else has this drug. We do have
many antidepressants, about 15 to be exact. Some are
stronger than others. However, only 70% of patients feel bet-
ter with the stronger ones, and quite a few feel better with
the weaker ones. At this moment in time, I cannot tell you
which will be the best for your son, and there is no scientific
way to predict which one will work best. I started with one of
the more effective drugs, and it resulted in increased appe-
tite and sleepiness. Let us try another one that does not have
these two particular side effects, but like all drugs, it has
some. In the case of this drug, the side effects would be in-
somnia and possible restlessness.

CHAPTER SEVEN

How to Talk About Suicide and Deal With Emergencies

According to the American Foundation for Suicide Prevention, suicide is the fourth-leading cause of death in American adults ages 18–65 (AFSP Web site). Every year, 33,000 Americans die by suicide, 60% of whom succeed on their first attempt (O'Connor, Sheehy, & O'Connor, 1999). Over 90% of suicide victims have an identifiable psychiatric diagnosis (Centers for Disease Control and Prevention, n.d.). Conversely, 5%–15% of those with a diagnosis of bipolar mood disorder, schizophrenia, recurrent major depressive disorder, or borderline personality disorder eventually commit suicide (Meltzer, 2001; AFSP Web site; NIMH Web site).

A suicide attempt is either an action taken with the intent to die or an action that makes death a real possibility but not a certainty (Posner, Oquendo, Gould, Stanley, & Davies, 2007). Taking an overdose of a large quantity of pills while alone without telling anybody is an example of the former, while turning on the gas and putting your head in the oven at 2:45 PM, knowing that your sister is coming at 3 PM is an example of the latter. Whether suicide is or is not successful depends not only on intent but also on the lethality of the method. Jumping off a high-rise building or using a gun is likelier to result in successful suicide than taking a prescription drug overdose.

Not all self-injurious behaviors are suicide attempts. People with severe personality disorders, most often borderline personality disorder, sometimes cut themselves to get others' attention or to relieve almost intolerable inner tension. Death is not the goal of such behavior, and although cuts may require stitches, they are rarely life threatening. This type of behavior is called a suicidal gesture. Suicidal gestures may still be fatal, but that is not the intention. Patients with borderline personality disorder often threaten to kill themselves, and often do, but sometimes because their suicidal gestures turned out to be more lethal than they anticipated.

Recent advances in the treatment of psychiatric disorders have not resulted in noticeable decreases in suicide rates. Traditional chronic risk factors for suicide attempts are having a psychiatric diagnosis, a history of previous suicide attempts, feelings of hopelessness, alcohol abuse issues, recent losses or major blows to social and financial status such as job loss or eviction, and lack of social support, as well as being a white professional male over 50. More recently, insomnia, panic, and overwhelming anxiety were identified as other risk factors (Goodwin & Hamilton, 2001; Kilbane, Gokbayrak, Tross, Cohen, & Galynker, 2009).

Some clinicians, including myself, believe that there exists a specific mental state, a "suicide trigger state," that triggers a transition from suicidal thoughts or suicidal ideation to actual suicidal action. In my experience this suicide trigger state involves a particular thought process experienced as a confusing, uncontrollable, unmanageable, or unstoppable profusion of ruminative thoughts—in effect, an overwhelming flood of ruminations. We have termed this phenomenon "ruminative flooding." These ruminations are accompanied by feelings of hopelessness and panic about being trapped in a no-win situation, doomed to failure without any good options or solutions. The best description for this conglomerate of feelings and thoughts is "frantic hopelessness" (Yassen, Johnson, Fox, & Galynker, 2009).

A person with the highest risk of imminent suicide attempt

would be a successful Caucasian professional man in his 50s who has recently and publicly lost his job, been evicted, or suffered another public humiliation. For young adults a common scenario leading to suicide attempts involves not living up to family expectations or having just transitioned to a more challenging level of education: from high school to college, from college to graduate school, or another similar transition. Particularly at risk are college students who both perceive themselves as failing and feel lonely and isolated. Finally, the painful breakup of a romantic relationship can also lead to suicide attempt. In all these cases, those who have recently stopped sleeping, who are telling their family and friends that they feel that they are trapped in a situation from which there is no escape, and who are drinking heavily would be the likeliest to attempt suicide.

There seem to be two types of suicide attempts: premeditated with a plan, and impulsive with little or no plan. Premeditated attempts involve choosing a specific method, a specific plan, and a specific date, and purposefully deceiving and misleading both friends and medical professionals so that the planned suicide cannot be prevented. Such planning can go on for weeks and months. Impulsive or little-planned suicide attempts can occur as little as 10 minutes after the first thoughts of suicide (Deisenhammer et al., 2009). The suicide trigger states for these two types of suicide attempts are probably not identical, but both involve an urge to end the state of frantic hopelessness and ruminative flooding.

Some families are not psychologically minded and need to be alerted that their relatives may be suicidal. Others are aware of the suicidality of their relatives but are not certain how to broach the subject. For many people, talking to a close friend or relative who may be suicidal about the latter's suicidal urges and plans is very difficult for a variety of reasons. Unless you are a trained professional, which most family members are not, you may be afraid to insult a person by intruding into his or her most private thoughts. Some families may believe that openly talking about the possibility of suicide can increase the chances of a suicide. However, bringing the possibility of a suicide attempt into the open in a caring way may actually reduce the risk of suicide because it makes the suicidal person feel less alone and gives the concerned friend or relative an opportunity to clarify the level of danger and call for help if necessary.

FOLLOWING AN UNSUCCESSFUL SUICIDE ATTEMPT

When talking to families after a patient's unsuccessful suicide attempt, your most important goal is to make sure that the family is not in denial of the gravity of the suicidal act, regardless of how seriously their suicidal relative was harmed as a result of the attempt. The other issues to address are the family's understanding of the circumstances leading to the attempt and then ensuring appropriate psychiatric follow-up for the patient. Finally, it is important to speak with the family about their loved one's suicide trigger state and make sure they recognize the warning signs when they see them. The following dialogue is an example of a conversation with the mother of a 17-year-old girl who took a near-lethal drug overdose after being transferred from a small private school to a public school. The mother, Pam, was questioning the seriousness of her daughter's suicide attempt.

I said: "Yes Pam, this was a really dangerous suicide attempt—she is lucky to be alive." Pam is still disbelieving: "But she called me." I persisted: "Yes, but even though she left a message on your cell phone telling you that she took the pills, this was really serious: There was no guarantee that you would not forget your cell phone in your car." Pam was beginning to understand: "I never saw it coming—she was such a happy girl." I used this as an opportunity to ground her understanding with facts: "You really did not see it coming—she was always such a happy girl? Let us go over the recent events in her life. What was she saying about her new school?" Pam responded: "She said the coursework was hard and she was having a difficult time making new friends. She was obsessing about wanting to go back to the old school and worrying that she had lost all her friends and would never have any friends again." I asked: "Is she shy?" Pam answered: "She has many friends at her old school, but they are the same friends she's had since kindergarten. She gets anxious at large gatherings." I paraphrased her thinking and agreed with her, putting us on the same side: "So being in a large new school could be really rough for her." I then concluded with a recommendation: "Pam, she needs to see both a psychiatrist and a therapist. She should have no pills in her possession; you should be giving her medications yourself. If she starts talking again like there is no hope, no way out, and if she is not able to see things clearly, try to dissuade her. However, if you are not able to, she may be feeling suicidal again and not telling you. If this is the case, you need to ask her if she feels safe or if she is thinking about taking an overdose or of hurting herself in some other way. If you have any shadow of doubt, call her therapist or her psychiatrist."

FOLLOWING A SUICIDE

Sometimes clinicians face the unenviable task of talking with the families of suicide victims. This may happen either when family members are the patients or when the suicide victim was a patient. It is hard to imagine a worse personal tragedy than the suicide of your spouse or child or another close relative. The devastation and the grief that follow are hard to imagine. Relatives of suicide victims are often scarred for life. For genetic reasons and for reasons related to the traumatic stress associated with the suicide of a loved one, these people may be at a higher lifetime suicide risk themselves. They invariably carry the burden of guilt of what might have been if they had done something differently. The best and really the only agenda for these talks is offering supportive listening, relieving ruminations involving constant second-guessing, and identifying family members who may need help themselves.

Some family members may express anger about the pain the suicide has caused them and others. They may blame the suicide victim for deceiving them, for being selfish, for being callous. It is hard to find the correct response to these statements. Most suicides occur in persons with mental illness. To help the family with their pain under these circumstances, it is helpful to redirect the family's anger away from the suicide victim and toward the illness. Ultimately, it is usually a psychiatric disorder that deprived the family of their loved one. The following vignette concerns the mother of a 25-year-old young man with bipolar disorder who committed suicide by drowning.

> I started by equating serious mental illness with terminal medical illness: "Do not blame yourself, you did everything possible. You have been doing everything possible to get him into treatment and have him stay in treatment. Patients with bipolar disorder are addicted to their highs and are notoriously noncompliant with their medications and treatments. Andrew had a very serious mental illness and he had very severe depressions. Most bipolars are not as sick as he was. This was his fourth serious suicide attempt. With somebody this sick, unfortunately, it was just a matter of time. Life was just too painful for him." The next step was to directly evaluate and support the family member: "You must be in shock. How have you been sleeping?" The mother answered: "Not well, I keep imagining him as he was, you know." I then validated her feelings and offered a referral for treatment: "You know, grief knows no schedules. It may be a good idea for you to try to get some help dealing with this loss. Taking medications to help you sleep for awhile should help you feel better."

FAMILIES WHO WORRY THAT THEIR LOVED ONE MAY ATTEMPT SUICIDE

Families who worry that a loved one may commit suicide usually have reasons to do so. One possible reason is that the person they are worried about has just suffered a devastating loss, such as an engagement broken over an affair or a career-ending disaster at work. Under these circumstances the two most important tasks for worried family members would be to remove any possible means of achieving a quick and violent death, such as firearms or bottles full of pills, and to have an open discussion about possible suicidal thoughts and plans. This discussion reduces the risk of suicide and opens the door to the possibility of treatment.

> *You do have some reasons to worry, Marie: The failure of your husband's business and the financial losses of his investors who, as I understand, were his friends, were severe blows to his self-image as a successful and near-infallible*

businessman. While the risk of him harming himself is hard
to assess, under these circumstances, it is much better to
overreact than to do too little, even if you may feel awkward
or ridiculous in the process. Trust me: Do not feel ridiculous,
because doing what you are about to do may save his life.
He hunts, so please hide or get rid of all his live munitions if
you can. Then talk to him about his business options, and if
he sees none, tell him that under these circumstances people
sometimes do stupid things, like shooting themselves, and
very gently ask him if he has been having thoughts like that.
If he does, stay with him until he can see a professional, and
get in touch with me or his therapist.

Another reason for such worries can be the skillful manipulation of an individual who is trying to prevent a real or imagined breakup with his or her spouse or partner. Even if he or she never expresses suicidal thoughts or intent, the ill individual, who often carries a diagnosis of either dependent or borderline personality disorder, can provoke strong feelings of guilt and responsibility on the part of the healthy partner. The latter then faces a false choice of either carrying on a painful and unworkable relationship or being responsible for his or her partner's certain death. If the possibility of a breakup is real, then both partners need support over the critical time. If outpatient support is inadequate, then the suicidal person may need hospitalization. If no breakup is being planned, then the ill partner needs reassurance and the healthy partner needs education about the etiology of the former's guilt and fears.

David, you have been very unhappy for a long time and
this is unlikely to change. She tells you—and she also makes
you feel—that she cannot live without you. Are you prepared
to spend the rest of your life feeling the way you have been
feeling for the last 5 years? Nobody should be asked to sacri-
fice every possibility of happiness for someone else for fear
of what he or she might do. After the initial pain, both of you
are going to feel much better. You may need to find a good
couples therapist and talk though your fears in his office.

She may need to be hospitalized for a period of time as she was in the past, but as in the past she should recover.

FAMILIES WHO MINIMIZE OR DENY THE POSSIBILITY THAT THEIR LOVED ONE MAY COMMIT SUICIDE

For somebody who does not deal with mental illness on a daily basis either in themselves, in their close relatives or friends, or as a professional, suicide is an inconceivable and unnatural act beyond the realm of possibility. The majority of people belong to this category and are therefore unlikely to believe that somebody they know may actually kill themselves. Their denial allows them not to deal with the stigma of having a mentally ill relative and all associated feelings and actions. When dealing with somebody without known history of mental illness or suicide attempts, a lot of families would consider a suicide inconceivable even in the face of recent overwhelming stress and even explicit suicidal statements. However, 60% of suicide victims succeed on their first attempt, and more often than not the response from friends and relatives is, "I just saw him last week and he was laughing and looked totally normal." When talking to families of those who, in your opinion, may be at suicide risk you should gently but firmly alert them to the possibility of suicide.

Talking to the sister of a recently retired teacher who now lives alone because he has sent his demented mother, whom he had lived with all his life to a nursing home: "Carol, Ed has been complaining of insomnia recently. To tell you the truth, I am worried about him. I am specifically worried that he may do something to himself. You think he would never do something like that but I am not so sure. He had two important things in his life, his job and his mother, and he has just lost both. He has been looking lost lately, calling you three or four times a day, asking you what to do with himself. He told you he does not know what to do now that he is retired. These are really drastic changes in his behavior fol-

*lowing two really devastating losses. You need to understand
that it is not business as usual for him. You may need to get
him a psychiatrist or if you are not sure how to deal with this,
bring him here. We'll talk to him together in my office."*

TALKING TO THE FAMILIES ABOUT REPEATED SUICIDAL THREATS

Some families face repeated suicidal statements or threats from
ill family members. Typically the latter carry diagnoses of schizophrenia, bipolar depression, unipolar depression, or borderline
personality disorder. Families ALWAYS need to take such threats
seriously and assess them in the context of current and recent life
events. The most dangerous and harmful response on the part of
the exhausted family would be to challenge the ill family member
about the seriousness of their suicidal thoughts and plans such as,
"You will never do it . . . You are only saying it. Go ahead make
my day, etc." Such responses will only increase alienation on the
part of the patient and will result in a series of increasingly serious
suicidal behaviors until they either feel that somebody cares, or
until they become incapacitated (in the case of an overdose), or
die. If a chronically suicidal person has suffered recent setbacks,
such as a worsening of their condition or a conflict at home or at
work, they need to be taken even more seriously than usual and
may need an emergency intervention. Family should always probe
for hidden stressors and setbacks as they may not be immediately
obvious. If there has been no acute setback, then a supportive
statement of hope, caring, and understanding can help reduce
suicide risk. The next vignette involves the husband of a bipolar
woman who has been diagnosed with treatable breast cancer and
has been talking about wanting to go the Brooklyn Bridge and
"escape."

*Tony, you need to take this seriously. You are tired of her
saying it, and you are asking me if she is actually going to
jump off the bridge. You know that she is extremely dependent on you, and last year when you started having chest
pains and needed a stent, she actually took a handful of*

pills. Now she is even more scared. You or somebody else
needs to watch her all the time, and if this is not possible,
she needs to be hospitalized. It's better to be safe than sorry.

REPEATED SELF-INJURIOUS BEHAVIOR

People with certain personality disorders engage in repeated
self-injurious behaviors that do not threaten their lives. The most
common of these behaviors is cutting or scratching, most often the
wrists but at times also the legs and abdomen. Another common
self-injurious behavior is burning oneself with cigarettes. These
behaviors are typically not life threatening but are extremely disturbing to family members and indicate fairly serious mental illness (Nock et al., 2008; Skegg, 2005). You as a doctor need to get
enough information to differentiate self-injurious cutting from a
suicide attempt. Families need to know not to confuse these with
suicidal actions and to remain composed. Cutting and burning
behavior is usually episodic and becomes more frequent with increased loneliness and worsening dysphoria (low mood) and depression. Families must know that when cutting gets worse, this
usually reflects either increased stress or worsening depression, or
both. If the family has a good relationship with the patient, they
can try to uncover the source of the stress themselves. If not, they
need to either involve the patient's psychiatrist or, if the "cutter"
has no psychiatrist, get one. In the following example, I tried to
help a woman get a better understanding of her 15-year-old
daughter's cutting.

"Janine, do not worry about her dying—what she did is not life
threatening. However, cutting herself is obviously not a healthy
behavior and really tells us that something is wrong. Did something
happen recently—did she break up with her boyfriend?" Janine
answered, "Yes she did. I didn't think it was serious; they have only
known each other for 2 weeks." I then underscored how serious the
problem was and urged a referral for treatment. "Her boyfriend of
2 weeks? There are much healthier ways to deal with such a
breakup. At this moment, there is no need to worry about her taking
her life, but you should really get her a therapist to help her process
her emotions in a more adaptive manner."

RECEIVING A CALL ABOUT
A PSYCHIATRIC EMERGENCY

This can happen to all doctors, not only to mental health professionals. Someone might call, sometimes in desperation, because of a relative's suicide attempts or threats, violence or threats of violence (although in this case families most often call 911), or sudden changes in behavior, including agitation, withdrawal, bizarre behaviors like disrobing and striking strange poses, or saying things that do not make sense. When you receive such a call, the most important thing to remember is that it is danger, not craziness, that constitutes grounds for involuntary admission to the hospital. The potential danger can be to oneself (a suicidal threat, or neglect in the form of not eating, not drinking, or neglecting self-care and hygiene to the point of a fire hazard or the threat of infestation) or to others (aggressive behavior).

In practice, this means that when a person says, "I can't stand this, I'm going to kill myself," even once, even in a whisper, and does nothing harmful, the police or EMS still have grounds to bring him or her to a psychiatric emergency room for evaluation against the person's will. They can use similar tactics with somebody whose apartment is so messy that things are spilling out into the hallway, or so smelly that it bothers the neighbors. On the other hand, that same person may be saying that he is Alexander the Great and Abraham Lincoln combined, planning to democratize Iran, and legally the person cannot be brought to the ER if he or she refuses to come. Your task when receiving such a call is to distinguish between these two scenarios and to help the family either call 911 or try to convince the mentally ill person to seek help.

What follows are two examples of frantic phone conversations with a desperate family member. The first describes a true emergency that requires immediate intervention; the second is typical of a desperate individual who is exhausted from caring for a chronically mentally ill relative. These examples are intended to give an idea of what type of questions need to be asked in order to differentiate a true emergency from a difficult but not dangerous situation.

Debbie, his threats may or may not be serious, but taking a lot of clonazepam while drinking alcohol can be lethal. Your husband has told me that he has two bottles of 60 pills. I can hear him screaming in the background. In this state you cannot count on him to be rational. The danger of him overdosing, whether intentionally or accidentally, is very real. You should immediately call 911 and tell them that he is suicidal and needs to be brought to the nearest emergency room. If, when EMS enters the room, he starts saying he was never suicidal, you need to tell them that he has a serious mental illness and that in this state he does not have the capacity to make decisions. Tell them they need to take him to the psychiatric ER and let the doctor there decide what to do next, to admit him to the hospital or to let him go.

I started by asking: "Tatiana, how bad is the smell and how messy is his room? Can you smell him from outside the apartment?" She said: "Really, really bad. You can smell it outside when you open the door." I suspected that this was not an emergency and continued asking questions to confirm my suspicion: "So, you are telling me that you are able to convince him to change his clothes twice a week and to sit in the kitchen while you clean his room. This is good for you and for him but it does make it more difficult to put him in the hospital. It must be really difficult for you to have lived this way for so many years. However, this is a chronic condition, and he is not violent, suicidal, or malnourished (he is, in fact, obese). For these reasons, if you call the police to bring him to the hospital, they will enter, assess the situation, and then turn around and leave. It sounds like you will need to either work more closely with his psychiatrist or stop cleaning the apartment until it becomes hazardous to live in. Only then will EMS take him to the ER."

Part III
COMMON DISORDERS

CHAPTER EIGHT

Schizophrenia

Schizophrenia is a serious and chronic mental illness that starts early in life and often results in severe impairment to all aspects of intellectual, emotional, sensory, social, and occupational functioning. Characteristic positive symptoms of schizophrenia include hallucinations, delusions, thought disorder, and grossly disorganized and bizarre behavior. The other group of symptoms is deficit, or negative, symptoms such as lack of motivation and will, lack or decline of quality of speech, and lack of emotion and of emotional expression. For a diagnosis of schizophrenia to be made, these deficits need to persist for at least 6 months.

BEFORE THE FIRST SCHIZOPHRENIC BREAK

Although the illness "officially" begins with the first psychotic break, schizophrenia is a neurodevelopmental disorder that starts in childhood. Researchers can differentiate children who will develop schizophrenia from healthy children by watching videotapes made of the children when they were 5–7 years old (Schiffman et al., 2004). Children with premorbid schizophrenia play alone, look odd, and have observable neurological signs.

Similarly, pre-schizophrenic adolescents tend to be isolated and often are teased by other children because they are perceived as odd. These adolescents already may have negative, or deficit, symptoms and therefore lack initiative and will. "Ultra-high risk for schizophrenia" is a phrase used to describe these adolescents, who often have unusual ideas and interests (called magical thinking) and may also daydream (Nelson, Sass, & Skodlar, 2009). These children rarely misbehave and rarely get into trouble. "He was such a good kid" is a comment frequently made by devastated parents.

Parents of these children may blame themselves for not noticing the illness early enough and for being too hard on them. They also often feel guilty about not paying enough attention to the sick child or not loving him or her enough because the child was distant or strange. Relieving the family's guilt and framing their future relationship with the ill child can help the patient and is also a means of forging a therapeutic alliance with the family.

> *Your daughter's illness probably started in childhood. Some believe it starts even before the child is born. Most often you see them gradually getting ill in adolescence— having few friends, having unusual ideas, and just looking and sounding different. Of course you were treating her differently because she was different. Let me assure you, however, that nothing you think you could have done would have prevented this illness.*

ADJUSTING TO THE CHRONIC COURSE OF THE ILLNESS

Although there are exceptions, schizophrenia typically manifests itself with the first psychotic episode in the late teens or early 20s. Men develop the illness several years earlier than women. The difference in the age of onset, together with the fact that women reach sexual maturity earlier than men, means that when they have their first break, women with schizophrenia may already have families and children. This means that with male patients, both at the beginning of the illness and throughout its course, you will be communicating mostly with the parents. In the case of women, in addition to the parents, you will have to work with their husbands and children. Parents are generally concerned about the patient's financial support in the future, when they are gone. With larger families, concerns include possible heritability of the illness and the impact of the ill person on his or her children. Your main concern here is giving hope and directing them to social services agencies:

> *It is understandable that you are worried about the future. There are both social and psychiatric services for the mentally ill in the community. They are extensive and complicated and not very well organized. Patients with schizophrenia can get disability, Medicare and Medicaid, home help, and housing. These can vary in quality, so you will need to get information to choose the best ones for your son. I suggest you contact local social services agencies and organizations for the mentally ill, such as NAMI.*

Schizophrenia is a chronic lifelong debilitating illness that is treatable but not curable. Schizoaffective disorder is similar to schizophrenia but has more pronounced mood swings and carries a somewhat better prognosis. When the first psychotic break occurs, families are devastated. At that time all communications with the family about the illness need to balance some degree of a realistic perspective on how the illness is going to affect their loved one with hope for his or her improvement and relief of suffering (see Chapters 4–6). After the first psychotic break, the illness takes a chronic course. In contrast to bipolar disorder, acute episodes in schizophrenia are all fairly similar in their symptomatology and response to medications and therefore are more predictable for the family.

> *Schizophrenia is a tough illness, but fortunately, after the initial adjustment, there is no further worsening of the symptoms. If he stays on his medications, he will not get worse than he is right now. You can help him by knowing what*

*happens to him when he gets better or worse, and in what
order. All patients with schizophrenia are different, and the
first signs of an episode are unique for each person. You can
learn about them and become an "early warning system" so
that you can help him adjust medications early.*

Some patients with schizophrenia learn to accept and understand their illness and adjust fairly well. They can control their
symptoms to some extent and are able to work and have relationships. Their lives and level of functioning may not be on par with
the family's expectations, but patients can be content, in part because they eventually develop an understanding and acceptance
of what they can realistically achieve and, correspondingly, what
makes them happy. Other schizophrenic patients never gain insight and forever remain noncompliant with medications. These
patients are frequently hospitalized and sometimes spend more
time in hospitals than in their homes or residences. A discussion of
the differences between the patient's and the family's realities can
help the family understand the ill person's behavior.

*I understand that you can get frustrated with her lifestyle
and that the way she lives may not be what you imagined
when she was a child. The things that make her happy are
different from what makes you happy and from what makes
healthy people happy. Her cat is very important to her and
makes her happy. Do not push her to accomplish what a
healthy person would. This will make both of you miserable.*

PSYCHOSIS

Patients with schizophrenia exhibit two kinds of symptoms: positive and negative (also known as deficit symptoms). Positive symptoms are hallucinations, delusions, and thought disorder, which,
either together or separately, constitute psychosis. The first two
refer to abnormal thought content (i.e., abnormal sensory experiences such as hearing voices and abnormal ideas such as a conviction that a certain movie star is sending personal messages through
the TV). Thought disorder involves abnormalities in the thinking

process regardless of its content. In its severity it ranges from very subtle, when a listener might doubt his or her ability to comprehend what seems to be coherent but for some reason is incomprehensible speech, to outright gibberish, often called "word salad." For families, some of these symptoms are more noticeable and bothersome than others. Families may not be aware of many subtle but consequential symptoms. Educating families about the symptoms of psychosis and how they may manifest in their loved ones can help them understand how to react in individual situations.

Your brother has a lot of symptoms of schizophrenia but, fortunately, when he is taking his medication, they do not interfere with his social life and he is even able to work. This should not be taken for granted, because in many cases the disease is so serious and debilitating that neither serious relationships nor employment is possible. You can still see his symptoms: He stares into space at times when he hears voices, he still believes that Cameron Diaz is sending messages to him through the television on a weekly basis, and his vocabulary is a little different from yours and mine. However, although it is difficult, he manages to handle these symptoms well. You can help him by keeping an eye on him and calling me when, for instance, Cameron Diaz starts talking to him daily. At that point we may need to increase the medications.

Positive Symptoms

Hallucinations and delusions are called positive symptoms because they represent abnormal brain activity that develops *in addition* to regular thinking (Sims, 2002). Although much more obvious to outsiders than negative symptoms, they often present less of a problem for patients and their families because they are treatable with antipsychotics. Moreover, when stabilized on medications, patients learn how to live with them and to some extent how to control them. In the acute stage, both hallucinations and delusions, however unusual, are very real to patients with schizophrenia. The most dangerous positive symptoms are hallucinations and delusions that urge patients to engage in violent behavior and to attempt suicide (see the previous chapter on how to talk to families about suicide). In general, the more abrupt the onset of positive symptoms, the better the prognosis. Families should know that, as this feature of the illness can be very comforting to them.

Families should be told that they should not argue with delusions during an acute episode. This is generally also true with regard to residual delusions when patients are functioning and are at their best. When one is dealing with delusions, it is best to speak not to their content but to the distress they may cause the patient, or to disrupt the patient's behavior. Finding the right framework is not easy but can define the atmosphere in the family in a positive or a negative way and also help with treatment compliance.

In the following example, I explained to a family how to circumvent delusions by talking about behavior:

> *Ed has this delusion that all electronic and mechanical equipment, including his washer and dryer, is under the influence of conspiring forces that are plotting to destroy New York and him. That is why he does not wash his clothes, even though they are pretty dirty and smelly. Please do not try to dissuade him, because you will just become part of that conspiracy. You may have more success if you work around his delusion. You can try turning on the washer for him and allowing him to put in and take out his own clothes. (In Ed's mind, touching the equipment is safe; it is turning it on that is a problem.) If this is not feasible, you can have him use the Laundromat, and if it gets "infected," you can ask him to throw out his underwear on a regular basis.*

In the second example, I instructed the patient's husband to talk about her anxiety around her delusions rather than about the delusions themselves:

> *Jenny believes that you will be killed because she is a sinner. She always says to me, "Why do they have to kill him? I am the one who is bad." This delusion makes her very anx-*

ious, but she does not want to take medications that will help reduce its intensity. You may be able to convince her to take the medication not because she is "sick" but because the medications will help her worry less about you and help you worry less about her.

Despite the fact that psychiatrists ask about "voices," patients learn to recognize that these voices—which they find to be very real—are considered abnormal by others, and they are often hesitant to share their content, let alone existence. Voices often say very intimate things—sometimes flattering (e.g., "You're so pretty, George Clooney is in love with you") or insulting and threatening (e.g., "You fat pig, if you tell them about me you will die"). Revealing these messages to others can be embarrassing and shameful. Patients often try to diminish the impact of their hallucinations by being with others, listening to music, sleeping, or pacing (Nayani & David, 1996). Families can tell that the patient is hallucinating when his or her eyes are rapidly darting or he or she stares into space when talking or blinks rapidly when stressful subjects are broached in conversation. Families can often help loved ones diminish the impact of hallucinations by doing something concrete together (cleaning the house or the yard, going for a walk, or shopping) or talking about mundane issues.

As you know, your son hears voices. When he has an episode, they are there constantly and they call him names. When he gets better, he hears them several times a day and they just comment on what he is doing. Listening to his iPod all the time, even when it seems inconsiderate to the people around him, helps him to drown out the voices. Keep that in mind when you ask him to turn off his MP3 player for one reason or another.

Delusions range from mild to outright bizarre, and are not as easy to spot as one would think. Even bizarre delusions that create realities that could not possibly exist in the real world are sometimes hard to spot because they may be "encapsulated" outside the main stream of consciousness. For example, I once treated an elderly patient who had a delusion that all her internal organs were missing. You would only become aware of the delusion if you were to ask a pointed question such as "How is your stomach?" Then she would respond: "I have no stomach." Mild delusions involve imaginary realities that are possible but still clearly false, for example, that one is being watched by the CIA.

Mild delusions may be even harder to identify because the boundary between delusional and normal thinking can be unclear. One typical example is when a patient believes that people are talking about him or her at work and that his or her job may be in danger. This suspicion may be based on the patient's poor job performance recently, or past or ongoing inappropriate behavior, and may reflect real staff discussions about the patient's future at his or her place of employment. On the other hand, this belief could be delusional if no discussions about the patient's work performance or employment are actually taking place.

Overvalued ideas are an in-between clinical phenomenon that is common in schizophrenia but is seen even more often in mood disorders (Mullen & Linscott, 2010). A person with overvalued ideas thinks obsessively about things that are real but loses control over how much he or she obsesses about that particular topic. This loss of control is a psychotic or a near-psychotic process that often responds to antipsychotic drugs. Families often know that their loved one obsesses about "that woman" or "that job" but may not realize that this is a treatable syndrome, particularly if the person feels head pain or pressure from thinking too much. A good example of overvalued ideas that lead to a psychotic break is given by Chekhov at the beginning of "Ward No 6." In the following example, I explained overvalued ideas to a patient's father.

At times your son thinks too much about what people think of him at work. He worries that the Chinese guy next to him is looking over his shoulder. He also thinks that because he is new, everybody is carefully watching him and maybe even talking about him behind his back in e-mails. You can talk to him about this and try to persuade him that maybe not everybody is watching him. However, he may still remain anxious and may even become depressed. You were very astute in picking up that this type of thinking is not healthy. It is called an overvalued idea and may develop into a full-blown psychosis. Overvalued ideas often respond to antipsychotics, so feel free to call me if you feel that they are increasing in intensity or making your son more emotional.

Many psychotic patients with schizophrenia know on some level that their delusions are the product of their illness and that they are not real, even though they continue to believe that they are. Other patients, while firmly holding onto their delusional ideas or when hallucinating, fully understand that other people think that those ideas and experiences are abnormal and see them as part of an illness. Nevertheless, these patients cannot force themselves to lie about their abnormal experiences. This happens because lying is much harder than telling the truth and requires a lot of willful effort and concentration. Patients with schizophrenia have impaired will, initiative, memory, concentration, and abstract thinking in general. These deficits improve with treatment, which makes it possible for patients with schizophrenia, as they get better, to start concealing their hallucinations and delusions. Families should know that the ability to lie about the symptoms and to hide them from others is a sign of improvement and generally should not be challenged.

You think that she is lying to you and she is still hearing them? You know, lying is a pretty complicated process: You need to be able to discern the truth from a lie as well as to know when to lie, and to whom. When she was really sick, she was not capable of lying; now that the voices are quieter and less threatening, her concentration is better and she can. So she is improving!

Negative Symptoms

Negative or deficit symptoms represent a loss of normal brain function. They include lack of initiative, motivation, and will; emo-

tional and social withdrawal; decreased vocabulary; and impover-
ished and stereotypical thinking (Velligan & Alphs, 2008). Schizophrenic patients also have a decreased range of emotion and its
external manifestation, affect. Negative symptoms that result from
the illness itself are called primary negative symptoms and do not
respond to current treatments. Negative symptoms that result from
medications, depression, and lack of stimulation are called secondary negative symptoms and are treatable. In general, the slower
the onset of the negative symptoms, the worse the prognosis. Although negative symptoms were initially described in schizophrenia, they are also present in patients with dementia and those who
have experienced a stroke (Eisenberg et al., 2009; Galynker et al.,
1998).

In everyday life, families encounter their loved ones' negative
symptoms in subtle and not-so-subtle ways. The subtler manifestations are various degrees of indifference and loss of connection
with the outside world, which manifests as insensitivity and lack of
empathy and the general ability to put oneself in another person's
shoes. The less subtle ones are an obvious lack of social skills, such
as the ability to maintain a two-way conversation with another
person or fit in at a family gathering. Other, often irritating behaviors that are also negative symptoms include staying in bed or inside the house all day, watching TV, not taking showers, and living
in a mess.

THOUGHT DISORDER

Thought disorder refers to a disrupted process of thought that
can manifest itself regardless of the thought content. Thought disorder makes patients with schizophrenia hard to understand and
can be extremely severe, to the extent that the person cannot form
words into sentences, or even syllables into words. During acute
episodes some patients lose the ability to speak altogether and just
utter sounds. On the other hand, thought disorder can be very subtle, and a family member might have trouble understanding what
the person with schizophrenia is saying without realizing that he
or she may be thought disordered. Families may blame themselves

for their difficulty identifying thought disorder as a syndrome of the illness, often doubting, perhaps, their own ability to comprehend speech.

In almost all patients, thought disorder gets worse with complicated and abstract subjects and improves when the conversation turns to everyday events. Thought disorder can disappear altogether with pointed questioning that requires yes or no answers. Since our thoughts are manifested externally through speech, thought disorder often manifests itself in tandem with speech abnormalities such as the inappropriate use of words or the use of made-up words that have significant meaning to the patient. These words are called neologisms. *Saturday Night Live's* "strategery" (instead of "strategy") would be an example of a neologism.

Families of patients with schizophrenia need to know how to talk to their loved ones when they are thought disordered and how to recognize early disorganization as a warning sign of a developing psychotic episode.

When your wife takes medications, she is very easy to understand and she speaks and thinks as logically as you and me and uses the same words. However, during her recent hospitalization after she stopped taking her medications, she was nearly incomprehensible. This type of shift from coherence to incoherence usually does not happen overnight. With your wife, she first starts speaking more rapidly and in longer sentences, which become more and more complicated and at some point nearly incomprehensible. Faster speech is one of the first signs that she is getting sick and a signal to act: When she starts speaking faster, call her psychiatrist, make sure she takes her medications, and if she is already doing so, increase the dose.

When one is communicating with somebody with thought disorder, the simpler the conversation is, the better. Complicated discussions can make a person with thought disorder very uncomfortable and give the person a headache. Talk about mundane everyday things: food, laundry, sleep, going for a walk. Avoid talking about ideas, art, religion, philosophy; avoid asking questions starting with "Why?" or "How?" Questions requiring yes or no answers such as "Did you sleep well?" and "Are you hungry?" are much easier to answer.

COGNITIVE DECLINE

Patients with schizophrenia also suffer substantial cognitive decline, which, together with their psychiatric symptoms, results in the loss of their ability to function at the level at which they functioned before the illness. Cognitive deficits also prevent them from developing the normal social and living skills that we all develop with age and experience. Schizophrenic patients have difficulty concentrating, understanding complex social relationships and appropriate social behaviors, understanding and remembering relevant information, and with abstract thinking in general. These deficits appear at the beginning of the illness but, after the initial phase, stabilize and may progress at the same pace as those normal to aging. A number of experts believe that schizophrenia is fundamentally a disorder of cognition (Andreasen, 1999; Green & Nuechterlein, 1999).

Cognitive deficits often determine how patients with schizophrenia function in society. Patients with more profound cognitive deficits are admitted to psychiatric hospitals from emergency rooms more often and stay hospitalized longer than those who are less impaired (Galynker & Harvey, 1992; Kato, Galynker, & Miner, 1995). It is cognitive deficits that prevent schizophrenics from fulfilling expectations and achieving life goals set by their parents. Families need to understand and accept the realities of cognitive decline in schizophrenia.

You have asked me if she will be able to return to Harvard. Brittany's diagnosis is not yet certain; however, it is clear that her illness is one of the schizophrenia spectrum disorders. Regretfully, these disorders impair your ability to think, concentrate, memorize, and pay attention. In fact, Brittany's difficulties with school and her poor grades before she got sick may have had something to do with these cogni-

tive deficits that were already present and interfering with
her studying. We will not know the full degree of her impair-
ment until she recovers from this episode. So we need to
wait. Harvard or some other less demanding school is not
going away if college is what she will need in the future.

ISOLATION

Those with schizophrenia spend most of their time alone and
are uncomfortable with people. This happens for a variety of reasons—some of them psychotic, some not. The psychotic reasons for
isolation are voices telling them not to talk to anybody, visual hallucinations of humans that are hard to differentiate from real people, and paranoid delusions and fears that people in the street
could harm them or are part of a conspiracy. They also may feel a
painful physical sensation or as if there is a bright light shining in
their eyes when they look somebody straight in the face. Families
must know which one it is so they can work with it.

> *Margie does not leave the house . . . Do you know why*
> *that is? She told me that people in the street are controlled*
> *by the Mafia and are sending her messages that the Mafia is*
> *waiting to kill you and her. Remarkably, the Mafia's influ-*
> *ence does not extend beyond the city limits! What do you*
> *think about taking Margie to Long Island for the weekend?*

Other reasons do not directly involve psychosis and involve a
lack of social skills, fear of being perceived as inadequate, prior
experiences of stigma, or just plain lack of need to be with people.
When families are ashamed of having a mentally ill person in their
midst, they do not encourage their communication with strangers
and, in some cultures, actively hide the ill family member from the
outside world. Parenthetically, this is a good example of stigma
starting in the family (see Chapter 5). These families encourage
patients' isolation, which may result in apathy and secondary negative symptoms and worsen their condition. Your task is often to
find out how much the family can accept the patient's presence in

social situations and to modify their behavior, if possible, to better meet the patient's needs, as in the following example.

> I started by focusing on the issues surrounding Ari's social isolation: "Ari is staying in the house all the time, playing video games. When was the last time he went somewhere that was not a doctor's appointment, either with you or on his own?" The mother said: "He doesn't go anywhere, and I can't take him to family events or outside because he looks like a zombie." I then inquired about the family's feelings when they are seen in public with Ari: "Does this make you feel ashamed?" They admitted: "Yes, it is very hard to be with him." I then suggested some ways to reduce Ari's isolation while relieving the parents' caregiving burden: "You know, some parents of mentally ill persons become their advocates, and that makes them feel good because they are doing something useful for their child and others like him. Not everybody has the inclination or time to get this involved, but this is something you may consider for yourself. On a different note, it would be good for Ari to talk to other family members. You once told me that Rebecca understands and likes him best. If he likes her, maybe Rebecca could take him to a movie."

Some relatives of patients with schizophrenia expect them to be as active as healthy people. They may attribute failure to meet their expectations not to the illness but to the patients' unwillingness to try hard. It is important for such families to know what limits the illness can set on the patient's ability to function, even with optimal medication treatment. Deciding what the patient can do and how it differs from what he or she wants to do and what the family wants him or her to do is one of the most common problems such families encounter. In other words, they struggle to differentiate what is the illness and what is the patient's personality (see Chapter 10).

Encouraging people with schizophrenia to function at a higher level and to socialize is the main task of various outpatient treatment programs. Some of them are affiliated with psychiatric hospitals; others are freestanding. These programs offer group psychotherapies on several levels that vary in the complexity of social demands placed on participants. Patients progress from low-functioning groups requiring little participation to higher-functioning groups, then possibly to sheltered employment, and finally to independent living and (for some) competitive employment. While trying to achieve a higher functioning level is an admirable goal, it often becomes subject to a modified Peter Principle (Peter & Hull, 1969).

The Peter principle humorously posits that in a business hierarchy every employee tends to rise to his/her level of incompetence. People are promoted so long as they work well. Eventually they are promoted to a position at which they are no longer competent (their "level of incompetence"). They forever remain working at their level of incompetence because they will never earn further promotions. Amazingly, this principle can be modeled mathematically (Pluchino, Rapisarda & Garofalo, 2009). Similarly, psychiatric patients reach a functional level they cannot handle because of limitations placed on them by their illness, and then they get sick and need to be hospitalized. It is important for families to know what their loved ones can realistically achieve.

> *I know you would like her to attend the day treatment program. But you know that she was discharged from three already for missing appointments and not showing up. This might mean that going to the day program on a daily basis is just something she cannot do. Right now she is in stable condition and I do not think that I have ever seen her in such good shape. She does keep herself clean and goes for walks on her own. Maybe this is the best she can do in terms of social activity.*

HYGIENE AND DRESS

For a variety of reasons, patients with schizophrenia often have poor hygiene. Negative symptoms make them indifferent to their appearance, so they cannot appreciate when their appearance is sloppy. Negative symptoms and cognitive impairment prevent them from noticing other people's reactions to their poor hygiene.

Hallucinations and delusions may directly prevent them from washing. For instance, they might have a delusion that the shower is bugged. Schizophrenics may have an impaired sense of smell and may not know when they have body odor. Even if they do know, fatigue from antipsychotic medications and disorganization makes it difficult for them to wash and clean. Some medications, particularly the first-generation antipsychotics, exude an odor through the skin. Almost all medications cause dry mouth, which eventually leads to poor dentition.

It is poor personal hygiene and grooming that often make families ashamed to bring their mentally ill loved ones to family events or to be with them in public. With regard to personal hygiene, families need to know how to pick their battles. At minimum, they need to address poor hygiene and grooming habits that become offensive to other people and that could be dangerous to patients themselves. Fortunately, even the sickest patients understand the need for a shower every 2–3 days, and for weekly laundry.

If poor hygiene is the result of delusions or hallucinations that are not improving with antipsychotic treatment, the patient may need to be hospitalized. Otherwise, because schizophrenics feel best when their life has a stable routine, the best way to help patients stay clean and neat is to make hygiene and grooming part of patients' daily routines. This can be an ongoing battle, particularly before a routine is established, and negotiations may be tough. As always, in negotiations, it is best to use the carrot and stick approach.

I agree with you, Michael does have body odor. Because of his illness he does not feel the need to stay clean, so he will not stay clean without your encouragement and help. You may need to bargain with him a little. I understand that he likes to play video games. You can try to make video games conditional on his daily shower. Is there a particular barber or barbershop that he likes? You can make sure that the same barber does his hair every time, and in exactly the same way. Once this becomes part of his life routine, he will be taking showers and getting haircuts as a matter of habit.

SOCIAL SKILLS

Actually, this heading should be "Lack of Social Skills" because patients with schizophrenia are severely impaired in their social interactions. Emotional and social withdrawal are two negative symptoms that are universal in schizophrenia. Lack of social skills is most damaging to newly diagnosed young people because social skills are essential for dating. For that reason a lot of young women and men with schizophrenia are not sexually active, do not get married, and do not have children. In that regard women are much less affected because their illness often has later onset and a milder course (Häfner & der Heiden, 1997).

Lack of social skills also plays a role in the social isolation of those with schizophrenia. To healthy outsiders, schizophrenics appear odd, mechanical, awkward, and either very aloof or just the opposite—intrusive. Appreciating subtle differences in how to behave with different people is a very demanding task and requires an ability to put oneself in the other person's shoes. This ability, called "mirroring," is lacking in patients with schizophrenia (Buccino & Amore, 2008). Hence they may also appear distant and insensitive.

As with other symptoms, families need to be realistic about what their ill relatives can and cannot do. They can encourage and reinforce appropriate behavior, although such feedback is often complicated by a family history of high expressed emotion and rivalries (Brown & Rutter, 1996). Most social skills training is done in a group setting in community mental health centers and day programs. A lot of patients with schizophrenia are able to connect better with other mentally ill individuals with whom they have a lot in common. Therefore families should encourage attendance of such programs.

Families often feel embarrassed, ashamed, and stigmatized when they appear in public with their mentally ill loved ones. The best cure for that is openness about mental illness, which goes a long way in eliminating stigma. I discuss this issue in more detail in Chapter 5. Because patients with schizophrenia have difficulties with abstract thinking, all coaching on social skills need to be conducted in the simplest and most concrete terms. For example, expressing positive feelings should be taught in three simple steps:

1. Look at the person while you are talking.
2. Say exactly what the person did that made you happy, for example, "You took a shower today."
3. Tell the person how it made you feel. "It made me want to go to the movies with you."

AGGRESSION

During acute psychotic episodes, patients with schizophrenia can become aggressive and even violent. Aggressiveness, together with suicidality, is the most dangerous feature of schizophrenia, and the one most frequently leading to inpatient hospitalization and involuntary commitment (Fazel & Grann, 2004). Aggression and violence in people with mental illness frighten the public at large and create the inaccurate perception that all mentally ill individuals are randomly violent. Acts of violence by untreated mentally ill people in several states have led to outpatient commitment laws, which in New York is called Kendra's Law, after a woman who was pushed onto the subway tracks by a person with mental illness. Outpatient commitment laws allow the involuntary hospitalization of mentally ill individuals with histories of violence who become noncompliant with their psychiatric treatment. Family members are probably the most frequent victims of such aggressive acts and, as a result, often are in a position to detect early warning signs of decompensation that may lead to violence. For that reason, advising families on this issue is extremely important.

Patients with schizophrenia can become aggressive for several reasons, and the appropriate response to an aggressive or violent patient depends to some extent on what those reasons are. At present, when most patients with schizophrenia are in treatment and taking antipsychotic medications, the most common reason for agitation and violence is worsening paranoid psychosis due to noncompliance with medications. Stopping medications leads to reemergence of hallucinations and delusions, and increased physical agitation due to resurgence of disorganization or a rebound in energy from discontinuation of sedating medications. The best strategy for controlling aggressiveness due to active psychosis is early detection and treatment.

Another reason for aggression, agitation, and violence is akathisia. Typically akathisia manifests itself as a need to get up and move one's feet constantly while standing in one place. However, in some cases the anxiety-like feelings can be intolerable and patients get agitated and aggressive and are unable to express what they feel inside. Akathisia is at times hard to recognize and is very difficult to treat. The best strategy is to contact the patient's psychiatrist and change medications. Temporarily one could give the patient a large dose of sedating medications because patients do not feel akathisia when they are asleep. Sometimes hospitalization may be necessary.

Families need to learn the very early signs of an impending acute episode. They should also know both their maintenance daily medications and those prescribed to use "PRN" (as needed) in emergencies. The early signs are very idiosyncratic and unique to each patient. Some examples are using brighter lipstick, speaking negatively about old friends, speaking out inappropriately at work, drinking, and worrying about somebody breaking into one's house. When patients get treatment at this early stage before they become agitated and aggressive, such behavior can be prevented.

If early detection and preventive treatment are not possible, families need to know the signs of escalating agitation, which may result in imminent aggressive acts. In contrast to early warning signs, these are similar for many patients with different diagnoses. Patients who are close to losing control are restless, pacing back and forth; have poor eye contact, staring away and down; and may raise their voices and clench their fists. When that happens, the best approach is to reduce stimulation in all possible ways: Stay away (5–6 feet) and do not invade the person's personal space, speak very little and quietly, make no abrupt movements, and sit rather than stand.

Regardless of how ill the patient is, no amount of violence can be tolerated, for the sake of both the patient and the family. It is harmful for the patient, because violent patients are invariably undertreated and, without proper response, will continue to be so. It is harmful for the family, because, among other things, tolerated aggression will lead to more violence. Aggressive and violent patients can become very different people when treated: pleasant, quiet, and compliant. The family needs to be instructed to try to be preventive, to quiet the patient down, and to give PRN medications. However, if the patient does not take medications or does not respond to talking down, the family needs to call 911 and report, "I have an ill person with schizophrenia who is aggressive and dangerous. Please send an ambulance; he needs to be hospitalized *immediately.*"

> *I really feel for you—you have a very tough situation with Karen. It is great that she is living with you and you give her filing work in the office. However, you have been bearing the brunt of her illness: She has not been taking her medications consistently, she has been violent with you, and you have been tolerating it. This is obviously not good for you, but it also is not good for her because she is being undertreated.*
>
> *You can prevent her from becoming violent if you watch her carefully and give her medications preventively, just as she starts getting worse. Fortunately, when Karen starts getting sicker, she starts blinking rapidly and sharply. I have seen that in the hospital and I am sure you have noticed that too. Given the fact that when she is relatively well, she tries to hide her delusions, the best way to monitor her condition is not by her delusions but by the rate of her blinking. You need to act when she begins to blink faster—either give her PRN medications or call the psychiatrist. If you do miss the beginning of the episode, you need to watch out for increased hostility toward you. This is a sign that she may become violent. At that point you need to call 911 and get her to the psychiatric emergency room.*

CHAPTER NINE

Bipolar
Mood Disorder

Although the boundaries of the diagnosis of bipolar mood disorder (BMD) are controversial, there is general agreement that the illness involves alternating or co-occurring extremes of mood. Depressed mood is present at one end of the spectrum, and the other is characterized by mania, which is its exact opposite. Episodic and unpredictable mood swings are the core manifestation of this disorder.

A major depressive episode in BMD is characterized by either the patient's subjective report of feeling sad, depressed, or empty or the objective observations of others that the patient looks sad or down or has been tearful. Other features of a depressive episode are diminished interest or pleasure in activities he or she used to enjoy, substantial weight loss or weight gain, loss of appetite, increased or decreased sleep, loss of energy, and fatigue. Depressed individuals often feel worthless, hopeless, helpless, and guilty of real or imaginary transgressions. They have difficulty concentrating and remembering and have trouble making decisions. Finally, they have persistent thoughts about dying, suicidal thoughts without a plan, and/or suicidal plans and attempts. To meet criteria for a depressive episode, symptoms must not result from drug and alcohol abuse or from bereavement. This last point is controversial because on a symptom level, depression is indistinguishable from bereavement.

A manic episode in BMD is characterized by a distinct period of abnormally and persistently elevated, expansive, or irritable mood lasting at least a week. During that time, patients with mania have several of the following symptoms: inflated self-esteem or grandiosity that can become delusional, decreased need for sleep, excessive talkativeness, rapid speech, and racing thoughts. They may also be easily distracted (i.e., attention too easily drawn to unimportant or irrelevant external stimuli) and experience an inability to focus, hypersexuality, and psychomotor agitation. A hallmark of mania is excessive involvement in pleasurable activities that have a high potential for painful consequences (e.g., engaging in unrestrained buying sprees, sexual indiscretions, or foolish business investments). Mania is usually severe enough to cause marked impairment in occupational functioning or in usual social activities or relationships with others, or to necessitate hospitalization to prevent harm to oneself or others. There may also be psychotic features. As usual in the *DSM-IV-TR*, the diagnosis is sustainable if the symptoms are not due to the direct physiological effects of substance use or a medical illness.

The *DSM-IV-TR* recognizes hypomania as a milder form of mania. Patients with hypomania and depression are given a diagnosis of bipolar mood disorder II or BMD II. Hypomania is defined as a distinct period of persistently elevated, expansive, or irritable mood lasting for at least 4 days, which is clearly distinguishable from the usual nondepressed mood. Symptoms of hypomania are exactly the same as those of mania but not as severe. Typically hypomania results in less functional impairment than mania. Still, hypomanic episodes are associated with a change in functioning from when the person is in a healthy state. These changes may be evident to others.

Paradoxically, symptoms of depression and mania are not mutually exclusive and often happen at the same time, constituting "mixed mania." In a mixed manic episode, the criteria are met both for a manic episode and for a major depressive episode nearly every day for at least a week. This short definition does not do justice to mixed mania, which is very common and more difficult to treat than either depressive or manic episodes of BMD.

BMD is the most confusing diagnostic entity used by present-day psychiatrists to describe a serious mental illness. In recent years the number of American adults carrying this diagnosis has increased to 4.4% (Merikangas et al., 2007), and the number of children with childhood bipolar has increased 40-fold over the last decade (Moreno et al., 2007). The public image of bipolar disorder is that of alternating episodes of horrific euphoria or hostility and deep depression, a Dr. Jekyll–Mr. Hyde sort of dichotomy. This picture is very far from the reality. Today a diagnosis of bipolar disorder encompasses over 10 categories ranging from mood lability to severe classic mania with psychosis.

It is unclear to what extent these nosological changes reflect the evolving phenomenological thinking of modern-day psychiatrists or to what extent they result from the changing clinical picture of bipolar disorder. The latter may be related to early treatments with psychotropic drugs or the changing nature of the human environment, or may have other unknown etiologies. In either case, bipolar disorder is currently a "fashionable" "diagnosis du jour" given to many people with mood fluctuations. The majority of patients given this diagnosis either are misdiagnosed or do not manifest the illness in its classic manic-depressive form.

Both clinicians and families need to know that those who have at some point been diagnosed with bipolar disorder (correctly or not) are often the most challenging patients to treat. For those who are correctly diagnosed, this happens because of their poor insight into the illness, frequent medication noncompliance, and unpredictable and varying symptoms during acute episodes, as well as the treatment resistance of bipolar depression. Most patients who are misdiagnosed as bipolar have severe depression or mood swings due to an equally challenging combination of severe personality disorders and alcohol or drug abuse. The following pages address specific topics of interest to families of those with bipolar illness.

DIFFERENT SUBTYPES OF MANIA
AND DIAGNOSTIC CONFUSION

The diagnostic confusion and diffusion of diagnostic boundaries occur at the two extremes of the illness: mild and severe. With regard to a boundary between BMD and generally more severe schizophrenia, recent genetic studies indicate that more relatives of schizophrenics are ill with bipolar disorder, and vice versa, than would be the case if these two illnesses were genetically unrelated (Craddock & Owen, 2010).

This phenomenon revives the very early "unitary theory of psychosis" that posited the existence of just one major psychiatric disorder with varying degrees of severity (Lapierre, 1994). A good analogy would be chicken pox that manifests itself with a rash that can spread differently over the body. The lesions can differ in number and in location, but they are all still chicken pox. Families often worry about whether their ill loved ones have BMD or schizophrenia, particularly when they were previously given the latter diagnosis or a diagnosis of schizoaffective disorder. Unfortunately misdiagnosis of schizophrenia as bipolar disorder and vice versa happens about half the time. Anxious families need to be reassured that response to treatment and adherence to medications are more important predictors of the future course of illness than diagnosis.

> I started the discussion. "Your son is currently very ill. At the moment he needs reduced stimulation and consistency of the environment and even seeing you will be stressful. You cannot see him, but you can talk to me. I think he is having a pretty severe acute manic episode. He has been pretty agitated all day and was bothered by these thoughts that his neighbors want him to be evicted so they can take his apartment."
>
> The father asked: "Is this psychosis?"
>
> I answered: "Yes, you could call this psychosis. Was he given a diagnosis of schizophrenia in the past?"
>
> The mother said: "During a hospitalization 3 years ago . . . And after that he did pretty well, working and living alone, and he even had several girlfriends."
>
> I continued and concluded with a positive statement: "See, this

is a very good demonstration that in psychiatry, treatment response is more important than diagnosis. He responded well to medications last time. This means that regardless of whether he is bipolar or schizophrenic (which is less likely), as long as he is taking his medications, he should be able to work, to live independently, and even to have a love life!"

Today, almost any illness that involves changes in mood might be diagnosed as what is called a "bipolar spectrum disorder" (Akiskal, 2007). This catchall term unites all clinical entities that involve both depression and periods of heightened activity, regardless of whether the latter in itself is abnormal. Some specialists go even further and label any serious treatment-resistant depression bipolar disorder with mania that has not yet occurred.

Moodiness and mood labiality are frequent symptoms in patients with borderline personality disorder and in cases of the abuse of drugs, particularly cocaine and cannabis. A lot of families would prefer that their loved ones carry a diagnosis of bipolar rather than borderline personality disorder, because in recent years bipolar has become more accepted and somewhat less stigmatized. Many families also find it easier to accept a diagnosis of bipolar disorder than that of substance abuse and also underestimate the disastrous effects of smoking marijuana on mood. As a result, patients with borderline personality disorder and cocaine and cannabis users are, at present, most frequently misdiagnosed as bipolar. The most important issue for families to understand is the difference between classic bipolar disorder and bipolar spectrum disorder and its implications for treatment.

Jim, you and your wife came to me because you were told that she is bipolar and because you are confused and scared. I have only seen her for 2 hours in consultation, so you need to take what I say with some skepticism. Nevertheless, in my opinion, you do not need to be scared. Your wife is not bipolar in a classic sense but most likely is "bipolarish" in the sense that she has an illness that belongs to what current psychiatry calls the bipolar spectrum disorder. This term describes almost anybody who has depressions intermixed with periods of greater-than-average activity. According to this definition, any workaholic who gets depression is bipolar. And you, a highly successful man, are also bipolarish in this sense. In practice, this means that you need to be careful in several ways. In terms of your lifestyle, you need to sleep regular hours and avoid working nonstop, however intoxicating this may be. In terms of medications, you need to be very careful when taking antidepressants, because they can make you manic in the true sense of the word.

Confusion also stems from the concepts of mixed bipolar and rapid cycling bipolar disorder. Since all depressed individuals with bipolar disorder have truly depressed mood and most manic individuals with bipolar disorder have elevated mood, it is easiest to conceptualize the illness as involving mood swings along a single mood dimension from low to high, from depression to mania. This is not the case. A better analogy is two parallel dimensions like railroad tracks: one for depressed mood symptoms and the other one for manic symptoms. These two dimensions are fairly independent. Therefore it is possible for somebody in the middle of a manic episode to also have enough symptoms of depression to be diagnosed as experiencing a major depressive episode (Dilsaver, Chen, Shoaib, & Swann, 1999).

It is also possible for somebody who is profoundly depressed and suicidal to have several symptoms of mania, such as high energy, agitation, and restlessness. Any disease state that presents itself as a combination of both depressed and manic symptoms is called a mixed manic state. In fact, the majority of acute and subacute manic episodes are mixed mania. The depressive and manic components of mixed mania respond to treatment differentially, and mania is much easier to treat than depression. Families need to understand this, because this uneven treatment response often leaves patients depressed.

Allison is having what is called a mixed episode or mixed manic episode. She has not slept for 5 days and she has been frantically trying to keep her business going and get new clients through the Internet 24 hours a day. She thinks that this new marketing strategy is so shrewd that it is going to turn her business around in a week, and she is going further into debt to pay for it. This is unrealistic and grandiose and is a sign of mania.

On the other hand, she starts crying easily at the slightest mention of the burden she may be putting on her girlfriend. She feels depressed, and she is. Here you have it: both mania and depression. Unfortunately, mania is much easier to treat than depression and it is likely that she will become depressed after we treat her mania. After that we'll have to treat her depression.

Rapid cycling bipolar disorder is defined as an illness that manifests in four or more acute episodes per year. Recent research has shown that rapid cycling bipolar could be seen as a more severe form of the illness with more frequent episodes (Nierenberg et al., 2009). Both in depression and, to some extent, in mania, changes in mood associated with both the onset and the resolution of acute episodes are not smooth but come in waves. Specifically, patients experience improvement in mood with antidepressant treatment as having more and more good days among the bad days of depression.

If you were to graph improvement in mood with antidepressant treatment, the chart would have a sawtooth pattern. For that reason, partially treated bipolar depression may feel and look like rapid cycling. More severe bipolar illness is often only partially treated and is therefore experienced as alternating good and bad times. Alternatively, patients with bipolar depression who are in partial remission may feel waves of depressed mood over a background of fair mood or experience good days while feeling generally depressed. The mood waves can be triggered by specific events or can occur endogenously with no discernible external reason.

Julie, you must feel like you have been riding a roller coaster. Over the last two months, Everett has been lying in bed on weekends, depressed, then on late Monday mornings he has been dragging himself into the office. By Wednesday he feels and looks more or less like his usual self, and on Fri-

day morning, he sounds like he is high and becomes abrupt and irritable. Then his mood plunges on Friday afternoon and he sleeps all weekend again. Yes, you could call this rapid cycling. However, in reality, this is undertreated bipolar depression. His current condition is a pretty dramatic improvement from where he was before the ECT treatment: staying at home, despondent and suicidal, and not able to function either at home or at work. We'll try to improve his mood even more by adding a new medication.

LEARNING TO RECOGNIZE EARLY SIGNS OF ACUTE MANIA

Manic episodes, whether euphoric, irritable, or depressed, are unique to bipolar disorder, and I will address them here. Some of the material covered here may also be useful in talking to families of those with schizoaffective disorder and with schizophrenia. Signs of bipolar depression are not very different from those of severe unipolar depression. For that reason I will discuss both phenomena in the chapter on major depressive disorder (Chapter 10).

The telltale sign of a severe manic episode is a reduced need for sleep. However, this is a late sign of mania. By the time a bipolar person stops sleeping, the episode has almost always escalated out of control and hospitalization is imminent. By that time a bipolar patient has probably done serious damage to his or her family and children; personal relationships, if he or she does not have a family and children; and work and career. At that time the bipolar brain enters a pathological loop that, even with medication treatment, will require 6 to 12 months for full recovery. During that time the mind is just trying to find its bearings and no maturational process that typically comes with life experience is possible. This is one of the reasons why bipolar patients often appear immature and behave as if they are younger than their biological age.

In order to prevent an acute decompensation, families need to be proactive in recognizing the very early symptoms and signs of mania (i.e., early warning signs). These can be very idiosyncratic and subtle. Recognizing these signs and ensuring that ill individuals trust the judgment of healthy (or healthier) family members is one of the most important things a doctor can do.

Most early episodes of mania start with a subtle or not-so-subtle elevation in mood or increase in irritability. To those who do not know the patient well, his or her behavior would appear normal. Some early signs of an impending episode may involve changes in appearance. Similar to schizophrenia, telltale signs or indications that an individual is about to have an episode in bipolar disorder include wearing a brighter shade of lipstick or clothing, changing hair color, and becoming increasingly unkempt. For example, at the very beginning of a manic episode, one of my patients would wear purplish lipstick, whereas another would stop wearing makeup altogether. Patients in the early stage of mania also can show subtle changes in behavior such as bursts of creativity or being unusually confrontational at business meetings; for example, one patient would uncharacteristically begin playing several musical instruments in the early stages of a manic episode. This would be his only change in behavior; his sleep and activity level would still be normal for several days.

Not all family members are psychologically minded, and not all are shrewd enough observers to notice these early signs. They need to be taught how to observe an ill relative in the way that a psychiatric nurse would, and how to do so tactfully and unobtrusively. This is not easy and can be emotionally draining. Some family members find this "patient monitoring" intrusive and burdensome and withdraw. Others feel just the opposite and become overinvolved and controlling.

I have found that the best strategy is for family members to compartmentalize their brains into two fairly independent parts: that of a relative and that of a nurse or doctor. When the ill individual is in a stable condition, the relative part is in the functioning mode and the nurse/doctor part is in an observing mode. If the observing nurse/doctor part registers an alarming sign of the illness, the roles reverse and the nurse/doctor mode takes control, while that of the relative takes the backseat. Most families understand this analogy and find it very useful.

Let us talk about possibly the most important thing you can do for your wife. I don't need to tell you that her previous mixed manic episodes were severe and lasted for months. You usually bring her to the hospital when she stops sleeping; unfortunately, by that time her symptoms have been evolving for months and are likely to worsen before they get better. In the future, we could be more successful if we take more proactive preventative measures and agree to increase her medications at the very first sign that something is not quite right. These signs are different among patients and are usually recognized only by the people who know them well. It could be something as subtle as a different eye shadow, or more pronounced, like resentment of an old friend.

With Jane, the first sign of mania is that special little smile she gets on her face once in awhile. Now that I have treated her through three manic episodes, I can recognize it. It is a little mysterious, as if she knows something important she is not going to tell you, a smile that indicates that she has a secret, a bit like that of the "cat that ate the canary." When you see that smile, it is time to up medication.

DISCOURAGING RISKY AND HARMFUL BEHAVIORS

Bipolar patients' lives are often dangerous, risky, exciting, colorful, and full of twists and turns, ups and downs. They can strike great fortunes and just as easily squander them, start multiple projects they never finish, and make commitments they cannot keep. These same people can also have love affairs in the wrong place, at the wrong time, with the wrong people. Their destructive behavior— toward themselves and others—is often obvious to all around them, most clearly to the family, but they themselves can remain wholly unaware of this unflattering reality. Their lives are very stressful, but leading a stressful life is a poor prognostic sign (Altman et al., 2006).

When you are talking with families about the risky behavior of bipolar individuals, it is important to identify a particular behavior as a symptom of the illness. This approach, "blaming the illness," is much more productive than blaming the patient—or seeing risky behaviors as character flaws (see Chapter 5). Once the behavior is identified as a symptom, it can be dealt with like any other symptom (i.e., a doctor can be consulted, medication can be taken, treatment can be complied with).

Risky and harmful behaviors include using drugs and alcohol, getting involved in fights, having impulsive or unprotected sex, traveling alone to dangerous and unsafe areas, gambling, and engaging in activities that are generally perceived as harmful to oneself and to others. These behaviors can be so bizarre that one would assume that someone just made them up (for example, a patient dressing in a red leather bathing suit and provocative makeup and attempting to pay a bridge toll because she believed she was a red Ferrari).

More common risky behaviors can occur in many spheres of life and thus may be harder to identify as resulting from mania. Typical risky and harmful behaviors at work include frequently missing work, misusing one's power and being insubordinate to superiors, engaging in conflicts and arguments, having sexual affairs with subordinates, and misusing funds and perks. Working long hours without sleep is a behavior that is specifically harmful and risky for people with bipolar disorder.

Harmful behaviors at home are often financial, such as out-of-control spending, gambling, making foolish investments, going into debt, and starting multiple unrealistic projects with family funds. Manic episodes can lead to infidelity, aggression, and verbal or physical abuse at home. Needless to say, family members are often affected and develop anxiety and mood disorders of their own (Steele, Maruyama, & Galynker, 2009). Since the onset of the first manic episode is insidious and can take years, all these behaviors can be mistaken for character traits or changes in character. Not infrequently, spouses of people with bipolar disorder ask, "What happened to the person I married?"

Some individuals with bipolar disorder have no understanding that they are living in a different universe than everybody else, including their loved ones, and cannot appreciate the effects of their behavior on others. Moreover they cannot feel changes in their mood and cannot assess changes in their appearance, attitudes, behavior toward others, and even sleep patterns. This lack of insight is difficult to treat. Families often become very frustrated at seeing the same destructive patterns repeated again and again. I once had a patient who, when noncompliant with medications, would become mistrustful of other women and would become hostile and confrontational with her female coworkers and friends. She had done that many times and yet each time felt justified in attacking yet another coworker.

Clinically, individuals with bipolar disorder who have a biologically driven lack of insight and flatly deny that there may be anything wrong with them are the most difficult to reason with and resistant to treatment. Those who want to succeed in living normal lives need to rely on the judgment of others, usually family members. This is absolutely essential to a good outcome in bipolar illness but can be perceived as infantilizing and is often resisted by patients. In these cases, sensible or "sweet" talk is unlikely to result in patients' acceptance of the need to rely on others to tell them how they are behaving. In order to foster such acceptance, tougher measures may be necessary, such as calling the police, arranging for an (often involuntary) admission to a psychiatric hospital, cutting off financial support, or threatening divorce in the event that the risky behaviors do not stop (and meaning it).

Mr. Goldstein, it is hard to for you to believe, but your son has no understanding that when—for the umpteenth time—he stops his medications and goes to another resort to pick up women, he will be arrested for inappropriate behavior. All this is highly stressful and usually results in him being hospitalized. Regrettably, neither you nor I will be able to teach him otherwise.

As long as he lives alone, there is nobody there to pick up on the early signs of yet another episode or to watch over him to ensure he takes his medications. I know that he is an adult, but the illness makes him behave like he is a child who just never learns. He cannot live alone. He needs to live either with you or in a residence and to trust someone else to give him medications and to tell him when he is sick. I see, while you are open to the idea and understand the benefit of him living with you, you think there will be resistance on his part. You are paying for his apartment—you have leverage.

Other people with bipolar disorder understand that their conduct is different from that of others and may even understand what effect their conduct has on other people. They might have a conscious or unconscious belief that common rules of behavior—whether social, ethical, or moral—do not apply to them, that somehow they can get away with what other people can never get away with, and that they are immune to the consequences of their own actions. For instance, one young man with bipolar disorder would indulge in periodic work "binges" when he would not sleep and would "run around all the time" to make money. He would then use this money to buy expensive jewelry for his fiancée because he believed that would make him a bigger man and would make her very happy. He did not understand that she was furious about his absences and the mess in his home office and was ready to break the engagement and leave because she saw no future in the relationship. He would argue that, in working 24 hours a day, he was doing everything he could for their family and was not being appreciated.

Such essentially narcissistic pathology is another striking core feature of mania and can have a damaging effect on families. Such bipolar individuals, even when they are not manic, behave in a way that can result in the spectacular collapse of a career or a marriage. When confronted, these individuals typically try to justify their behavior and engage in defensive arguments with family members. For them, the treatment of choice is psychotherapy, which unfortunately often comes after the damage has been done.

Elena, he needs both medications and therapy. Medications help him sleep, make him less impulsive, and, most importantly, prevent his hypomania from turning into mania. His workaholic behavior is risky and dangerous, because one day, after working for 3 days straight, he is likely to have

*a full-blown manic episode that will require hospitalization.
In addition, as I understand it, he experiences a great deal
of stress over the prospect of losing you or risking another
depression.*

*He has a pretty distorted view of what he needs to be
happy and of what makes you happy. He thinks that only
money can bring happiness. You will need to help him
change that. He has a full understanding of his actions, but
he does not understand the consequences. I will help him
(and you) gain that understanding through psychotherapy. It
will take some time to "rewire" him, but he should be able to
change. He needs you and will do it for you.*

ENCOURAGING PROTECTIVE AND HEALTHY BEHAVIORS

It would not surprise anybody that encouraging healthy behaviors among the families of bipolar patients is no easier than talking about healthy diet and exercise with the families of those with cardiovascular disease and diabetes. Multiple epidemiological studies and randomized clinical studies have shown that obesity increases the risk of diabetes mellitus and cardiovascular disease and that diet and exercise work toward reducing that risk and improving cardiovascular health. Despite this, the obesity epidemic in the United States has reached the magnitude of a major public health issue. It would be fair to say that many obese individuals are aware of this, and yet they do not engage in healthy behaviors that would reduce this risk. The main reason could lie in the fact that it is difficult for patients to trade instant the gratification of pleasurable but harmful behavior (e.g., eating cake) for the distant benefits of difficult and unpleasant healthy behaviors (e.g., staying on a diet).

Health-related behaviors for people with bipolar illness are less researched, less developed, and less obvious, so the benefits of, for instance, reduced workload and less ambitious career goals may not be obvious. For bipolar patients, doing the right thing is even more difficult because of their poor impulse control and impaired judgment during the manic state and poor motivation and low energy in the depressed state. Drawing parallels between bipolar illness and common medical disorders is very helpful when one is dealing either with patients or with their families. Similarities between cardiovascular disease and bipolar illness are the easiest to understand. Bipolar illness, diabetes, and cardiovascular disease resemble each other in that they are chronic lifelong illnesses that have a strong genetic component. People inherit not the illness but a vulnerability to developing the illness. Whether the person actually gets sick depends on a combination of genetic factors and his or her health behaviors. Diet and exercise are the main health behaviors for diabetes and cardiovascular disease. Stress management, both at work and in one's personal life, sleep hygiene, and abstinence from illicit drugs are the three most important protective behaviors for bipolar disorder. Therefore, the best strategy when talking to families is to make these and similar parallels as clear as possible.

You have no problem telling Jessica that playing squash is good for her: It keeps her weight down and her body toned, helps her look pretty, helps her confidence. You should be as clear about her taking medications and keeping regular sleep and study hours, which makes her mind sharp, and her personality attractive, so she will be beautiful both inside and outside.

MOODINESS AND IRRITABILITY

Mood changes are the main symptoms of bipolar illness. Similarly, some irritability may be part of the illness even at baseline. Ideally, it should be minimized with a proper medication regimen, although this is not always possible. Under those circumstances the side effects may outweigh the benefits of the drug, which would then need to be changed. Families should learn enough about the moods and irritability of their ill loved ones to tell the difference between ordinary fluctuations and early signs of a developing episode. Having learned these distinctions, families should learn how not to overreact to regular moodiness and how to intervene sensibly at the earliest signs of developing mania or depression. I have said that early mood symptoms are very individual to each patient. Family members need to be both good observers to see them and good communicators to identify them to the patients.

> You are right, his moodiness in general is pretty difficult to deal with. It is part of his illness that even when he is stable, he has mood fluctuations. Overreacting to them and criticizing him for his moodiness will create an atmosphere of high expressed emotion at home, and that is a predictor of a poor outcome for him. So you need to take a deep breath and let it go. If you are able to do that, it will be easier for him to accept what you say when you notice the first signs of his depression, when it really matters.

SEXUAL BEHAVIOR

Even in families without mental illness, sex and sexual behavior is probably one of the most difficult issues to talk about. For people with bipolar disorder, inappropriate and often promiscuous sexual behavior during manic episodes can become the most damaging aspect of the illness. Among the catastrophic consequences of sexual indiscretions during manic episodes are broken marriages, ruined careers, and STD infections, including HIV. The divorce rates in bipolar families are high (over 50%) but not much higher than in the general population. Families' responses to manic hypersexual loved ones can range from complete intolerance to acceptance and forgiveness—which may be incomprehensible to an outsider. Counseling and advising families on a proper course of action in these cases can be very difficult, especially because some families' moral standards and tolerance for betrayal and promiscuity may be very different from your own. Bear that in mind when initiating a conversation of this kind, and resist making judgments. The following example is of such a conversation with the wife of a well-off man with BMD II caught spending thousands of dollars at questionable massage parlors:

I started by sympathizing: "Some of his behavior is clearly due to his hypomania. I cannot imagine how terrible you must be feeling."

She said: "I am so tired, I don't know if I will be able to stay in this marriage . . . I have no idea what to think about the way he has been acting. At this point, even after all this time, I can't tell if he's just a cheater or if this is caused by his illness. How can you tell what is the illness and what is the person?"

I responded with an educational statement and a suggestion: "It is hard to say. If this behavior is either clearly out of character or episodic, it is more likely illness related. If it is continual, it is more likely due to his character. In the United States, many marriages would not survive such stress, illness related or not. Your husband is willing to comply with treatment and take medications. If you are able, you might consider postponing your decision until we have treated the hypomania."

On the other hand, bipolar depression, just like unipolar depression, can lead to decreased libido and sexual activity. Although this is a less distressing problem in many relationships than the hypersexuality experienced during mania, it also has implications for relationships. Bipolar individuals are, on average, depressed 90% of the time (Thase, 2005), and the lack of sexual activity can strain relationships and marriages. The spurned partner often perceives the lack of physical intimacy as rejection and feels a lot of pain and resentment. As a result, many couples are most compatible when the patient is in either a euthymic (neither manic nor depressed) or hypomanic state but not during mania or severe depression. Because bipolar illness is cyclical, partners find themselves intermittently compatible.

You know that when your husband is depressed he has a hard time even getting out of bed. In this state it is very difficult for him to step outside himself and think about your needs. I suspect that even if he tried to be tender with you, it would feel more like neediness. When he gets this depressed, having a discussion with him about his being distant will just make him feel like he is worthless. If he is still distant when he feels better, you may want to give the discussion another try.

Families of patients with severe bipolar, similar to those of patients with schizophrenia, encounter another set of problems. With those who are severely ill, the choice of sexual partners can be limited by patients' low functioning and cognitive deficits. Such patients either do not have relationships or form intimate relationships with other severely mentally ill individuals. Under these circumstances families need to learn to lower their expectations for a suitable match for their children and understand that for some just having a stable relationship with anybody may be a great accomplishment.

Congratulations! Your son has a girlfriend. It is true she is bipolar, but he seems happier lately and he is definitely less lonely. He has been alone for a long time. With his illness, it is difficult for him to have any relationships. Some people with his illness are barely able to take care of pets. It is actually a serious step for him. I would even call it an accomplishment.

CANNABIS USE AND BIPOLAR ILLNESS

Over the course of my career, every 2 to 3 months I have hospitalized young marijuana smokers presenting with either an episode of psychotic mania or the first episode of psychosis. After THC in a pill form was approved as Marinol for the treatment of intractable pain and for "failure to thrive" in cancer patients, I also began treating a number of patients who became psychotic while taking this drug.

Until very recently this experience was at odds with the commonly held belief that marijuana smoking, though illegal, is generally not a serious concern. However, recent studies show that in some individuals marijuana can cause psychosis and permanent decline in cognitive abilities—notably memory and concentration. Moreover, several years ago British researchers demonstrated an association between marijuana smoking and schizophrenia (Arseneault, Cannon, Witton, & Murray, 2004; D'Souza, Sewell, & Ranganathan, 2009). Other studies have shown that marijuana smoking may cause mania as well. The risk of developing a mental illness while using cannabis is higher for those who started smoking before age 14 (Rubino & Parolaro, 2008). Given the recent findings of geneticists that patients with bipolar illness and schizophrenia share the same genetic pool, it is only a matter of time before it is demonstrated that in some people cannabis can also cause schizophrenia.

Thus it appears that although the majority of marijuana smokers can indulge in their habit without developing a major psychiatric disorder beyond cannabis addiction, a distinct genetically vulnerable minority can become psychotic. The future of individuals who develop psychosis in this way is uncertain. Some never recover and proceed to have either schizophrenia or bipolar disorder; in others, with cessation of marijuana use, the symptoms may resolve completely but return with resumption of the habit. For these people, with each future psychotic episode, the symptoms are harder to reverse with treatment, and if marijuana abuse continues, the drug user is likely to develop a major psychiatric illness.

Most marijuana smokers coming down with an acute episode of mania or psychosis are young adults. Their parents, probably remembering their own fairly benign experiences of getting high in college, or being marijuana smokers themselves, often do not take this addiction seriously. You cannot be too emphatic in explaining to parents the harm of cannabis use by their ill children.

Fortunately Lily is feeling better. She makes sense now when she talks, she is much calmer, she sleeps better, and she is no longer hostile, and that includes her behavior toward you. I am not sure if you know that she has been smoking pot daily for close to a year. I cannot overstate this to you: She ended up in a psychiatric hospital—psychotic and manic—because of pot. You have told me that depression, and possibly bipolar illness, runs in your family.

Most likely Lily's genetic makeup makes her vulnerable to developing mood disorder and psychosis, and, to add insult to injury, the THC in her brain has brought it out. I can-

*not tell you at this time whether she now has a full-blown bi-
polar illness or this is still a cannabis-induced episode that
will resolve completely with medications that eventually
could be stopped. However, for her pot is poison, and I guarantee you that if she continues to smoke, her mind will not
come back.*

This chapter has addressed most issues facing families during
manic and mixed manic episodes of bipolar illness. Bipolar depression, which typically has an overall longer duration than bipolar
mania, will be addressed in the next chapter.

CHAPTER TEN

Major
Depressive
Disorder

Written with Michelle Foster

Major depressive disorder (MDD) is an illness characterized by either single or recurrent major depressive episodes similar to those described for BMD, but without any periods of mania or hypomania. As in BMD, a major depressive episode in MDD is characterized by either the individual's subjective reports of feeling sad, depressed, or empty or the objective observations of others that the individual has been looking sad or down or has been tearful. Other features of a depressive episode are diminished interest or pleasure in activities that the patient used to enjoy, substantial weight loss or weight gain, loss of appetite, increased or decreased sleep, loss of energy, and fatigue. Depressed individuals often feel worthless, hopeless, helpless, and guilty of real or imaginary transgressions. They have difficulty concentrating and remembering and have trouble making decisions. Finally, they have persistent thoughts of dying and suicidal thoughts, some with a plan and some without a plan; some have attempted suicide. To meet criteria for a depressive episode, symptoms must not result from drug or alcohol abuse.

According to the World Health Organization (2004), MDD is the leading cause of disability in the United States. The lifetime prevalence of major depression is 10%–25% for women and 5%–12% for men (Oquendo et al., 2005). Probably because it is so common, depression entered the American consciousness earlier than other mental disorders and is one of the least stigmatized. Major depressive disorder, as it is now called, has been identified as a phenomenon in many ancient cultures, including ancient Greece, where it was described by Hippocrates. It was well known by the name of melancholia during the Renaissance. In the 17th century, Dürer created a very well-known lithograph that depicts Melancholia as a woman staring pensively into space.

A popular myth regarding depression is that it is a passing condition and can be fairly easily cured with antidepressants. Depressed patients seeing a psychiatrist for the first time often believe that there is a "happy pill" that they can take—a pill that will take care of all current and future depressions, causing their ailments to disappear without a trace. The reality is far less rosy. Antidepressants are effective only in two-thirds of patients having an episode of major depression. The remission is often incomplete, and depression is often recurrent.

The term "subsyndromal depression" describes a pattern of depression that typically presents as low energy and anhedonia (lack of pleasure) but does not meet criteria for a major depressive episode. "Double depression" is a popular term that is used to describe a person who, even at his or her best, has low mood (dysthymia) and develops episodes of major depression at his or her worst. These two terms can be very useful when one is discussing depression with patients' families because they are colloquial terms often used by laypersons and psychotherapists.

Some prominent psychiatrists in the field, notably Hagop Akiskal, believe that MDD is a form of bipolar illness without mania. This school of thought emphasizes mood cyclicity rather than discrete episodes of mania or depression as the main syndrome of the illness (Akiskal & Benazzi, 2006). According to Akiskal's conceptualization, all mood disorders can be located on a "bipolar spectrum," with manic and depressive symptoms varying in their relative manifestations from person to person. This formulation can be very useful when one is discussing both MDD and BMD with families.

ENDOGENOUS VERSUS REACTIVE DEPRESSION

Depression and other mood disorders run in families. However, as is the case with most psychiatric disorders, it is a vulnerability to the illness rather than the illness itself that is inherited. Also as with other disorders, the heritability of depression is multifactorial; there are several and possibly many genes that give one an increased vulnerability to depression. The extent to which somebody is prone to developing depressive episodes depends on both nature (genes) and nurture (environment). Nature determines how many "depression-proneness" gene variants one inherits. The environment, particularly childhood stress, determines to what extent the neurochemical pathways underlying depression are susceptible to actually crossing the threshold that allow the illness to manifest itself. In this way, a person's genetic composition is akin to a suspension bridge. Some bridges are much more durable and less susceptible to the wear and tear of daily use and to corrosive environmental influences. In keeping with our analogy, a person with high genetic loading for depression will probably develop the disorder over his or her lifetime, regardless of the course that life takes, much as a wooden suspension bridge shows signs of day-to-day weathering. Persons with this kind of endogenous depression most often require treatment for life. On the other hand, patients with a low genetic loading for the disorder tend to develop depression reactively, that is, in response to an extraordinary and clearly identifiable event—much as an earthquake destabilizes even the sturdiest bridge. Persons with reactive depression almost always recover and, barring another catastrophic event, may not develop another depression.

RECOGNIZING AND DEALING WITH MILD DEPRESSION

Symptoms of depression can range in severity from very mild to completely incapacitating. Both depressed individuals and their families can confuse mild depression with the usual ups and downs of life. Mild and moderate depressive episodes usually begin with changes in behavior, whereas changes in mood come later, and people tend to identify their struggles as depression even later, if at all. Some realize they have had a depressive episode only after it is over. Others may not appreciate the nature of their depression until much later in life. For example, it is not uncommon for people to confide in their friends something like: "I had a hard time when I moved to Washington. I was probably depressed. I just didn't know it."

Persons with mild depression tend to have low energy, withdraw from their friends, reduce their social activities, and experience anhedonia. Their family, close friends, or coworkers may notice these differences, but individuals with mild depression either do not see a change or explain their behavior by saying that they "just don't feel like" doing things they used to enjoy doing. They just do not feel like going to a movie today, are not in the mood to see a friend, feel too tired from work or school to go to a party, or do not feel like taking their weekly bike ride in Central Park. Those who are mildly depressed sometimes also have changes in concentration and memory but similarly ascribe those symptoms to fatigue or too much work. This attribution may not be entirely inaccurate, as being overworked is a frequent cause of depression.

Families are rarely able to identify the signs of a first depression, whether it is mild or severe. On the other hand, they often can recognize the early warning signs of even a mild *subsequent* depressive episode and therefore are in the best position to help in its early stages. Early behavioral signs of a depressive episode can be very idiosyncratic but tend to follow a predictable sequence for each individual. Some examples are listening to music rather than to news in the car on the way to work; wearing a darker shade of lipstick; asking oneself, "Am I getting depressed?" while feeling well; or watching basketball on TV if this is not something one usually does. Some of the more common early signs of incipient depression are less frequent workouts and careless attire. Close family members and friends are often best positioned to notice these changes early on and should alert the depressed individual to their observations so treatment can be adjusted.

Some researchers have argued that mild depressions serve an

adaptive function in that they change people's behavior to their advantage when they face unachievable goals or unwinnable social situations (Nesse, 2000). For example, more passive depressed individuals with little initiative are less likely to waste precious years of their lives pursuing hopeless romantic involvement or unfeasible careers. However, even if this were true, it is clear that under almost all circumstances, there is no benefit to being depressed. In fact, prolonged depression can harm careers, families, and interpersonal relationships and, in addition, cause lasting deleterious effects on memory and concentration. Therefore even mild depressions need to be identified and treated.

However, at this early stage, families of patients who are in the best position to see early signs of depression tend to either miss or minimize symptoms. Often they deny them altogether, explaining them as a passing phase, or as a reaction to a particular set of circumstances. Depressed patients themselves are often of little help because they are still not knowledgeable of depressive symptoms. Thus at this stage, educating the family about early symptoms of depression can be crucial both to getting the depressed person into treatment and to the treatment's success. The following is an example of such an education: A successful businesswoman is trying to understand early signs of depression in her 18-year-old daughter.

Esther, if you are able to recognize the first subtle signs of Rachel's depression, then you can alert her psychiatrist and he can adjust her medication and prevent a serious episode. In the earlier stages she feels fairly well—the same or almost the same as usual, and for that reason she cannot tell that an episode is about to begin. You know her very well. You have told me that when she starts getting depressed, she starts taking naps after school. This is a very astute observation— make sure you call her psychiatrist when this happens.

In this example, I validate Esther's observations of changes in her daughter's behavior and frame them as the first signs of her depression. As a result of this discussion, Esther has learned when to ask Rachel about her mood and when to contact a psychiatrist.

RECOGNIZING AND DEALING WITH WORSENING DEPRESSION

The main signs of worsening depression are increased irritability and sensitivity as well as a negative outlook on life. As depression becomes more severe, in addition to lower energy, fatigue, and other symptoms, the person starts experiencing depressed mood, sadness, physical exhaustion, and hopelessness about the future. Moderate depression is also characterized by feelings of guilt over real or imaginary transgressions. Repetitive thoughts of past mistakes, deemed irrevocable by the depressed person, often further aggravate a sense of hopelessness about the future. Some people feel increasingly lonely; others feel that they either have failed or are failing in life. Many develop somatic symptoms such as back pain, headaches, and flu-like body aches.

As their condition deteriorates, patients may experience strange sensations like numbness, ringing in the ears, and sometimes heavy or burning eyelids. Some may develop increasing anxiety and panic attacks. As depression becomes increasingly serious, the afflicted individual often reveals his or her his or her symptoms to family members. Some start telling family members and friends that they are depressed, ill, or tired. Others start complaining about their jobs, parents, children, spouses, or friends. Worsening depression is much more noticeable to outsiders. Moderately depressed people may look sad and withdrawn, may cry, may have glassy or red eyes, or may have less-than-perfect hygiene. Depressed patients often are not as careful in choosing their clothes or in putting on makeup as they usually are.

Although loved ones may notice that the person has not been him- or herself lately, they often do not recognize the symptoms as depression. As a treating clinician, you can both help them to distinguish symptoms of depression from healthy behavior and encourage them to remember such symptoms for future reference in case depression recurs. You can start this conversation by asking what exactly "not being himself" means: it may mean worrying slightly more than usual or it may mean profound changes in behavior. Some family members can be shy or inarticulate and may need several probing questions to help them arrive at an answer.

> A vague "he's just not himself" was offered by the girlfriend of a 50-year-old patient who was slipping into a depressive episode following the loss of his job on Wall Street. I asked, "What do you mean by 'He's not been himself?'" She elaborated, "He is not working on three different projects, as is usual for him, and does not believe he will ever get a good job again. This is not like him." I probed further. "Does he look different?" She responded, "He sometimes forgets to shave, which is so unlike him." Reflecting back the valuable observations she had shared, I told her, "You know, in somebody for whom this behavior is out of character, like your boyfriend, all these could be signs of depression, and your boyfriend may be getting seriously depressed. It would be good if you could remember these symptoms so you can recognize his depression if it happens again. Now let us talk about how to get him help."

In this example I needed two follow-up questions to obtain a clear picture of the patient's depression.

Although at this stage, some families are still unaware that their loved ones are depressed, if you have a discussion similar to this one, at least one family member will know that the depressed person is not well. However, even in cases in which family members are able to recognize symptoms, individuals with depression still may be reluctant to seek treatment. Patients often cite a fear of the stigma surrounding depression, a dislike of medications, and a fear of becoming dependent on them, in addition to a feeling that they should be able to will themselves out of the depressed state, as reasons for their reluctance. These families need reassurance that a psychiatrist is just another specialist MD to be consulted just as one would consult an endocrinologist. However, in exceptional cases, if neither the depressed patient nor his or her family is willing to see a psychiatrist, antidepressant treatment can be initiated in a general practitioner's office with the goal of eventually transitioning the patient to a psychiatrist's office.

As I discussed in Chapter 4, I believe that psychiatric medications should be prescribed by psychiatrists whenever possible.

This belief is mainly based on my frequent encounters with unde-
sired and unrecognized manic episodes, panic attacks, and ex-
trapyramidal symptoms that resulted from psychotropic drugs
prescribed by internists, family doctors, and even surgeons. Psychiatric differential diagnosis is not a trivial matter, and recognizing subtle medication-induced changes in psychiatric presentation
can be particularly difficult. For that reason, treatment with antidepressants or other drugs ideally should be initiated only after a
thorough mental status examination and history-taking, followed
by frequent office visits. Typically, only psychiatrists have proper
specialized training and practices that are dedicated to providing
this type of care. Examples of how to talk about referring to a psychiatrist can be found in Chapter 6.

RECOGNIZING AND COPING
WITH SEVERE DEPRESSION

Severe depression is a potentially life-threatening condition.
Suicide rates in the depressed population (unipolar and bipolar)
can be as high as 15%. Anxiety and panic attacks increase suicide
risk (Kilbane et al., 2009). When a family recognizes that a loved
one is severely depressed and refers him or her for psychiatric
consultation, they may be saving that person's life. Unfortunately,
however, as previously discussed, families often misjudge the severity of depression in their loved ones and may appreciate it only
retrospectively after a failed suicide attempt or, tragically, a completed suicide.

Most tellingly, people with severe depression have difficulty
functioning in one or more spheres of their lives: at work, at home,
with their relatives and friends, during leisure time. Those who are
severely depressed may often be late for work or miss work entirely, may have trouble completing assignments, and may have
difficulty dealing with routine work activities and politics. At
home, they may stay in bed on weekends, may stop cleaning the
house, and may not be able to do even routine house chores. They
may become withdrawn, apathetic, and even lethargic. People
with this severe depression "disappear." For example, they stop

seeing and calling friends or coming to family functions. When they do come to family gatherings, they may look withdrawn and ill.

Alternatively, they may also become very irritable and have a short fuse. As a result, they may start having conflicts, both at work and at home, which may lead to job loss or marital strife. Little irritants, everyday frictions that occur in all families, get to them, causing frequent arguments. In individuals with severe depression, soothing and stress-reducing techniques such as watching TV, reading, going to movies, or playing sports may not work.

People with severe depression can become suicidal. I deal with this issue at length in the chapter on suicide. Here it should suffice to say that families are in the best position to identify the suicidal individual and guide him or her into much-needed treatment. Persons at high risk are professional white males age 50 and up who have suffered a public setback or failure in their careers, or a job loss with drastic decrease in income and social standing. Individuals who begin to vocalize hopelessness about the future, talk about not seeing any good solutions or options, or are tense, anxious, and even confused are at high risk of suicide. Clinicians should develop a sensitive ear for such a narrative, as it can often belie serious depression and may warrant an urgent psychiatric referral. The following is an example of such a conversation with the wife of a businessman who lost a lot of his and his friends' money after the collapse of his Internet startup.

> I asked: "How is he reacting to this disaster?" She responded: "He's been lying in bed all day and has not been returning phone calls. He hasn't been to the gym in 2 weeks, which is unheard of for him." I then inquired: "Has he talked like his life is not worth living?" She said, "Sometimes." Then I replied: "You know, this sounds pretty serious. Your husband is behaving like he has a very serious depression and may be having suicidal thoughts. Has he seen a psychiatrist? He needs to be evaluated for depression, and soon. Here is the phone number of the psychiatrist I work with. Please call him today."

A discussion like this takes 2 minutes but can bring somebody into treatment and sometimes avert a suicide.

Families must know that talking to suicidal loved ones can prevent suicide attempts, however difficult such conversations may be. By talking to them and telling them that the family needs them alive and well (and by not being critical!), families can make them feel needed, wanted, and understood. When talking to suicidal and depressed relatives, family members can try to reduce their anguish about their real or imagined failures. Finally, by discussing possible suicidal plans, families can better understand the seriousness of a suicidal threat and can hospitalize the depressed family member before the attempt actually happens.

PSYCHOTIC DEPRESSION

Some people with severe depression develop a distorted sense of reality that can reach levels of psychosis. The transition from reality to psychosis can be gradual and difficult to notice or abrupt and obvious. Typical examples are delusions of guilt such as an erroneous belief that an insignificant past mistake resulted in irreversible damage to them, their families, or somebody else. Other frequent psychotic symptoms include disorganized thinking and behavior, often with catatonia and mutism and somatic delusions of having an incurable illness or unusual and bizarre bodily sensations: feeling blood rushing in one's veins or hearing sounds and noises. Naturally, psychotic depressions can be even scarier than depressions without psychosis for families. The good news is that depressions with psychosis respond to treatment as readily as those without. When given an opportunity, you should reassure families that this is the case, as in the following conversation with the wife of a depressed superintendant who thought he was being watched by an Albanian secret service because he immigrated.

Do not worry. His ideas about the secret service do not make sense because, as a result of depression, his thinking got distorted. These ideas—we call them delusions—are a part of his depression and should improve quickly with medications.

SNAPPING OUT OF IT

Many families unfamiliar with mental illness believe that people choose to be depressed in response to stressful events in their lives and can "snap out" of depression if they want to. To some degree, this attitude is not uncommon even in families who have experience dealing with depression. This belief persists because persons with depression are not able to act in ways that might help them improve. People with depression tend to isolate rather than see friends, lie in bed rather than exercise, sleep too much rather then get up early and go to work, and stop participating in pleasurable activities rather than increase such participation. Depression deprives one of the ability to do what is needed to get cured. Families often get frustrated with what they perceive as lack of effort on the part of depressed individuals to do what it takes to get better. They need to be educated that the behavior they see in their depressed relatives is biological and "snapping out of it" is not feasible.

Barbara, he cannot just pull himself out of depression, which is a biological illness. He can do certain things that will help him improve with medications—exercising, socializing, and not drinking can go a long way in helping him improve faster. However, for him, doing all this is like running 10 km with a 104 degree fever—painful and difficult. Let us have a little more patience and give medications and therapy a chance to work.

ANTIDEPRESSANTS AND OTHER MEDICATIONS

With direct-to-consumer advertising and the recent negative publicity regarding the effectiveness of drug treatment for depression and suicide warnings on drug labels, many families are confused about the effectiveness of medications for depression. Most families of depressed individuals have heard of SSRIs and have been influenced by TV advertising for the latest antidepressants and for second-generation antipsychotics. Many families

are Internet savvy and read information posted by drug manu-
facturers, keep up with the many relevant blogs, and participate in
chatrooms. Your main challenge in talking with families about
medications for depression lies in explaining their similar rates
of effectiveness, addressing differences in side effects, and discussing any degree of increase in a risk of suicide. Another important issue to bring up is the duration of treatment. All these issues
are pretty standard and can be addressed in one brief conversation.

All antidepressants have pretty similar effectiveness:
About two out of three people respond on the first try. Psy-
chiatrists recommend an antidepressant based on which side
effects the patient finds least objectionable, and she should
stay on it for about a year after the depression resolves. The
additional risk of suicide with antidepressant treatment is
not significant but anything that she says about killing her-
self or not wanting to live should be taken seriously.

ELECTROCONVULSIVE THERAPY

Electroconvulsive therapy (ECT) is a valuable treatment for
depression similar in its effectiveness to that of a typical antidepressant (Sackeim et al., 2008). I believe that because it is used
mostly for treatment-resistant cases, its usefulness is underrated.
Aside from side effects affecting memory, which are real but do
not cause functional impairment, ECT has fewer side effects than
antidepressants. Antidepressants' side effects affect many body
systems and include rashes, electrolyte imbalance, and liver function test elevations, to name a few. Side effects from ECT are related almost exclusively to the short-term anesthesia needed to
properly administer the treatment. Nevertheless, most families of
patients with depression are fearful of ECT and use it as the treatment of last resort only after failures of single antidepressants and
their combinations. There are two reasons for this reluctance: the
difficult-to-eradicate public image of ECT as torture, exemplified
by the movie *One Flew Over the Cuckoo's Nest,* and the need to

interrupt the patient's everyday life for either inpatient or outpatient ECT treatment. When talking with families, physicians should advocate its use as a treatment option rather than as a last resort, while emphasizing its safety and debunking the myth that ECT is a form of torture. I also acknowledge and discuss families' concerns about memory loss and disruption of patients' lifestyle. The following vignette is an example of a discussion with the boyfriend of a 35-year-old woman with psychotic depression who has been refusing the ECT treatment recommended by her psychiatrist.

> *There is a reason why her psychiatrist is suggesting ECT: Although Nancy does not have severe depression, after several months on antidepressants, she has not improved. Yes, with ECT there is some memory loss, but there are none of the side effects not uncommon with antidepressants—weight gain, dry mouth, decreased sex drive. Neal, ECT is safe, and depression improves quickly, sometimes after one treatment. Think about it.*

HOW DEPRESSION IMPROVES AND RESOLVES

Families often ask how long it takes for depression to improve but think that they know how it improves and do not ask questions about this aspect of the illness. In my experience the course of improvement of depressive symptoms is not straightforward and is neither abrupt nor smooth. Before having the patient start the antidepressant treatment, I often describe to families (and patients) how depression may resolve. Typically, mood changes with antidepressant treatment are experienced as sudden improvement for a day or so, almost back to baseline, followed by return to depression, followed by another good day and then up-and-down staggered recovery until finally good days far outnumber the bad days. Patients' functional improvement when they return to their old levels of activity and productivity is typically smoother than their symptomatic improvement. An explanation of how depression improves in concrete terms might help some ambivalent family members feel that they are part of the treatment team and help them accept antidepressant treatment for their loved ones. This description of improvement can be used verbatim:

Typically, mood changes with antidepressant treatment are experienced as sudden improvement for a day or so, almost back to baseline, followed by return to depression, followed by another good day and then by up-and-down staggered recovery until finally good days far outnumber the bad days. Eventually she will have mostly good days with an occasional bad day, like all of us.

RISK OF FUTURE DEPRESSIONS

According to research studies, if medications are discontinued, the risk of a second episode of major depression after resolution of the first one is about 50%. The risk of a third episode increases to 70%, and the risk of a fourth episode increases to 90% (Solomon et al., 2000). One study indicated that after 15 years off antidepressants, 85% of patients will have relapsed (Mueller et al., 1999). For treatment purposes, this means that antidepressants can be stopped several months after the end of the first depressive episode but should be continued indefinitely from the second episode on. Families must be given this information at the outset so they can appreciate that depression, although initially episodic, is a whole-body illness that becomes chronic when it recurs.

Both patients and their family members sometimes have difficulty accepting the recommendation for ongoing and indefinite antidepressant treatment. To help them be more hopeful, you could say that none of us can see the future, and new, better treatments might become available that may actually cure depression. Still, in these cases they should be made aware of the wealth of research data regarding the harmful effects of untreated depression on cardiovascular health and even on the course of some cancers. Understanding this from the beginning helps families recognize depression as a serious biological illness, encourages treatment adherence, and improves chances for proper follow-up with a psychiatrist. As always, analogies with chronic medical illness such as hypertension and diabetes, and the reminder that all medications, medical and psychiatric, have side effects that sometimes are unavoidable, make understanding this easier.

Jane, because he just had his second depressive episode, his illness has become chronic and chances are 9 out of 10 that he will become depressed again if his antidepressant is stopped. Depression affects cardiovascular health, and given his recent cardiac bypass, it is even more imperative that he continue to take the drug. Please talk to the psychiatrist about sexual side effects, and maybe she can switch him to an antidepressant that does not have them.

PROTECTING THE EMOTIONAL AND PHYSICAL HEALTH OF THE FAMILY

Finally, depression can be contagious. Studies have shown that living with a depressed individual even for several months can lower your mood and even cause depression. This applies to populations as different as American college roommates and peasant families in rural Mexico. Living with a depressed close relative—a spouse, a child, or a parent—and being his or her caregiver can be very stressful. Whether stress is the only mechanism by which the depressed mood "contagion" occurs is unclear. However, regardless of the etiology, I warn close family members of depressed individuals that they need to take care of themselves and watch for signs and symptoms of their own depression (Sheffield, 1999, 2003; Steele et al., 2009).

Caregivers often hide their depression from the "designated" depressed person in the family. Sometimes both spouses hide their depression from each other either in order not to burden the other person or because they are afraid to be labeled mentally ill and stigmatized. Alas, as I mention several times in this book, stigma starts in the family. It is not uncommon for spouses to hide their antidepressant bottles from each other. Ironically, sometimes they are hiding the same antidepressant in the same bedroom without knowing it. I recommend discussing these scenarios with family members with a sense of humor.

> *Steve, you really need to take care of yourself. You are burning the candle at both ends, trying to keep a full business schedule and also respond to your wife's every need. Do you seriously think you can take every business trip and make every business meeting and be home at 6 PM every day to help your wife take her daily walk in Central Park? If this continues, you are going to run out of your stress hormones. Watch out for your own depression! How about getting some home help?*

MDD is a complicated illness. There is simply no way to cover *all* its aspects and how to discuss them with patients' families. Nevertheless, the material in this chapter, together with that covered in Parts I, II, and IV, should cover most of what is needed to confidently talk with families about MDD.

CHAPTER ELEVEN

Generalized Anxiety Disorder and Panic Disorder

Although not as serious as schizophrenia and bipolar disorder, both generalized anxiety disorder (GAD) and panic disorder (panic D/O) can be quite debilitating for patients. GAD and panic D/O are considered by some to be milder disorders than major depression, but this is not quite true. After experiencing a single episode of major depression, half of patients will never have another depressive episode. In contrast, GAD and panic D/O are lifelong illnesses that do not improve if left untreated. The two disorders are clinically and neurochemically related, and their pharmacological treatments are similar. For that reason I discuss them in the same chapter.

Generally, families are much less concerned with anxiety and panic than with schizophrenia and mood disorders, and your discussions with the families of individuals with these illnesses will not be as frequent. However, because GAD and panic D/O can have severely impairing affects on patients' functioning, it is still important to address all aspects of the disorders with family members. Moreover, both disorders have been recognized as factors that make the course of other psychiatric illnesses more severe and increase the risk of suicide (Goodwin & Hamilton, 2001, 2002;

Kilbane et al., 2009). Thus both disorders deserve to be taken seriously.

In the *DSM-IV-TR*, GAD and panic D/O both fall into the category of anxiety disorders but are classified as two separate illnesses. Recent studies of twins suggest that genetically, GAD is much closer to MDD than previously thought (Gorwood, 2004). Similar studies for panic D/O are lacking. Clinically, many patients with panic D/O have GAD, and many patients with GAD never develop panic attacks, although some do. The severe anxiety that can precede panic attacks is sometimes experienced as physical discomfort, for example, as nausea, sweating, and the frequent need to urinate, so the two phenomena can be confused. However, panic D/O can be clearly distinguished by the patient's overwhelming fear of dying or losing his or her mind, which is absent in severe anxiety.

Although GAD and panic D/O are clinically related, conversations with families about them tend to be different. Discussions with families about GAD tend to start with "He is just so nervous" or "She is such a worrier" and focus on anxiety as if it were a character trait. Whether a particular behavior is a character feature or a symptom of a mental illness is a fascinating subject that is beyond the scope of this book. In discussions with families, however, a symptom can be defined as a feature treatable with medications, whereas character can be changed only with long-term psychotherapy, if at all. On the other hand, discussions about panic D/O usually focus on panic attacks as a distinct and often disturbing syndrome, similar to asthma attacks, that relatives are hopeful can be diminished or eradicated with medication. Conversations about panic D/O usually center on whether medication treatment is needed and, if so, for how long.

GENERALIZED ANXIETY DISORDER

According to the *DSM-IV-TR*, for a person to be diagnosed with generalized anxiety disorder, he or she needs to experience excessive anxiety and worry on a regular basis about a number of events or activities, for example, at work, in school, or in his or her personal life. A person with GAD finds it difficult to control his or her worries, which have physical symptoms such as restlessness or the feeling of being keyed up or on edge, fatigue or irritability, muscle tension, difficulty falling or staying asleep, difficulty concentrating, or the feeling that one's mind has gone blank. In some cases GAD may result in nausea, vomiting, and chronic stomachaches. GAD is different from specific phobias or fears in that the anxiety and worry are not confined to a specific issue, such as being uncomfortable in public (as in social phobia), gaining weight (as in anorexia nervosa), or having a serious illness (as in hypochondriasis). As always in the *DSM*, the symptoms are not the direct physiological effects of a substance (e.g., a drug of abuse, a medication) or a medical illness.

GAD is twice as common in women as in men. The disorder often starts in adolescence and continues chronically. The majority of patients with GAD are acutely aware of their anxiety. In its milder forms it can manifest as an episodic but easily identifiable feeling of nervousness, worry, or inner restlessness with some queasiness—similar to the feeling of having butterflies in one's stomach—feelings most people experience before a presentation or big exam. For people with GAD, however, these symptoms are present much more frequently and are often inhibiting. Despite the disorder's chronic nature, its course varies, depending on life stress and family and other emotional support systems. Furthermore, GAD is treatable both with medication and psychotherapy.

The anxious feelings that are characteristic of the illness can take varied forms among patients. Also, as with any mental illness, different patients can have different levels of insight into their illness. In fact, in a minority of cases, people with GAD may not think that their anxiety is excessive and are surprised when their loved ones tell them that they should not be worrying so much. It is surprising that awareness of their anxiety may not be related to its severity. In other words, some people with severe and debilitating anxiety may not even know that they are anxious, whereas those with very mild anxiety may be acutely aware of their symptoms.

Some patients may be so anxious and tense that others, including members of their family, have difficulty being around them because they start feeling anxious (and often angry) themselves. Patients like these often cannot appreciate repeated requests from their families that they calm down because they are making everybody "crazy." In these instances, the loved ones of people who suffer from GAD may ask for your guidance on how to tell their anxious relatives that they have a problem and need to seek help. Nevertheless, before you suggest a possible course of action, you should familiarize yourself with the patient's and relatives' attitudes toward and beliefs about mental health practitioners and psychiatric medications. Your response should then be tailored to the family's attitude regarding a diagnosis of GAD and treatment of it. Patients and families with no previous experience with psychiatry may be more receptive to the terms "nervousness" and "nerves." Alternatively, those who have previously been treated by psychiatrists and therapists may actually find it a relief to be told that they have an identifiable and treatable psychiatric illness.

When talking with the families of patients with GAD, your first task is to establish whether the patient in question does have GAD or the family's concerns are overblown. If a GAD diagnosis is plausible, your main goal is to frame it as a treatable biological entity, particularly when family members think that it is just his or her character. Your secondary goal is to suggest to the family an appropriate treatment modality, which typically is supportive psychotherapy for a mild disorder and medications for more severe anxiety. Because anxiety symptoms in GAD, like anxiety symptoms in general, are stress dependent and increase in stressful situations, it is prudent to be conservative in recommending pharmacotherapy for adolescents and young adults, whose symptoms may improve without medications in a less stressful situation or environment. The first of the two following vignettes involves the family of an 18-year-old high school student with mild GAD, whereas the second involves the father of a 40-year-old teacher with a personality disorder and severe untreated GAD.

> I started with a clarification: "Anxiety is not necessarily a bad thing. Being anxious before exams gives you some extra adrenaline,

which usually helps you perform better. What makes you think that her anxiety is a problem?" The mother answered: "She can't sleep and gets even more high strung than usual during exams." I responded with a conservative suggestion: "I understand: She is worrying about her performance all the time, making herself miserable, as well as everybody around her. I understand why you are concerned. Although I could prescribe her medications, I am reluctant to do so for someone this young. We need to understand better exactly what pressure she thinks she is under. My suggestion would be that she see a psychologist or clinical social worker who can give her support as well as help her to gain some perspective on the importance of good grades in her life."

I hear you saying that she is very hard to be around and that none of the therapists she has seen over the years seem to be of help. From what you are telling me, and from what I saw in my office, she has a pretty serious illness. The name of the illness is generalized anxiety disorder, or GAD, and it is treatable. It is a chronic illness, so the fact that she has always been like this does correspond to its natural course. People who have it are always anxious about something. That "something" or the subject of their worry changes, but the anxiety remains. Because psychotherapy has not helped, it is likely that her GAD is quite severe and requires medication, possibly more than one. Let me give you a referral to a psychopharmacologist.

In many cases either the GAD sufferer or one or more of his or her loved ones are opposed to treatment. In mild cases, the patient is often encouraged by the family to tough out the symptoms on his or her own. The best way to overcome this reluctance is to emphasize that seeking treatment is not a sign of weakness, and that in many cases its duration can be short, until the stressful time in the patient's life is over. I find an analogy between GAD and allergies very helpful in making my case:

I would just like to emphasize that GAD is a real illness that needs treatment. You would treat allergies, wouldn't you? GAD is not that different. The symptoms come and go

depending on stress, and sometimes medications are needed
when stress is high, just as a person with allergies would
need medications when the pollen count is high.

In severe cases, resistance to treatment often comes from the inability to recognize the symptoms of the disorder as psychological. Severe GAD can be quite debilitating, but the most disabling symptoms can be perceived as physical symptoms. Many patients experience somatic anxiety, which manifests as though something is amiss with one or several body parts or internal systems. Different areas of the skin, most often the face, may feel tight, numb, or tingly. Gastrointestinal symptoms most often take the form of nausea and even vomiting, although frequent bowel movements and constipation are also possible. People frequently report irritability, dizziness, or headaches. Dry mouth and burning eyelids are also possible. Finally, a person with severe anxiety usually feels overall malaise, as if he or she has the flu. In cases like these, although the person may be willing to seek treatment, he or she may not view psychiatric treatment as the most appropriate approach. Patients and family members in this category require very straightforward psychoeducation to help them overcome their skepticism and recognize that a mental disorder can take the form of a physical illness. In these cases it usually pays to speak directly to the body-mind relationship. The level of discussion depends on the family's level of interest in and familiarity with the neurobiology of anxiety. The following example illustrates how to start the discussion in general terms and then go into specifics, if the family is interested.

The psyche and the body are not separate entities, in
truth. The brain is part of the body—do you accept that?
With GAD, anxiety spills over into your body on a continual
basis, and this can be harmful to both the body and the mind
if left untreated. If you find this explanation helpful, I can be
more specific. Chronic anxiety, as in GAD, is your mind and
body's fight-or-flight response to danger or stress that has
gotten out of control. In cases of acute stress, it is controlled
by the hypothalamus and pituitary gland in the brain, which

*send neurochemical signals to the adrenals, which in re-
sponse release cortisol, insulin, and norepinephrine. These
hormones mobilize your body's resources in the short term
for faster overdrive action: Your heartbeat becomes faster,
the blood supply is richer, metabolic rates are higher, the
senses become more acute, and concentration improves. In
the long term, they exhaust these resources—it becomes difficult to concentrate, people become restless or fatigued, the
senses become dull or process information incorrectly. We
can talk more about this, but the bottom line is that your
daughter is suffering from a neurochemical illness. If she
takes the right medication, she may feel better in as little as
24 hours.*

PANIC DISORDER

A panic attack is an episode of intense fear that occurs suddenly
and with distinct physical symptoms such as palpitations, a pound-
ing heart, accelerated heart rate, chest pain or discomfort, sweating, shaking, shortness of breath or a sense that one is choking,
nausea, dizziness or lightheadedness, feelings of unreality (de-
realization) or detachment from oneself (depersonalization),
numbness or tingling sensations (paresthesias), and chills or hot
flashes. The presence of two or three symptoms may be considered a limited-symptom panic attack. Panic D/O is diagnosed in
cases of recurrent panic attacks that are not due to either a physical illness or specific phobias, such as claustrophobia (fear of
closed spaces) or social phobia (fear of social situations).

Simply put, panic attack is a state of extreme fear with physical
symptoms. The fear is either of dying (because these physical symptoms reach an intensity that feels dangerous) or of losing one's
mind (because it can no longer process the troubling thoughts). In
the latter case, one's thoughts can either be racing or feel blocked.
Panic D/O can be viewed as a more severe form of GAD, when
somatic manifestations of anxiety become so severe that they appear life threatening. Indeed, most patients with panic D/O also
have concomitant GAD.

Panic D/O can be categorized as early and late onset. Early-onset panic attacks appear when a person is his or her late teens or early 20s. These attacks tend to be more severe and more persistent and are a sign of a more severe psychopathology. Of all the associated psychiatric problems—depression, bipolar disorder, OCD, and phobias included—early-onset panic D/O is associated with the worst prognosis. For this reason, early-onset panic D/O needs to be treated upon diagnosis, and aggressively. Late-onset panic D/O develops typically when people are in their 40s with increased life stresses, responsibilities, and burdens. These tend to be more episodic and come and go with stress. Under the right circumstances, patients with late-onset panic D/O can be symptom free and off medications for long periods of time.

The first panic attack, also called a herald panic attack, can be indescribably frightening, partly because the person who is having it has never experienced anything like it before and has no point of reference. I would imagine it feels similar to being waterboarded. Later panic attacks can be as severe, but the patient may at least understand the cause. Some panic attacks continue to feel like imminent death, despite multiple reccurrences, just because the symptoms are so painful. Sometimes fears can reach delusional intensity, resulting in panic attacks with psychosis (Galynker, Ieronimo, Perez-Aquino, Lee, & Winston, 1996).

The most frequent presentation of panic D/O seen by non-psychiatrists is crushing chest pain that feels like a heart attack. The medical workup is invariably negative, but it does not make the feelings any less real. Since the pain is sudden and intense, most patients do not see their regular doctors for it and instead go directly to the emergency room. Eventually—typically after several negative workups, some of them invasive—they are referred to a psychiatrist. Unfortunately, some patients may also have mild to moderate coronary artery disease and may get unnecessary invasive procedures, including stents, before they are properly diagnosed. Under these circumstances a good approach is to suggest the need for a psychiatric consultation. In doing so, I suggest equating it with a consultation by another medical professional that is unlikely to lead to intensive procedures, as in the following example.

> *You have been helping your husband get the right treatment, but you did not take him to see a psychiatrist! Chest pains could be a symptom of a panic attack, which is a lot easier to treat than angina, and you will not need an invasive procedure. I strongly recommend that he see a psychiatrist to rule out panic attacks before he sees a cardiologist who is a stent specialist.*

Difficulty breathing and hyperventilation, or globus hystericus, is another frequent symptom. Generally, patients more readily recognize this occurrence as psychiatric in nature and do not go to the emergency room, and instead make an appointment with a psychiatrist. A time-honored medical treatment for panic attacks with hyperventilation (which by now also is a folk remedy) is breathing into a paper bag. You can recommend trying this first if the family is resistant to medication treatment for panic D/O. If the ill individual has panic D/O, the paper bag is unlikely to help, but trying it first will make the family more receptive to psychopharmacology.

Nocturnal panic attacks are also common and may or may not be associated with nightmares. Sufferers typically wake up in the middle of the night in cold sweat and fear. They experience difficulty breathing and thinking, nausea, and even vomiting. For some, these symptoms are combined with tingling, numbness, and dizziness. Because the connection between the mind and the gastrointestinal system is more obvious than that with other body systems, patients are usually aware of the mental origins of their gastrointestinal upset. Sometimes, however, patients and their significant others cannot differentiate nocturnal panic attacks from nightmares. Patients' partners may tell you that they cannot sleep at night because the patients wake up screaming in the middle of the night. In this case families can benefit from considering panic attacks as a possible cause of their nocturnal distress, and from a little psychoeducation, as described in the following example.

I asked a series of questions: "Could you tell me in more detail what happens when your wife wakes up at night screaming? Is she very scared? Is she breathing rapidly? Is she sweating?" The husband said: "She is terrified, and all of the above." Here I mention the possibility of panic as a diagnosis: "I know that she has always been a very strong woman, but it is very possible she is having nocturnal panic attacks. Has anything happened in your life recently that is making her feel stressed out?" The husband mused, "Maybe selling the house." I then concluded with a diagnosis and a referral: "This stress may be too much for her, and since she is not one to easily admit that she is overwhelmed, nocturnal panic attacks are doing it for her. They are treatable—I can give you a referral to a psychiatrist."

Panic attacks are easily treatable with benzodiazepines, and less so with SSRIs. It is worth mentioning to patients and their families that these classes of drugs can have similar complicating effects when used for long-term treatment. In panic D/O they can engender physical dependency in that when they are stopped, the panic attacks return. In a sense, patients become dependent on psychotropic drugs to stay healthy. In contrast to SSRIs, benzodiazepines (lorazepam, clonazepam, alprazolam, diazepam, and others) also have addictive potential. They can make people euphoric, and some patients become addicted, getting into a vicious cycle of wanting and then needing higher doses of the drug to get the same effect. Drug addiction is a serious problem that is beyond the scope of this book but must be considered and discussed with families of those with panic D/O.

Given the addictive potential of benzodiazepines, they are not suggested for ongoing treatment. Chronic psychiatric patients are generally aware of this, and in my experience patients asking for benzodiazepines for ongoing treatment of anxiety and panic D/O are likely to have either a personal history of substance abuse or substance abuse in their families. Patients who are afraid of being addicted generally do not request benzodiazepines, and they can be reassured that as long as they take a steady prescribed dose, they will not become addicted. Most patients and families are also aware that benzodiazepine withdrawal can be quite severe. Few, however, realize that SSRI withdrawal syndrome can be quite difficult and equally debilitating. Although the current trend is to treat panic D/O with antidepressants, in terms of dependence and withdrawal, these two drug classes are more similar than many believe. All this can be explained to concerned families in a few sentences:

> *Your daughter may become dependent on her medication for not having panic attacks in the same way you depend on your antihypertensive pills to have normal blood pressure. When you stop medications, symptoms return. She will not get addicted as long as she takes them as prescribed. You can get withdrawal, so when the time comes, medications will need to be stopped carefully. But we'll cross that bridge when we get there.*

In conclusion, my typical message to relatives of individuals with early-onset panic attacks is that the illness is fully treatable, without residual symptoms, and that with proper psychiatric follow-up, either benzodiazepines or SSRIs can be used long term. For families of those with late-onset panic attacks, the message is the same, except that in cases of infrequent panic attacks, single doses of benzodiazepines can be used to interrupt a panic attack just as it is starting to develop, particularly if there is no history of substance abuse in the family. As always, I encourage family members to be helpful and involved. A typical example of such a conversation is given here.

> *Stella, we need to make sure George starts taking his medication. There is absolutely no reason for him to continue to have panic attacks when two pills a day can prevent them. He has never been dependent on drugs and there is little danger of him developing an addiction now. I would rather not give him SSRIs because they give him sexual side effects. Yes, he may need to take the medication for a long time, but he will probably be able to stop the medication once his business problems resolve. He needs your encouragement with this because the panic attacks sometimes prevent him from thinking clearly.*

CHAPTER 12

Obsessive-Compulsive Disorder

Obsessive-compulsive disorder (OCD) is diagnosed when a person has obsessions or compulsions that are seriously incapacitating. Obsessions are recurrent and persistent thoughts, impulses, or images that are experienced as intrusive and inappropriate and cause distress. These go beyond excessive worries about real-life problems. The person fails in his or her attempts to ignore or suppress such thoughts, impulses, or images, even though he or she recognizes that the obsessional thoughts, impulses, or images are a product of his or her own mind. Compulsions are repetitive behaviors (e.g., hand washing or checking whether the door has been locked) or mental activity (e.g., praying or counting) that the person feels compelled to perform according to rigid, ritualistic rules. Compulsions may or may not occur in response to obsessions. For the diagnosis of OCD to be made, the obsessions or compulsions must cause distress or significantly interfere with the person's normal routine, work, school, or usual activities or relationships.

OCD became relatively well known to the public after it was featured in two popular movies with two well-known actors. In *As Good as It Gets*, Jack Nicholson renders a fairly benign portrait of an infinitely obnoxious yet somehow very likable "neat freak" who, after considerable coaching by Helen Hunt, manages to evolve into somebody capable of an intimate relationship. *The Aviator* portrays a more malignant disorder that runs a relentless and deteriorating course.

Although the terms "OCD," "obsessive," and "compulsive" have become a part of the common vernacular, the colloquialisms applied most often do not align with the true diagnosis. At worst, people commonly described as workaholics or anal might qualify for a diagnosis of obsessive-compulsive personality disorder (OCPD). OCPD is one of 10 personality disorders currently recognized by the *DSM-IV-TR*. However, research indicates that very few people with OCD meet the criteria for OCPD (Fineberg, Sharma, Sivakumaran, Sahakian, & Chamberlain, 2007). In fact, an obsessive-compulsive personality may actually be advantageous for people living in the United States and other industrialized nations.

OCD is an illness that involves obsessions and compulsions. Classically, obsessions are thought to be ego-dystonic, that is, unpleasant or disturbing to the individual with OCD. Compulsions are thought to relieve negative emotions caused by obsessive thinking. A worry that one has left the stove on is an example of fairly benign obsessive thinking that causes a negative emotion of anxiety. Going back to the house to see if the stove is on is an example of a compulsive action that relieves the anxiety. When the syndrome of obsessive thinking followed by compulsive actions develops into a repeated pattern, it is called a ritual; having to check the stove multiple times would be an example of a checking ritual.

Public awareness of OCD, and particularly of washing, checking and ordering, is fairly high. Behavioral symptoms of OCD are fairly obvious. Because these are often physical rather than mental in nature, they are less stigmatizing. For all these reasons, families seek treatments for OCD more readily than for other disorders and actually tend to overdiagnose themselves and their loved ones. Talking to families about OCD often is very similar to talking about rashes and colds—the phrase "He has been obsessing all week" is used as easily as the phrase "He has been coughing all night."

The most common rituals involve checking, washing, ordering, hoarding, and over-immersing oneself in religious rituals. Of these, hoarding and washing are the most severe and can become extremely debilitating. Recent research suggests that hoarding in particular constitutes a more malignant form of the illness (Pertusa et al., 2008). Hoarding behaviors involve the accumulation of material things without regard to their usefulness. On the benign end of the spectrum are healthy people who do not throw out old things and keep them as mementos or "just in case." For example, I am sure you know a 30-something who is still holding onto his or her high school homework.

Hoarding becomes a symptom when it takes on a life of its own and begins interfering with one's functioning. As an example, let us consider the out-of-control buying and hoarding of jazz CDs. A hoarder with a penchant for jazz CDs might buy CDs he does not have time to open, let alone listen to. As a result, new CDs remain in boxes for months. At the beginning, the CD boxes could be confined to closets, but as hoarding progresses, the boxes might begin to appear in bedrooms and living rooms. At first they may remain on shelves and in corners, but over time, a hoarder will allow these boxes to pile up on the floor, eventually dominating his or her apartment. In more severe cases, opened and unopened delivery boxes and boxes of CDs could be lying everywhere, stacked or piled up on the floor for years, infested with rodents and insects. In this way, "collecting" can become haphazard and even bizarre. In the worst cases I have been directly exposed to, there were 5-feet-high piles of junk mail in the living room, and in the kitchen, plastic milk containers and both opened and unopened cans of food were stacked to the ceiling.

Hoarding is much more common than one would think. Because house calls are uncommon, doctors and even psychiatrists are often unaware that their patients or patients' relatives could have this problem. Unless you ask directly, it is possible to treat a hoarder for years without realizing there may be a problem beyond the patient's apartment being a mess. Interestingly, hoarders tend to normalize their behavior or even deny the existence of the problem and consider the state of their dwellings normal or, at the very least, acceptable. Nonetheless, this syndrome gets worse with age and may come to clinical attention when either the smell of spoiling food becomes too strong or multiplying mice and rats start disturbing the neighbors. If you suspect hoarding, the easiest way to determine the extent of the hoarding behavior is to ask to someone to describe the home of the potential hoarder in detail.

> I asked, "I am not sure what you mean when you say that your son buys stuff and keeps it. What does he buy?" The parents hesitantly answered, "CDs." I responded with several other questions: "Does he even take them out of the packaging? Does he open the boxes in which they are sent? Are the boxes confined to closets or does he also have them in the bedroom and in the living room?" "They are everywhere," replied the parents. I continued to ask for more detail: "How high do they pile up—ankle high, knee high, waist high, to the ceiling? Is there a path going from the entrance to the bedroom and to the bathroom? Is the kitchen usable?" The parents then said, "You can barely get to the bathroom and you can't even get into the kitchen—it is full of empty milk containers." I then wrapped up the conversation with a summary and a recommendation: "I see. It sounds like he has a serious hoarding problem. This is the bad news. The good news is that there are at least three medications effective for OCD with hoarding, and he has not tried any of them."

Hoarders often liken the accumulated junk to an extra body part or an organ vital to their survival. These patients react to the idea of putting a pile of old junk mail into a trash bag and taking it out with pain and devastation akin to that caused by an amputation or some other major surgery. Hoarded belongings, subconsciously, can become a symbol of one's work and accomplishments. Once they are taken out, usually because the apartment has been deemed a fire or hygienic hazard, the newly cleaned dwelling looks eerily empty. This emptiness can exacerbate low self-esteem, as if confirming one's failure in life. At the same time, piles of hoarded things are often a symbol of permanence, an irrational antidote to the transience of life. In this way, removing unopened boxes of CDs, knives, or coffee pots can feel like a death sentence. Because of the complex layers of the disorder, families of patients with OCD who, after organizing a cleanup, expect relief and gratitude instead find the hoarder experiencing intense grief similar to that experienced after the death of a loved one. They should be prepared for a negative reaction, as in the following example.

> *It is great that you are willing to pay for his apartment to be cleaned. Although you think his place is full of useless junk, he thinks otherwise and is therefore not thrilled. He feels the junk is part of his body. For that reason the necessary cleanup you are planning feels to him like the amputation of his leg. He will be missing his limb and will benefit from "painkillers" as well as a "prosthesis." It would be great if you can somehow reward him, say, by taking him on a trip and also fill the emptiness of the apartment with some new but necessary things, such as a new TV. His is ancient.*

A fear of contamination is another debilitating symptom of OCD. It can take different forms that result in different compulsions, such as frequently checking clothes for animal hair for fear of catching rabies or washing one's hands, the latter of which can be severe enough to result in bleeding hands and, at worst, complete incapacitation. Contamination fears and behaviors, though somewhat rooted in reality, are either irrational or vastly exaggerated. Most fears are rooted in a theoretically possible but highly improbable scenario.

The most common and "normal" fear is that of catching a disease by touching something used by many people in a public place, such as a door handle, hotel linens, or a toilet seat. An example of an OCD patient with contamination fears is an accountant who avoids touching door knobs, using tissues for protection when necessary, for fear of contracting HIV.

Checking and ordering are the least severe and troublesome symptoms of OCD. Families of orderly, driven, detail-oriented "compulsive" people may be unaware that their loved ones may have a mild form of the illness. Checking rituals usually involve verifying whether electric appliances, lights, or gas stoves have been left on or whether doors have been locked. Most of the time these are annoyances that do not result in much disability. Other fairly benign rituals border on superstition, such as following the same path to work or eating the same lunch in the same place for years. Other repetitive behaviors may be considered near-normal religious routines, such as saying a prayer 50 times after an argument. None of this usually results in family interactions of significance.

Although religion can be a secondary feature of the disorder, often when religious people develop OCD, their symptoms are religious in nature. Distinguishing obsessive and compulsive praying rituals from regular worship may in theory seem difficult. However, in reality, making this distinction is difficult only for those outside the cultural framework of the particular religion. Insiders (i.e., people of the same faith, parish, congregation, or community) can usually tell fairly easily who is praying compulsively. However, family members may or may not have this insight. For instance, in Jewish families it is very common for the children to become involved in a different branch of Judaism, either more liberal (e.g., Reform Judaism) or more conservative (e.g., ultra-Orthodox Judaism). In these cases, the person in the best position to judge whether the practiced religious rituals are appropriate, excessive, or bizarre would be an authority of the faith. This individual is often in the best position to convince the person with OCD to get treatment. Families may need help making these distinctions and finding their way to the appropriate religious figure, as in the following example.

> I started the discussion by agreeing with the family: "I have also noticed that Matthew has become very religious—he prays all the time when he is waiting for his appointment. This may or may not just be youthful rebellion against secular Jewish parents. However, being secular Jews—and, moreover, the parents he is rebelling against—you are not in a good position to make a judgment. Nether am I. Do you know his rabbi?" The father answered, "Not really," to which I responded, "It may still be a good idea to meet with him and tell him about your concerns. If Matthew is developing OCD or some other psychiatric problem, the rabbi is in the best position to make that judgment and to observe him more closely, if needed. You may disagree with his practice of Judaism, but on this issue he is your ally, and if Matthew needs help, at this moment in time he is much more likely to listen to his rabbi than to his parents.

In this example I identified the rabbi as an expert and an ally who could help the child and the family. By doing so, I validated the parents' needing to behave contrary to their secular principles and go to him for help for their son.

Compulsions are repeated behaviors that are undeterred by will or consequence. When this definition is used broadly, compulsive gambling, shopping, hair pulling, and other similar behaviors can be considered OCD. The term "obsessive-compulsive spectrum" describes a range of such behaviors. The broad spectrum of obsessive-compulsive-related disorders includes these behaviors as well as many others, such as somatoform disorders, impulse-control disorders, and tic disorders. Others, including drug-induced and non-psychiatric disorders, can overlap and show similar clinical pictures (Fornaro et al., 2009).

At present, both the very concept of OCPD and its boundaries are a matter of intense debate in the psychiatric community, which is well beyond the scope of this discussion. Patients who exhibit compulsive behaviors and their families, however, are likely to be confused about what is and what is not OCD and may need your guidance and reassurance. Newer pathological behaviors born from recent advances in medicine and information technology present particularly difficult challenges. Most of the newer obsessive-compulsive behaviors involve the Internet and smart phone. The most common problem I have seen in my practice is addiction to Internet pornography. Others include compulsive dating on online dating sites, compulsive online shopping, and compulsive gaming. The pathological consequences of these compulsions were highlighted recently by the lay press. In one such article, the *New York Times* reported how constant compulsive contact between teenage girls and their mothers, facilitated by mobile phones, leads to indecisiveness and an inability to make independent decisions on the part of the daughters.

Most likely you will be discussing compulsive phone use, texting, or similar behaviors with the families of anybody who they feel is doing something in excess. Although the jury is still out, common sense tells us that all current and future obsessive and compulsive behaviors are likely to have the same mechanism and

to be at least partially mediated by serotonin. My fairly conservative and reassuring message to families of OCD patients is as
follows: Any repetitive behavior that leads to disability can be considered a compulsion and an OCD. As such these behaviors should
be relieved by selective serotonin reuptake inhibitors and other
drugs that help relieve OCD symptoms. In the following example,
I convey this message to the father of a 26-year-old man who
spends hours every day after work playing video games and has
no personal life.

*I am not sure if he has OCD, but his gaming seems both
obsessive and compulsive: He thinks about his games a lot
and he cannot stop playing even though he wants to. Such
compulsive behaviors are treatable. It is a good idea for him
to be evaluated by a psychiatrist. He may need medication
or another type of therapy, and maybe help with some of the
other problems you mentioned to me, like shyness.*

CHAPTER THIRTEEN

Personality Disorders

Personality disorder is a persistent style of behavior in some or all spheres of an individual's life that is different from what is accepted in the person's culture. This pattern is manifested in thinking, affect (the range, intensity, lability and appropriateness of emotional response), interpersonal functioning, or impulse control. The behavioral style of people with personality disorder is inflexible and present across a broad range of personal and social situations and causes distress for them or people around them. Almost invariably, the behavior is stable and of long duration and started in childhood or adolescence. The *DSM-IV-TR* lists 10 personality disorders, grouped into three clusters.

Cluster A (odd or eccentric disorders) consists of three disorders. Paranoid personality disorder is characterized by irrational suspicions and mistrust of others, schizoid personality disorder involves lack of interest in social relationships, and schizotypal personality disorder is characterized by odd behavior or thinking.

Cluster B (dramatic or emotional disorders) consists of four distinct disorders. Antisocial personality disorder is characterized by persistent disregard for the law and the rights of others. Borderline personality disorder is characterized by a fear of abandonment, extreme black-and-white thinking, and instability in relationships, self-image, identity, and behavior. Histrionic personality disorder involves attention-seeking behavior that is often sexualized and is manifested in the context of shallow or exaggerated emotions. Narcissistic personality disorder is characterized by a pervasive pattern of grandiosity, a need for admiration, and a lack of empathy for others.

Finally, Cluster C (anxious or fearful disorders) is made up of three disorders. Avoidant personality disorder is characterized by feelings of inadequacy, extreme sensitivity to negative evaluation or real or perceived rejection, and avoidance of social interaction. Dependent personality disorder is manifested through excessive psychological dependence on other people. Finally, obsessive-compulsive personality disorder involves rigid conformity to rules and moral codes, and excessive orderliness.

The diagnosis of a personality disorder has pejorative connotations because it implies that the person's problem is not a treatable illness but a flaw. Since we are responsible for our own behavior, this also implies that the person is guilty of not being willing or able to change or improve—a personal failure. Furthermore, psychiatrists treat personality disorders not with medications but with psychotherapy.

Psychotherapy, in both theory and practice, involves active and willful changes in behavior rather than a passive transformation under the influence of psychotropic drugs. For the lay public, this may create an impression that personality disorder is not a real medical—or even psychiatric—disorder, but a personal failing. Finally, our own *DSM-IV-TR* puts personality disorders on Axis II, in a different category from depression and schizophrenia, which belong to Axis I. Such a hierarchy clearly indicates that Axis I disorders are more important and thus more biological. All this makes talking with families about personality disorders especially problematic.

To make discussions of personality disorders with families even more difficult, having any psychiatric disorder, including a personality disorder, can have implications in a court of law. The most obvious court cases involve violent crimes committed by mentally ill individuals while acutely manic or psychotic. There have been cases when a diagnosis of borderline personality disorder was used to excuse or justify heinous violent crimes, making perpetrators of such future crimes eligible for not-guilty pleas for reasons of insanity (Borderline Personality Disorder and the insanity defense). In much less trivial cases, personality disorders—either in combination with a history of childhood abuse or alone—can also be used as a defense in court.

For all these reasons, when talking to families about personality disorders in their relatives, I prefer, if possible, to avoid this term altogether and instead speak about features of character. I often talk about patients being shy, fragile, and vulnerable. These words have sympathetic and warm connotations and are not perceived as pathologizing or pejorative. For other symptoms and signs of personality disorders that are more disturbing to the family, I often use words and phrases such as "difficulty" and "a problem with," for example, "difficulty understanding how other people feel," "a problem with understanding what hurts other people," or "difficulty controlling emotions." Here is an example of such a conversation with the mother of a teenage girl with severe personality disorder:

> Patty, I understand why you are worrying about Jen: She is more emotional than other people. She also has difficulty being alone. When she is by herself, she feels that nobody cares about her and nobody will ever care again. The main reason she gets involved with all the wrong guys is because they are the ones who are around when she is lonely. This can be changed. It takes time and effort and a commitment, but with a good therapist, she can learn to deal with feelings of loneliness and to be less impulsive about starting new relationships.

Most patients with personality disorders seek treatment because they are either depressed or anxious, and this distresses their families. When talking to families in distress about diagnosis and treatment of their relatives with personality disorders, I try to separate mood, anxiety, and other symptoms—such as substance abuse—

from personality issues. I also stress that although all behavior is ultimately determined biologically, anxiety and depression are treated with medications. Personality change should, however, be forged through psychotherapy, and it is the patient's responsibility. A perfect example of this attitude is displayed by a poster near the entrance to a treatment facility for multiple personality disorder (or dissociative identity disorder): "It does not matter which personality did it: you are responsible." This discussion at the outset of treatment allows you to anticipate a frequent, though often unspoken, question: "If this is an illness, does this mean it is not her fault?" and preempts the statement "It is not my fault, I have a personality disorder." The following example illustrates how to talk about personality disorders in a situation ripe with possible legal ramifications without using psychiatric terminology.

> *Barbara, your husband has two sets of problems: The first lies in his neurobiology; the second has to do with his personality. Biologically, he comes from a family with a history of alcoholism and depression and has had both in the past. His brain was different to begin with, but now it is even more different. He has been depressed, even while in AA and sober, which indicates that he needs antidepressant treatment. His second problem is that he has difficulty feeling and even imagining other people's pain. He also feels that he is entitled to his angry outbursts. He is an attractive and charming man, but looks and charm can be deceiving. While antidepressants may make him less explosive, they will not change his belief that blowing up and screaming are his right. This can be changed, but it will require a lot of therapy with a tough therapist who will not be charmed by his looks—such therapists do exist.*

Personality, as defined in the *DSM*, is empirically postulated to remain stable through one's lifetime (Nestadt et al., 2010). This creates difficulties in explaining to families why and how psychotherapy can help their loved ones with personality disorders. Indeed, the goal of psychotherapy is to change personality characteristics from pathological to adaptive. There are many types of psychotherapy and their discussion is well beyond the scope of this book, but all of them have a stated goal of changing patients' fixed patterns of behavior that make them and others suffer. This is true of both individual and group therapies, couples counseling, and cognitive, dynamic, and analytic therapies, and their specialized and manualized variants, such as cognitive behavioral therapy and dialectical behavioral therapy. Fortunately, recent research has resolved this contradiction, because it has been shown that personality does change with treatment and time (Farrell, Shaw, & Webber, 2009; Gabbard & Horowitz, 2009; Nadort et al., 2009). Kenneth Kendler, one of the world's leading psychiatric geneticists, demonstrated in a series of papers and symposia that, genetically speaking, there are three groups of genes that convey a vulnerability to personality disorders. One group of genes controls a predisposition to develop *any* personality disorder. The other two genotypes render proclivity to only two groups of personality disorders, which could be termed internalizing and externalizing (Kendler et al., 2008).

Internalizing disorders are characterized by feelings of inadequacy, self-blame, and low self-esteem and include avoidant-dependent, schizoid, and schizotypal personality disorders (Kendler et al., 2008). People with these disorders may be likened to a man with a pebble in his shoe: He looks perfectly fine to everyone else but feels dreadfully uncomfortable, for reasons that are obvious, for the most part, just to him. Over the last several decades, the buzzword for these people has been "low self-esteem." They are often perceived as shy and lacking in self-confidence—seen as nice guys and nice girls who lack some essential ingredient preventing them from succeeding both personally and professionally.

In contrast, people with externalizing personality disorders tend to feel comfortable inside. However, they also tend to not take responsibility for their actions and to blame their misfortunes on external circumstance or other people. This group includes mainly narcissistic, borderline, and antisocial personality disorders. People with externalizing disorders are perceived as entitled and insensitive. In its extreme, externalizing personality disorders take the form of narcissistic sociopathy or psychopathy—a puzzling disorder characterized by a total lack of empathy for others, who are regarded and treated with no more concern than inanimate objects (Rogstadt & Rogers, 2008). Needless to say, psychopathy has always been fascinating and horrifying to non-psychopaths and has been portrayed and idealized in many movies and TV series, most recently *Dexter* and *The Sopranos.*

These research findings are new and do not agree with the diagnostic classification of the *DSM-IV-TR,* which recognizes 10 personality disorders grouped in three clusters (as described in the beginning of this chapter). This classification is not intuitive but, with minor modifications, has nevertheless been used by mental health professionals for decades. The diagnostic labels used in the *DSM* have entered the common vernacular and are being used without regard to their original meaning in print, on TV, and on the Web.

Unfortunately, the *DSM-IV-TR* classification has several serious shortcomings. Most of these arose simply because *DSM* definitions are not based on solid experimental data but rather are arrived at by the expert consensus. Once patients with *DSM*-defined personality disorders were evaluated with the latest scientific methods, such as extensive phenomenological description, longitudinal observation, sophisticated statistical analyses, brain imaging, and genetic studies, the research results raised questions about both the validity of *DSM* definitions and clusters and the whole concept of Axis I versus Axis II psychopathology.

According to new research studies, *DSM-IV-TR* personality disorders are highly comorbid (i.e., they occur together rather than in isolation). It is nearly impossible to find a patient who, for instance, just has a histrionic personality disorder. It usually co-occurs with borderline, narcissistic, dependant, or some other personality disorder and anxiety or mood disorder. One exception may be the obsessive-compulsive personality disorder, which in a milder form may be an adaptive personality trait, because such people tend to be both personally and professionally successful. I would venture even further to say that in our highly organized information-based society, it is impossible to become successful without some obsessive and compulsive traits. It is OCD (see Chapter 12) that can be a serious illness.

Avoidant personality disorder and dependent personality disorder overlap in the vast majority of cases and, most likely, are two sides of the same disorder. The same people who are shy, anxious, and afraid to approach others for fear of rejection tend to become dependent on those with whom they do connect (Leising, Sporberg, & Rehbein, 2006). Patients with avoidant-dependent personality disorder frequently have well-defined anxiety disorders or dysthymia and depression. Some exhibit schizotypal features and are perceived as different and a little unusual. They often engage in esoteric pursuits such as collecting violin bows, practicing Chinese archery, or studying ancient Sumerian culture, to name a few. Some become avid collectors and, in the extreme, start accumulating possessions and even become hoarders (see Chapter 12).

One of the complaints you may hear from the families of such patients is that they are not doing anything with their lives and are not going anywhere. They stay with their parents or nearby, both resenting their parents' interference and unable to break away. The best approach in this case is to identify the two main problems, in accessible and clear language, and to encourage a referral to psychotherapy. I often use the descriptors "difficulty being independent" and "shy" for avoidant-dependant behavior. With regard to odd pursuits and schizotypal features, the euphemisms "being different" and "speaking the same language as other people" usually help, as in the following example.

You have raised Eli to be a really nice kid. I am saying kid even though he is 30, because he continues to live like a teenager. He wants to be independent but is so comfortable at home that he cannot leave. He knows he really should be living on his own, he is angry that he cannot, and he takes it out on you. Because he is shy, he has not met the right girl yet, and living at home does not make it easier to meet girls. Yes, he saves a lot of money by living at home, but I think it might be at the expense of having a life! He spends all his free time working on his bodybuilding routine. He is so good, he should try to teach and share it—become involved in the culture and speak the same language as other personal trainers and people who have similar interests. Maybe he'll even meet somebody. But he will not do so without your help. You need to let him go. In your case, this means helping him move out of the house and getting him a good therapist who will help him to be independent. You cannot take on the role of a therapist and help him because this will only make him more dependent on you.

Borderline personality disorder (BPD)—with suicide rates and morbidity similar to those of MDD, bipolar mood disorder, and schizophrenia—is often found to be comorbid with narcissistic and histrionic personality disorder but is much more severe and probably deserves its own category. Initially BPD was conceptualized as a disorder that phenomenologically combined features of nearly all Axis I and personality disorders—in the most severe cases, it can be found on the cusp between more severe psychoses and less severe neuroses (Gunderson, 2008). The families of patients with BPD often live on an emotional rollercoaster punctuated by fears of self-injurious behavior or suicide. In recent years, BPD has entered the vernacular and is becoming accepted by the lay public. Dialectical behavioral therapy (DBT), created and popularized by Marsha Linehan (1993), has become the treatment of choice for this disorder. For these reasons, I make an exception to the rule of not naming personality disorders and explicitly discuss the diagnosis of serious-case BPD when chances of suicide are above zero and the family needs to refer the patient to DBT.

Your daughter does have borderline personality disorder. You how much pain you have been feeling over the last several months? Your pain is largely a reflection of the inner pain and turmoil she is feeling, only for her it is stronger and is not going away. Medications help these symptoms, but it is imperative that she start psychotherapy. She is a likeable and attractive person—which will serve as a great asset and strength. This means that with treatment and time, these

feelings of being on a rollercoaster will subside—she will
have a life and you will sleep at night. She needs DBT, and I
can tell you where to find it.

It is easy to recognize the presence of people with severe externalizing disorders by the destructive turmoil they create around them. However, their identity can be much more elusive, particularly in the community or even in a work environment. For instance, a stressful, unpredictable, backstabbing work environment may be created by just one person with severe personality disorder. However, this person might be so adept at covering his or her tracks that you may have no inkling of who is really behind the never-ending conflict and chaos.

A family business in which many siblings, in-laws, children, and stepchildren are involved is frequently the setting of such a continuous and self-perpetuating toxic climate. Because in a family business, people often cannot be fired or leave and feel trapped, clashes between family members with different personality disorders get ritualized and amplified. The best a doctor can do when presented with such a situation is to alert the family to the complexity of the situation and encourage them not pass judgment and try to break up the toxic environment. Having one or two people who "cannot be fired" leave usually drastically improves the situation.

Deliberate, non-impulsive narcissistic sociopaths are often impossible to recognize until it may be too late. They are supremely self-serving and indifferent to the needs of other people unless these other people serve their purposes. Surprisingly, social psychology studies have shown that such people are repeatedly promoted and get ahead in the work environment. The best end up running major corporations, perpetrating sophisticated white-collar crimes, and either never get caught or make headlines after they are discovered—often too late. The most famous recent examples of this phenomenon are Bernard Madoff (Creswell & Thomas, 2009) and the heads of Enron, AIG, and Tyco. As a doctor, you may be asked to explain how it is possible that "the man I have been married to for 40 years could do this to me," his children, his friends, and people in general. Many families asked me this question after the recent economic meltdown. The following can be used as a stock message in all discussions with family members who have been ruined by their relatives (or friends) with antisocial personality disorder or psychopathy.

> It is actually almost like they are "as if" people. They look like people, talk like people, eat, drink, and do things that people do, but they are a different species inside. They do not have empathy, remorse, or regard for you or anybody else. They are hard and sometimes impossible to recognize. Your most reliable guide to identifying one is just one thing: What that person does, offers, or makes you feel like contradicts your objective experience, but for unclear reasons, you feel so good around him or her that you act in a way that is exceptional or unprecedented. Examples large and small include investing out of character and unwisely, trusting the person with a large sum of money, starting a romance when you usually would not, and giving an exceptionally large tip.

I will end this chapter with this rather disconcerting statement, which demonstrates that personality disorders can be the most mysterious and difficult disorder to recognize. How to talk about them is a fascinating topic that deserves a separate book. Nevertheless, this chapter should help you both recognize the most common personality clusters and help the families of those with personality disorders do the same.

Part IV

REAL-LIFE ISSUES

CHAPTER FOURTEEN

Stress
Management

Much of the material in this chapter is based on a talk I once gave on stress. With an audience that consisted primarily of the relatives of bipolar patients, the talk attempted to synthesize many conversations I have had with the families of mentally ill individuals and addressed how one might strive for happiness in the otherwise stressful world in which we live. Any part of this chapter can be useful if you have the commitment and time required to successfully touch on its major points. I provide an outline of the most important points for discussion at the end.

What is stress? Stress is either a real or perceived imminent threat or danger that causes distress. In fact, the word "stress" is derived from the Latin word *distress*. Here is an example of an imminent perceived threat: A young man gets an assignment at work that causes him to have to work all day and night. He does so because he perceives a threat—that he will not be promoted and will be let go if he does not complete the assignment within 24 hours. This possibility could mean the end of his career and life as he knows it; whether this threat is real or imagined now becomes a secondary matter.

Family stress can be defined as a real or imagined imbalance between the demands on the family and their ability to meet those demands. Stress in the families of mentally ill individuals is quite real: both emotional and financial demands are high, the latter mostly because of medical bills. As emotional and financial demands increase, resources tend to decrease because mentally ill individuals often cannot maintain employment.

The current name for such a threat or demand is "stressor." Negative stressors for the families of mentally ill individuals include other illnesses in the family, job loss, and depleted resources. Stressors, however, can be either positive or negative. Examples of positive stressors are meeting the man or woman of one's dreams, the birth of a child, a marriage, a promotion, going to college, or getting a book published. Examples of negative stressors are, not surprisingly, the opposite: getting rejected by the man or woman of one's dreams, a divorce, and having a book proposal be continually rejected.

Many lists of the most stressful life events have been compiled; for the most part, they agree with the rank order shown here:

1. Death of a spouse
2. Divorce
3. Marital separation
4. Jail term or death of a close family member
5. Personal injury or illness
6. Marriage
7. Loss of job due to termination
8. Marital reconciliation or retirement
9. Pregnancy
10. Change in financial state

Some professions are more stressful than others. The least stressful professions have very little to do with people and a lot to do with animals, vegetables, minerals, and space. The least stressful professions are those of astronomers, geologists, and marine biologists. Lists of the most stressful professions are more varied than those of stressful life events because, among other things, not everyone agrees on what is a job and what is an occupation. According to JobBank USA (2006), IT is currently the most stressful profession, followed by medicine and other caring professions, engineering, sales and marketing, education, finance, human resources, operations, production, and clerical work.

Not all stress is bad—it can often motivate you. The saying "The less you work, the less you want to work" reflects this reality. If there is no stress, the brain is underperforming and productivity is lower. Therefore, in the absence of stress, there is little productivity. When one is dealing with stress, it is best to view it as a challenge. Perceived stress activates the limbic system, which in turn activates a set of emergency emotions. As a result of this activation, a signal is sent to the adrenals to release a stress hormone, cortisone, which floods the body and the brain, creating a state of emergency readiness. When cortisone crosses the blood-brain barrier, the brain responds by releasing norepinephrine, which mobilizes both men and women into a state of heightened alert: Mood is improved, energy is increased, new ideas are formed, and thinking becomes creative. All these components come together to meet the stressful challenge head on and create new memories to be used later. Under optimal stress, even the immune system works better, and people under such stress tend not to get sick.

However, both acute extraordinary stress and chronic severe stress are harmful. In both cases, too much cortisone is being secreted and excessive cortisone affects the brain adversely. Under the influence of excessive cortisone secretion, some adaptive responses turn into their opposites. Heightened memory may turn into poor memory, diminished concentration, and inattention. Anxiety that was once motivating may turn into paralyzing panic attacks. Heightened arousal and energy turn into fatigue. Good mood turns into depression, and aggression into apathy. The immune system may weaken and shut down, resulting in stress-related diseases—ulcers, heart attacks, infections, even cancer. Chronic stress can lead to unhappiness, depression, misery, and sometimes suicidality.

There are many ways to manage stress. Probably the first and most important thing to understand is the difference between happiness and perfection. Too many people confuse the pursuit of happiness with that of perfection. Those who pursue perfection will never find it and therefore will always be under stress. There is a saying that "Perfect is the enemy of good." More important, perfect is the enemy of happiness. The most important way to deal with stress is to make sure that it is not the result of the pursuit of perfection. A perfect spouse is an example of an unattainable goal that has caused immeasurable stress and harm to multitudes of people.

The second approach to stress management is employing both problem-focused and emotion-focused strategies (Bond & Bunce, 2000). The first step is to recognize whether the stressful situation presents a problem that can be solved by an action. If this is the case, solving the problem or removing the situation (or removing yourself from the situation) that causes stress should be the focus. This is not as obvious as it may seem, because strong emotions can sometimes interfere with the identification of solvable problems and the design and execution of the necessary problem-solving steps. Having a close relative with bipolar disorder who works two jobs to support a lifestyle that could be modified to make it less costly is an example of when you need to use a problem-focused strategy.

An example of an unsolvable problem is a setback at work that cannot be reversed, such as a citation or demotion. Such a setback is bound to cause a strong and often complex emotional reaction— one of anger, frustration, resentment, anxiety, and depression. The best approach in this case would be to concentrate on understanding and regulating one's emotions. Familial support and feedback are crucial here to identifying feelings, helping to relieve anxiety, regulating and rechanneling anger, and restoring self-confidence.

Interestingly, the well-known Serenity Prayer could be viewed as a guide to problem-focused and emotion-focused stress management.

> God grant me the serenity
> To accept the things I cannot change;
> Courage to change the things I can;
> And the wisdom to know the difference.

Some people and families collapse under stress that might seem trivial, whereas others survive stress that appears insurmountable. The survivors probably not only know the difference between happiness and perfection and correctly use problem-focused and emotion-focused coping strategies but might also carry genes that make them resilient to stress. Most likely, these genes relate to the stability of the hypothalamic-pituitary-adrenal axis as well as a personality style developed from previous experience, resources, and support in times of stress.

There are probably as many ways to describe resilient people as there are psychiatrists, but these descriptions have common themes that describe a certain type of person. These individuals work hard, but work and ambition are not the only driving force in their lives. They value and are dedicated to their families but find time to maintain a wide network of friends with whom they share interests other than work. Finally, they are spiritual in that they are cognizant that their lives have meaning beyond survival and the pursuit of prosperity.

I often envision these people as standing firmly on four legs: work, love, play, and spirituality. These legs are, of course, figurative, but this image, as if they are supported by the legs of a barstool, can be helpful. A barstool can stand firmly on four legs or three legs, but not on one or two. Four legs, however, are much better than three, because if one of the legs is weakened, you still have three others to support you. With a three-legged stool, if something happens to one of the legs, the stool is bound to collapse.

Obviously, work is something you do to make a living. The preeminent role of work and play in human happiness was purportedly identified by Freud (Ryan, 1995). However, work can also be an activity that you deeply care about and that occupies most of your time, even if you do not get paid for it. The most common examples of work for which one is not directly paid are charitable work, raising children, and taking care of aging parents.

Love most often takes the form of a romantic relationship that requires attachment, trust, and closeness. A fair description of a good loving relationship is when you can define it not as a conquest but as surrender—when you surrender your trust to the other person—trust him or her not to hurt you—and do not build defenses against a possible, or even inevitable, upcoming assault or betrayal. In return, the person you love does not hurt you.

Play is something that you like to do that does not provide a source of income. The view of play as one of the essential components of happiness was popularized by Shor (1992) in his book *Work, Love, Play: Self-Repair in the Psychoanalytic Dialogue*. Play is something you do when you have nothing else to do, because it is fun and it makes you feel good. It is something you care about, something you want to do well or better but would continue doing even if you were doing it badly. Play can be sports, gardening, travel, and many other things. Recent animal studies on emotional intelligence show that play and joy are essential even for the development of healthy rats (Panksepp, 2007).

The final theme is spirituality, a search for life's meaning beyond its material representation. Spirituality is most often associated with major religions. More broadly, spirituality involves multiple paths to understanding the spiritual connections on earth to the multidimensional reality we seek to understand and the meaning of life. For some people, spirituality extends beyond earth and involves a search for an understanding of our connections with the universe. For the purpose of stress management, spirituality is also a concern as to whether you are in the right place in the circle of life, even if you are an atheist or agnostic.

These four legs are not equal: The two main legs are work and love, and they usually have priority over play and spirituality. In practical terms, it means that when you are engaged in play (e.g., watching a baseball game on TV) and your love calls to tell you about some boots on sale that she just saw, you interrupt the game and listen to her talk about the boots. Or, if you are helping your friend choose the right boots and your loved one calls to ask you to drop everything to have a drink with some out-of-town friend he forgot to tell you about, then you need to have that drink.

In terms of emotional resources, the ideal ratio for work, love, play, and spirituality is about 40:40:10:10. If either work or love commands more than 60% of your emotional resources, you become vulnerable to severe trauma. If either play or spirituality (unless it is your field of work) takes up more than 30% of your energy, either your work or your relationship is deprived of your attention and is vulnerable to harm.

The most serious stressor in the arena of work is losing your job. This is a top 10 stressor. Besides creating a financial hardship, in our country, losing a job is a blow to the core of who we are. The second most serious chronic stressor is working in the wrong field. This typically happens when somebody destined to work in a caring profession works in a business environment instead, where profit—definitely not helping—is the primary motivation, or the other way around. Such major mistakes in choosing one's occupation can result in persistent, sometimes lifelong, dissatisfaction and chronic stress. Other work problems, such as insufficient compensation, being overworked, and having terrible bosses are relatively minor by comparison but still can be incredibly bothersome.

The biggest blow to love is the death of a spouse or divorce. Sometimes divorces are worse than death—they are often worse for the children. The second most serious stressor is being married to the wrong person. This is often *not* as obvious as one would think and could be—and is—the subject of an entire book. In my experience, men and women marry the wrong partners for somewhat different reasons. The most common reasons for getting into a bad marriage for women are marrying for safety in the absence of love and marrying for passion without thinking rationally about the decision. For men, the most troubling scenarios occur when they marry somebody they do not worship because they feel pressured to marry, because they marry out of guilt, or because they did not get to know the person well before deciding to get married. Most domestic disputes are the result of these preventable mismatches. The third stressor is the Blackberry, the iPhone, and other smart phone devices. Blackberries have infiltrated our love, our play, our spirit, our bedrooms, and our time to be close, to hear, and to understand.

The biggest hurdle to play is not playing at all. This often happens because one has no friends outside one's family or no time for friends because of the demands of both work and love. Friendships need to be nurtured, fed, watered, and fertilized. Another problem is the complete lack of a hobby. Hobbies can be competitive, individual, pleasurable pursuits—for example, yachting and golf. They can also involve networking and relationship building, such as working for causes, PTAs, or nonprofit boards. These activities are major coping mechanisms and most effective if actively and frequently engaged in.

Finally, the main problem with spirituality is a lack of awareness of its importance. Spiritual people are on average less stressed, depressed, and anxious (Chatters et al., 2008; Maselko, Gilman, & Buka, 2009). Again, I define spirituality broadly as including all types of concerns and an understanding that one is in the right place and in a relationship with something bigger than oneself. It may be God, the universe, humanity as a whole, or a circle of life. The major problem is uncritical involvement with fringe cult movements, which can sometimes lead to tragic results, the most extreme example being Jonestown.

In essence, a poor response to stress in one of life's domains is trying to fix it while neglecting the others. The most typical example of such a response is that of a workaholic who is overinvested into his work, neglects his family, has no time for friends and no spiritual life, and is under constant stress in his effort to do a perfect job. His response to critical feedback at work is often a feeling of failure ("Perfection is the enemy of happiness") and as a result he spends even more time at work and less time with his family and friends. Another example, in which the problem is in the love domain, is when a codependent couple in a tumultuous relationship decides to spend more and more time with each other to work out their power struggles.

In contrast, the best response to stress is to rely more on the functioning domains in one's life and to draw strength from them—to see it as a challenge rather than a personal failure. Using this strategy, a man let go from his job might try to regroup and look for another, using this opportunity to reassess the situation and strengthen the other domains of his life. He would spend more time with his wife and children and try to understand how the change affected them and how he might help. He would discuss his work strategies with his wife and take her input seriously. He would do things that he previously never had time to do with his children; reconnect with friends, including those he hasn't seen in awhile; and keep in "fighting" shape by running and playing basketball. Finally, he would use his spirituality to understand the meaning of recent changes for his life in the grand scheme of things.

COPING WITH STRESS AS A FAMILY

A happy family consists of happy people. However, it can take just one unhappy family member to shift the entire family toward unhappiness. These families are often aware of the shift in mood and, unfortunately, tend to hold a particular individual responsible. This person is often the one who is mentally ill. Notably, many happy families may be unaware of their happiness and become conscious of it only when periods of unhappiness do happen.

Unhappy families often seek help from family therapists. Although I talk to families all the time, I am not a family therapist and do not engage them in extended treatment. To the extent that I discuss family dynamics, I provide guidance on how to interact with mentally ill family members and among themselves in a way that will reduce family stress.

In dealing with such families, I use an eclectic set of rules developed by several specialists in family dynamics that families find clear, intuitive, and useful. I discuss anywhere from one to all of them, depending on the complexity of the family dynamics, the issues at hand, and how much time we have.

Emotional Bank Account

It is important to have a surplus in the family emotional bank account. The concept of an emotional bank account was created by Stephen R. Covey and popularized in his book *The 7 Habits of Highly Effective People* (2004). All families, whether or not they know it, have an emotional bank account. Each time you say or do something caring or generally positive, you make a deposit; each time you say something critical, or generally negative, you make a withdrawal. Families among whom positive statements predominate have surpluses in their accounts and are happy. The content of positive statements or emotions is not important. A positive interaction can range from telling a good joke to buying your spouse a mansion. This is why, beyond poverty, happiness is only marginally related to income. The main difference between an emotional bank account and a real one is that emotional deposits and withdrawals are not equal. One critical statement negates five praises or other positive statements. Therefore, just to break even (and breaking even is far from being happy), the ratio of positive statements to criticisms has to be at least 5:1. Here is a startling illustration of this point: When you say, "Honey, I love you, but you should not talk like this to my mother," you've just put yourself in 4-point hole.

Low Expressed Emotion

It is important for families to have low expressed emotion (Butzlaff & Hooley, 1998; Barrowclough & Hooley, 2003). The idea of expressed emotion was conceptualized by Brown and Rutter (1966). EE (expressed emotion) describes negative patterns of family interactions consisting of hostility, overinvolvement, and criticism. Hostility is generally expressed in the form of direct negative statements about a person such as "I hate you" or "You drive me crazy." Overinvolvement is a less intuitive term and describes two types of interactions. The first implies that a mentally ill person cannot be successful or even competent, for example, "He's so sensitive, there is no way he can do it without me." The second is an invasion and interpretation of somebody's unexpressed thoughts and feelings, as in, "You didn't clean your room just to be oppositional." Criticism is a negative comment on somebody's actions, such as "You're gaining weight." Critical comments that demonstrate overinvolvement, although well meaning on the surface, can be particularly toxic: "You are not doing this right—let me help you!"

High EE in families is associated with poor prognosis for the whole family and specifically the mentally ill. With high EE, there is more stress, anxiety, depression, and substance abuse, and frequent relapses for those with schizophrenia and bipolar disorder.

Help Versus Support

On the surface, the words "help" and "support" are synonyms that mean to aid or assist. However, when applied to relationships, they have nearly opposite meanings: "Support" indicates that you are confident in another person's ability to do something on his or her own. A supportive statement aims at bolstering the other person's strength, as in "You are so resourceful, you can do it." "Help" is when you step in because the other person's abilities are insufficient and implies the other person's failure to do something on his or her own. In family interactions, it is best to offer support first and offer help *only* when asked. To help without offering support makes the other person feel undermined and makes the person offering help look critical and controlling.

After a Conflict

It is very important to care about the feelings of the other side after a conflict. All families and couples have conflicts and fights and go on to coexist afterward. There are two general ways couples can behave after an argument. One is to continue the argument in one's head and ruminate about what one should have said to make the point better and what one might do better next time (i.e., sharpening weapons for the future). One can also stew about how one was treated unfairly and taken advantage of, and how underappreciated one is in general. These ruminations usually lead to an aggravated adversarial stance, such as, "Of course I was right, how could she not see that! In fact, she should be grateful to me and say thank you." As a result, the fight resumes and escalates to new levels of hostility at the first opportunity.

The other way to behave is to think how the fight may have hurt the other side. Even Robert McNamara, the architect of the Vietnam War, by the end of his life arrived at the conclusion that for the sake of peace, it is best to empathize with one's enemy (Williams, Ahlberg, & Morris, 2003).

If you are able to empathize with a family member after a conflict, instead of stewing, you can say, "I am sorry I upset you"— now *that* ends the fight. For people who deeply love each other, this happens effortlessly. But even those families with more complex feelings can learn how to make these calls intentionally with the purpose of ending a conflict.

Following these four rules does not guarantee happiness but certainly maintains functional family life with some degree of contentment. In stressful situations, the individual domains of love, work, play, and spirituality can be hit or preserved fairly independently. In other words, work troubles may not directly affect the marriage or the tennis game but nevertheless can have indirect consequences. Families under stress tend to forget all these rules at the same time. Your best strategy, as a doctor, is to remind them what they are. Hopefully, on occasion your practice will allow you to do that.

CHAPTER FIFTEEN

School and Work

 SCHOOL

Children and adolescents who will later become ill with schizophrenia are often studious. For them, learning in isolation provides a safe haven—a retreat from the increasingly confusing and chaotic world of human relationships and the complexities of social life. They are often the "good" kids who never give their parents any trouble. Unfortunately part of the reason that they stay out of trouble is their evolving negative symptoms—difficulty with socialization and a lack of will, initiative, and motivation. These students often become sick either in the last year of high school or the first two years of college.

The pressures and stress that come with planning one's future and separating from home are extremely great; however, not all these pressures are negative. Choosing a college, visiting schools, moving away from home, and meeting new friends in college can be very exciting and a lot of fun. People often remember this time as the best years of their lives. However, for someone who has a genetic vulnerability to developing a major mental illness, this transitional period can precipitate the first major episode of the illness. The precipitating factors are a combination of the separation from supporting families, difficulty fitting into a new environment, increasing academic demands, lack of sleep due to irregular work hours and competing social needs, and exposure to illicit drugs, most frequently marijuana.

Because the United States is a meritocracy, for high school and college students, grades and school are the keys to a successful future. Parents sacrifice a tremendous amount to help their children get into the best schools possible. Some have several jobs; others deplete their savings and take out loans. Immigrants often take manual-labor jobs so that their children can fulfill their parents' dreams by becoming high achievers in their new country. Even when there are no financial sacrifices, often all the emotional and social resources of the family are directed at academic success.

In this context, when a student becomes ill, the first question is often "What is going to happen with his school?" More precisely, whether the ill student will be able to return to school, and if so, what school it will be. If the diagnosis is schizophrenia or schizoaffective disorder, further education may not be possible. With bipolar disorder, it is often possible to continue education but this depends on the severity of the illness. With MDD and anxiety disorders, further education, although often in a less demanding environment, is almost always possible.

The best strategy in talking to the distraught parents of a student who experienced a recent breakdown is to focus on the student's psychiatric disability and on the need to get well. It may be appropriate to suggest that the student take a leave of absence. Any psychotic or mood episode severe enough to disrupt one's school routine is likely to be followed by a recovery period lasting at least several weeks. When cannabis or other drugs are involved, a 4-week inpatient rehabilitation is often needed.

The best option for a student who is in the midst of or recovering from a breakdown is to take incompletes for his or her courses and to revisit the issue after recovery. When one is asked directly how the illness will affect one's ability to process information, it is best initially to avoid the potentially threatening term "cognitive impairment" and to talk instead about difficulties with concentration, attention, and memory. In the beginning of the illness, the extent and duration of these impairments are often unknown. Therefore, it is best not to be predictive but rather to give information.

One might wish to point out that although in general the sicker somebody is, the harder it is for him or her to concentrate, the relationship between mental illness and academic performance is neither direct nor absolute. With the families of patients who have recently had their first break, a proper stance is generally that of support, sympathy, and hope. To illustrate this approach, what follows is the discussion that I had with the parents of a 19-year-old woman with schizoaffective disorder. The patient had her first episode as a sophomore after a transfer from a state school to an Ivy League school.

> I told the parents the bad news: "She is really quite ill, and at this time thinking about how and when she is going back to school is premature." The father, who was not quite ready to hear me, asked: "Will she be able to study in the hospital?" "I do not think so," I said. "You see, in addition to having all these strange ideas, as you may have noticed, her attention and concentration are quite impaired. At present, it is difficult for her to read a newspaper or a book or even watch TV. She also told me that even when she reads, she does not retain information that well. These difficulties are often part of the illness. Her thinking should improve after she recovers. For the time being, she needs to take a leave of absence just as she would after major surgery. The school will always be there."

As illustrated by the father's question, parents frequently have difficulty adjusting their expectations to suit the current functional abilities of their ill child. Although this deterioration in the patient may be clearly marked by difficulty concentrating and an inability to complete academic and work-related tasks, some parents cannot accept that their expectations are no longer realistic. The parents feel that in the absence of acute mood symptoms or psychosis, their son or daughter should continue with college as if nothing happened. Their refusal to lower their expectations, sometimes drastically, heightens the sense of failure on the part of the patient.

The patient may then continue to try to work or study in high-pressure institutions, putting him- or herself in a position to receive direct or indirect feedback that confirms the feeling that he or she is damaged or inferior. This combination of pressure from home and failure at school (or work) makes people feel trapped, hopeless, doomed, and frantic. In rare cases, such entrapment results in heinous violence, as in the case of the Virginia Tech shooter (Galynker, 2007; Hodge, 2007). More often this state of mind is associated with suicidal thinking and attempts. In contrast to the previous case, with these families you need to be empathetic but also firm and clinical. To underscore the seriousness of this matter, it could be useful to set up a formal meeting with a specific agenda. The following example illustrates such a meeting with the parents of an adolescent with bipolar illness. He was attending a high-pressure prep school, and despite his hard work, he had always performed poorly. He had had two episodes of depression and had been suicidal in the past and recently.

> I opened the meeting with a rather dramatic statement: "Hello, Paul. Hello, Melinda. I asked you to come because I believe that your son's schooling has become probably the most critical issue that will determine how his life is going to develop in the future." I then elaborated: "It is not going to be news to you that he has been struggling for awhile. He is a hard worker, but because of his concentration and attention difficulties, which are part of his bipolar illness, he just cannot keep up with work. He is in a very difficult situation academically and socially. His grades are low, and both he and you are getting letters to the effect that he needs to improve his academic performance. This makes him feel, in his words, like 'damaged goods.' At his school, performance is everything, and he has been feeling like a failure for awhile. I do not see this getting better.
>
> "If he did not have bipolar illness, he could work longer hours, and sleep less. He has bipolar illness, however, and sleep is probably the single most important thing for his mental health. This, together with his poor academic performance, makes him different from others, and he has been feeling like an outcast. Again, I do not see this getting better at this school."
>
> Finally, as described in Chapter 1, I made several supportive statements focused on relieving the parents' potential guilt and

made a clear recommendation for a future course of action. "He is such a nice kid and he tries so hard. With bipolar illness, people often have trouble concentrating even when they are euthymic. This is a clinical reality you need to accept. It is not his fault that he has this illness, and it is not your fault. However, this school environment is toxic for him. Unless he changes schools, his depressive episodes and suicidal thoughts are likely to continue. There are many spheres of life and also many schools where there is less emphasis on academic performance. He will be a better-than-average student in many public schools. There are also private schools that have a supportive rather than competitive environment."

WORK AND CAREERS

Discussions about work also require a lot of effort to adjust families' expectations. Usually, the tone of these discussions is a little bit different. When talking with the parents of students, you have to work not only with reality but also with students' and parents' dreams about the future. These dreams and hopes can be realistic but frequently they exceed students' actual abilities. Thus when one is talking about schools, it makes more sense to put the emphasis of the discussion on stress. Stress is external and transitory and does not label the student permanently flawed as the inability to think and reason would.

By the time you talk to families about careers, you will be dealing less with their dreams and more with reality. Even at the start of their careers, individuals with psychiatric disorders have already finished or not finished college, have had a number of job interviews, and may have been working for some time. Once the true scope of patients' abilities and limitations becomes evident, you can discuss their cognitive function and cognitive limitations.

Cognitive function describes various aspects of the brain's ability to process information: long- and short-term memory, attention, concentration, vocabulary, visual-spatial ability, and abstract thinking. It is not surprising that schizophrenia and bipolar mood disorder, two serious illnesses affecting the brain, in addition to their signature symptoms of hallucinations, delusions, mania, and depression, also cause cognitive impairment. However, it is somewhat surprising that the ability to work, to have careers, and to function may depend more on patients' cognitive function than on the core symptoms of the illness (Matza et al., 2006). To a lesser degree, this may be true of MDD.

This paradoxical phenomenon explains the common clinical observation that some mentally ill people with intact intelligence can work while being floridly psychotic (see the film *A Beautiful Mind* for an excellent example of this). Alternatively, many patients in the post-acute stage who no longer have psychotic, manic, or depressive symptoms but have severe problems with concentration and attention are not able to work. This trend was described in two reports on admissions and discharges from psychiatric units (Galynker & Harvey, 1992; Kato, Galynker, Miner, & Rosenblum, 1995), and it has recently become the subject of extensive research.

Because the level of cognitive disability in mentally ill individuals is so important and underappreciated, any discussion of work and career planning with their families must include psychoeducation about how cognitive disability may affect their ability to work. Obviously, this discussion does not negate the need for a more customary conversation about the effects of psychotic, mood, and anxiety symptoms on work. This relationship is reciprocal. Work and, more specifically, work-related stress can precipitate a relapse in psychosis, mania, depression, and panic D/O.

Thus, discussions with families about work and career planning for their mentally ill relatives can be roughly divided into two categories. In the first category are debates about how much stress the patient can tolerate at work and how the illness-precipitating stress threshold can be modified by support at home and elsewhere. The second category includes conversations about what kind of career a previously promising and healthy individual can now have with much-reduced cognitive abilities.

Although work stress may become a key problem for patients with schizophrenia, stress issues are much more relevant for the families of patients with mood and anxiety disorders. Most individuals with these disorders work, and some hold responsible positions throughout the workforce. Work-related stress is very variable. There are several lists that rank jobs according to their stress level. The least stressful occupations are typically those that have the least to do with people (see Chapter 14). The highest stress is associated with professions in which employees are responsible for other people's functioning and well-being, such as in medicine, sales, marketing, finance, management, and information technology.

Stressful work conditions can precipitate depression, mania, anxiety, panic, and other symptoms in any field of work. Frequent travel, which disrupts the sleep-wake cycle, is particularly harmful. Other typical stressful events common to all professions are deadlines, presentations, competitive assignments, relocations, rigid and unreasonable demands, promotions, and expanding job responsibilities when one must fill in for coworkers or supervisors. The last two can be especially toxic because these stressful events are perceived as positive challenges. Yet for individuals with the proper genetic loading, getting a promotion or successfully doing the work of two people can be one of the best recipes for becoming manic.

Families usually want advice on their ill relatives' jobs and careers after one of these stressors leads to unbearable tension and turmoil at home, serious performance issues at work, or a breakdown leading to hospitalization. Families want to know whether the recent episode of the illness was an isolated incident or, if not, under what circumstances it could repeat itself in the future. They may want to know how their loved ones need to modify their behavior at work to reduce stress. They can benefit from direct advice on whether the current job or career path is tenable. Finally, they also need help understanding how they can support the patient to avoid future episodes. The following two examples of such discussions address all these issues.

The first example is a discussion with the successful parents of a very ambitious young man who is prone to developing severe depression under stress. The parents have invested a lot in his career, both emotionally and financially. They are having difficulties adjusting their priorities and expectations. Meetings of this kind most often occur in the early stages of the patient's career.

Mr. and Mrs. Green, first the good news: Your son is feel-
ing better and is not in danger. He is responding to treat-
ment, and with the right follow-up and discharge planning,
if he continues to take his medications and comply with
other aspects of treatment, there is a good chance he will not
get depressed again. Now the news you may not consider so
good: This job, and possibly this line of work, is too stressful
for him. There is too much pressure, expectations for his per-
formance are unreasonable, and the competition is toxic.
You may have been able to handle this type of environment
when you were younger, but for him it is intolerable and, I
would have to say, unsurvivable.

He has a different genetic makeup and he is a fairly sensi-
tive young man. You yourself just told me that. Yes, what-
ever does not kill you makes you stronger, but we need to
make sure he is on the "stronger" and not the "kill you" side
of this equation. He really does not like this type of work and
probably would rather not be here. So we have two strong
arrows pointing in one direction: He does not like this work
and he became severely depressed with psychotic features
while doing it. The arrows are pointing in the direction of a
job change or, better yet, a career change, preferably to a
less stressful occupation. You, Mr. Green, are in this busi-
ness. Is it possible for him to have a less stressful career in
the business? Please understand that this is not a matter of
intelligence but one of vulnerability to mood disorders and
stress tolerance. He is a gifted young man and he may do
very well in a less stressful field.

The second example involves the supportive and devoted wife
of an engineer who developed bipolar disorder with panic attacks.
She has been trying to talk him into working less for several years
and would welcome any outside support, particularly from a doctor. These types of discussions usually occur with regard to patients in the middle of their careers who previously were able to
work well under less stressful circumstances.

Dear Sasha, you have reason to be concerned. Bipolar dis-order does not get any better with stress, and if he continues in this lifestyle, he is very likely to have a breakdown, which will require hospitalization. Constant changes in time zones disrupt his sleep and make a future episode even more likely. This is my professional opinion, and I will be very happy to put it down in writing and send it to his employer. Next: What can you do? The best thing would be for you to clearly understand what I just said and also know that if he does have a serious episode, he will have to stay on disabil-ity for several months. You can also help him not to push himself so hard. As you intimated, there is no financial pres-sure to work so hard. My letter to his job will recommend a transfer to a position that requires no travel at all. He told me that he is a valuable employee and this should be possi-ble. You can help by encouraging and supporting this transi-tion, although it may result in lower income. I am afraid the choices here are either reduced income or no income, and the first is preferable to the second.

These vignettes are examples of what I would say, as a psychia-trist, about careers to the families of patients with mental illness. Primary care doctors and specialists may not have time to have similar discussions. However, if the situation arises, both the con-cepts and the terminology used in this chapter can be used in much shorter conversations.

CHAPTER SIXTEEN

Real-Life Relationships
and Planning Families

Almost all patients with mental illness have more difficulties with their relationships than do individuals without mental illness. These relationship difficulties permeate their interactions with close family members and caregivers as well as with outsiders. The nature of these difficulties depends on several factors: the closeness of the relationship, the patient's diagnosis, the severity of the illness, the patient's age, and his or her life stage. For example, young patients with depressive disorders who have parents and siblings may have several conflictual relationships at the same time. Arguments can arise between the patient and his or her caregiver or parent resulting from the patient's excessive dependency. Conflicts can also happen because when the patient monopolizes the parents' attention and resources, healthier siblings feel that the patient is getting all of the parents' affection. At the same time, young depressed people can feel isolated and rejected in their romantic and peer relationships and at work.

Families are usually aware of these complexities. To them, the effects that the malady can have on relationships can be as bewildering and confusing as the psychiatric illness itself. Therefore, I find it advantageous to help families deal with this complex issue

systematically. One approach I use is to help family members analyze the relationship issues in three steps. First I ask them to understand how the patient's behavior may be different from that of
healthy people. Once this is accomplished, I encourage family
members to identify realistic expectations for their relationships
with their mentally ill relatives. The final step is recommending
how the family can apply their understanding of the patient's behavior to their everyday life with the patient. The following is an
example of such a discussion with the parents of Isaac, a young
man with major depression and Asperger's syndrome:

> Identifying differences: "Isaac is different from you and
> me in that he does not understand the rules of social interac-
> tions nor does he understand when he does something
> wrong. He can talk to you nonstop about computers without
> ever asking what is on your mind and does not understand
> why you get annoyed. Even such basic concepts as how long
> to look at somebody are a mystery to him."

> Adjusting expectations: "Given these biological limita-
> tions, you cannot expect to have the kind of relationship
> with him that you with your other children. For the same
> reason, it is difficult for him to date, to work, and to have
> friends. For him, holding any job for an extended period of
> time or having a romantic relationship with anybody is a
> major accomplishment."

> Making a recommendation: "Keep in mind that he lives in
> a different world with different rules. Understanding what
> those rules are will help you and him. You cannot expect
> him to behave in a certain way toward you naturally and
> will need to do quite a bit of interpreting. Sometimes it may
> feel like teaching somebody to walk. For example, when he
> does not look at you when he is speaking, it is not because
> of defiance but because he does not understand or feel the
> need to do so. You may help him by telling him to look at
> you for 5 seconds each time he starts talking."

Living with a seriously mentally ill individual requires frequent
analysis of his or her behavior along these or similar lines. Often

this process is so stressful and threatening that families shy away from going through it purposefully and prefer to stay in denial of the extent to which their loved ones' illness alters their relationships with others. A particularly difficult task for each family member and for each current or potential caregiver is to decide how burdensome this and other caregiving tasks are for him or her. The decision about how close to be to a mentally ill relative, potential relative, or friend, and the extent to which one wishes to assume the role of caregiver, can be as personal and as important as the decision to get married or have children. In fact, some of the most difficult decisions specifically concern marriage and children. As a physician, you will need to be especially sensitive in providing information, guidance, and support in the journey along this challenging and often grueling road.

For example, even if after the first break of schizophrenia or bipolar illness, caregivers intellectually understand that their loved ones have changed, emotionally they may not be ready to grapple with the new reality that the mental illness presents. In a sense, they cannot be truly ready: It may take years for the illness to fully develop and for all the symptoms to surface. It can take years for the full scope of emotional and cognitive limitations or lack thereof to become obvious. To add to the problem, the course of any mental illness varies, and patients' functional levels change dramatically from an acute episode to partial remission to remission. The unpredictability, the ups and downs of the illness, can be very confusing and traumatic for the family. A woman with a mild form of schizophrenia, for example, can be completely incapacitated during an episode but can maintain a household and take care of her children during remission. A man with bipolar disorder might also function in close-to-normal range when in remission but be reckless and violent during manic episodes, and not able to get out of bed when depressed.

Healthy family members facing this uncertainty must make critical decisions. This can be very complicated. The simpler ones are: Which insurance to keep? The one with the best mental health coverage? Should we move closer to parents just in case we need help? Should the patient look for a less stressful job? What about disability? What should we say to friends? What should we say to our children? I have addressed some of these dilemmas elsewhere in this book (see the beginning of Chapter 4).

The most heart-wrenching decision involves the future of the relationship itself. In this chapter I will describe how to talk to families in four frequently occurring real-life situations when the family is at a crossroads. In each of these situations, a caregiver or family member has to make a difficult decision that is likely to have lasting consequences for the rest of his or her life. In all these instances the psychiatric diagnosis may influence the details but not the essence of these discussions.

WHETHER TO LIVE WITH AN ADULT CHILD WITH SCHIZOPHRENIA OR BIPOLAR ILLNESS

In schizophrenia, the illness typically manifests itself in the late teens for men and in the early 20s for women. In bipolar disorder, the onset may be a little later, in the early to mid-20s, and the gender differences are of less importance. Young adults often become ill in the first 2 years of college, while working at their first job after college, and, less frequently, in the last 2 years of high school. As a result they often move back home to live with their parents. This development sooner or later leads to questions as to whether the ill child will continue living at home and to what extent he or she will need to be supported by the parents.

The answers to these questions are not straightforward and depend both on the diagnosis and on the family's resources. Even if they get Social Security Disability, a majority of patients with schizophrenia and schizoaffective disorder are not able to live independently and will need to live either with their parents or a caregiver or in a psychiatric residence. Most often the parents' home is a safe, supportive, and caring environment. For the patient, it also has the advantage of two kinds of familiarity: The patient is very familiar with his or her childhood home, and the parents are familiar with all or most of the earlier manifestations of the illness and are sensitive to the early warning signs of an impending episode. Often parents can monitor medication adherence, help their ill child with hygiene, and help him or her with social interactions with more distant family members, whom they can, hopefully, educate about their child's disorder.

The biggest problem for the parents of young adults with psychosis is that when symptomatic, their children may not be able to take care of themselves and can be abusive. However, even for parents of schizophrenic children who are stable, living at home may present problems. One of them is that patients with schizophrenia can be very messy and can have poor hygiene. They may have no understanding that either is a problem and may constantly need someone to clean up after them, and there may be never-ending negotiations about personal hygiene and body odor. Another common problem is conflicts over medication adherence and treatment adherence in general, which can occur either sporadically or on a daily basis. The third is conflicts regarding the children's dependency on their parents. All these can lead to verbal and sometimes physical abuse and violence.

Bipolar disorder as a rule is less debilitating than schizophrenia, and only adults with the most severe forms of bipolar illness must live with their parents or in psychiatric residences for prolonged periods of time. The practical issues for the most severely ill bipolar patients are the same as for those with schizophrenia and schizoaffective disorder. The majority of patients with bipolar illness should be able to find some kind of gainful employment. Some young patients with bipolar are able to have permanent and even very demanding jobs. Even if they are not able to work, bipolar patients are more cognitively intact and have either no or less severe negative symptoms, allowing them to live independently. However, in the manic or mixed manic state, patients with bipolar disorder can be delusional, irritable, aggressive, and violent. When manic, they can "trash" their lives, sometimes with tragic consequences for both themselves and their parents. It is not unheard of for manic patients who are perfectly functional when euthymic, to break furniture or destroy property when manic. They may also engage in conflicts with neighbors and relatives that may require law enforcement to be called to the scene.

As a result of these major disruptions, parents' lives can be completely hijacked by the need to care for their mentally ill children. In the most heartbreaking cases, parents become trapped living with a sick adult child, with daily conflicts over body odor, medications, and going to day treatment programs, living in constant misery and battling their own depression but feeling too guilty to move the child to a psychiatric residence. When one is talking to the parents of mentally ill young adults, it is important to assess the clinical situation in its entirety and then support the family in choosing the plan of action that will maximally benefit all family members without breaking the family structure. In doing so with most families, you may need to alleviate either their guilt about placing the ill child in a psychiatric residence or their anxiety about letting him or her live independently. Abusive families whom you may consider incorrigible, like those with entrenched patterns of physical or emotional abuse and neglect, are an exception to this approach. In the cases of such families, it is better to promote residence placement, and sometimes it may become necessary to contact law enforcement or protection agencies. The legalities of doing so differ from state to state.

Here are examples of two discussions with parents of mentally ill young adults struggling with whether or not to live with their children. In both cases, there is no history of abuse on the part of the parents. They are sincere and well meaning, wanting to do the best possible thing. Their resilience and resources are different and so is the severity of the children's illness.

Michael has a fairly mild form of bipolar illness. He has been hospitalized only once and is able to work in the family business. Being ill delayed his maturation and growth. Some of the family conflicts you are having are about his need to become independent. Yes, he has never lived alone before but he has also never been 25 and in treatment and on medications before. Working in the family business provides a lot of support and security and also gives you an opportunity to see him every day so you can see for yourself how he is feeling and not be so worried about him all the time. Do you ever plan to let him live separately and have a family, or do you want to have a 50-year-old child living with you, and no grandchildren? Then there is no better time to help him become independent than now.

In this example, the family is resilient and has resources, and the patient's illness is fairly mild. Therefore my message to the family aims to help them find the optimal framework to support their son in a way that will reduce stress and buttress his self-worth. In the next example, the adult child is much sicker and the family does not have the emotional resources necessary to set behavioral limits and prevent violence. Consequently, my suggestion to them, framed in positive and supportive terms, is to place the daughter in a psychiatric residence.

Mr. Grinnell, I hope you realize that you could not have been a better father to your daughter. Although you have not literally given your life for her, you are doing so figuratively. I am afraid this sacrifice may be in vain because, for a number of reasons, living at home is not the best option for her. First, she needs the daily structure provided in hospitals and residencies through groups and activities. Second, she has delusions about you and others trying to harm her. Third, living at home is a constant reminder to her of how disabled she is, and this makes her angry and results in abusive behavior and violence. She should live in a residence, where she will have structure and will be surrounded by people like her and supportive staff. There is a good residence not too far from here that I can recommend.

WHETHER TO MARRY A BIPOLAR BOYFRIEND OR GIRLFRIEND

I have treated several bipolar patients who were in long-term relationships that led to marriage and children. Almost invariably the patients revealed their illness to their partners only several months after they started dating and with much trepidation. The main fear that the bipolar individuals had was that once they revealed their illness, their partners would leave them. In reality, most of them got married and their spouses were fully aware of their diagnoses and medical treatment. More often than not, partners of my bipolar patients based their decision whether to stay in the relationship on their own experience and did not press me for the full implications the diagnosis of bipolar carried for their future.

Whether on medications or not, young people with bipolar illness can be bright, attractive, and very charismatic. They can have exciting, emotional, sparkling, lively relationships full of emotional closeness, but also significant drama. Frequent fights, breakups, and reconciliations are not uncommon. Their relationships can be likened to the proverbial little girl who, "when she was good, was very, very good, but when she was bad, she was horrid." More prosaically, these couples can be described as intermittently compatible. If the fiancé of a bipolar patient is contemplating marriage, however hesitantly, he is certainly not turned off by such a diagnosis.

I find that the best strategy in talking to partners is to answer their questions in the usual supportive manner, to invite other questions, and to offer opportunities for them to ask questions they have not yet thought of by mentioning these issues. This strategy of course is applicable to any conversation with family members on any subject. When one is discussing major decisions about the future, however, it is imperative that this approach be taken. As always, it is important to remember that the future course of the illness is unpredictable and can be modified by changes in stress levels and medications, as well as social changes.

Specifically, when one is talking to ambivalent partners of bipolar patients, even more so then usual, it is important to listen and to understand what they want to know and what they are prepared to hear. Some have already made a decision to get married and want to know the risks of passing on bipolar disorder to their children, if they choose to have them. Others are truly undecided because they have witnessed one or several acute episodes and do not know whether they want to live for the rest of their lives with somebody who is at risk of becoming acutely ill. These hesitant partners just want to collect as much information as possible in order to make an informed decision. Yet others may have already chosen to end the exciting but already troubled relationship but are conflicted because of their deep love for their partner.

The following three examples are of family meetings roughly corresponding to the aforementioned situations, in which I use the strategy just described. In the first example, the future husband has made up his mind and is not interested in receiving information about his fiancée's prognosis or genetic risks to their children. Giving this unsolicited information would be perceived as an intrusion and could be met with resentment or hostility.

I started the meeting: "Congratulations on your engagement! You both look very happy today. I am ready to answer all your questions."

Asher then asked: "Will she always need to take medications?"

I answered: "Yes, my recommendation is that she should, even if she feels well, like she is feeling now. She is looking and feeling healthy because her medications are working. However, the likelihood of her having an episode within a year of stopping her drugs is very high."

Asher continued to ask questions. "Can her medications be harmful to the baby if she gets pregnant?"

I responded: "She can get pregnant, but her medications would need to be changed somewhat. Some of the older neuroleptics have been around for a long time, and there have been no problems with pregnancies."

Then Laurie joined the conversation: "Can I breastfeed?"

I continued to give information. "If you can have a baby, you can certainly breastfeed: Whatever exposure your baby is going to get to your medications will occur during pregnancy because their concentration in the amniotic fluid is much higher than in the breast milk. That's all? Please ask more questions!"

Then I made a provocative statement—with a smile. "To tell you the truth, your fiancée was afraid that you would leave as soon as you learned she has bipolar disorder and takes psychotropics. This is not an easy illness to have and to deal with." This statement was an implicit invitation to discuss the illness and the future.

Asher was not interested and answered simply, "I am not that type of guy."

I then concluded the discussion but left the door open to another one at some later date: "Best of luck to you. There are some strategies you can use at home to reduce the risk of her having an episode in the future. We can talk about those some other time."

In the second case the boyfriend actually has all the information he needs, from his own experience, from reading, and from years of therapy. He wants to leave the relationship. However, he is having trouble being decisive and wants more information to help him decide.

> Josh and Sarah have been living together for 6 years. She was hospitalized three times: twice for severe psychotic depression, and once for mania. When she is well, he wants to stay together but is afraid to get married out of fear that she will get sick again; when she is sick, he wants to leave but feels too guilty to do it.
>
> Josh asked: "When is she going to have another episode?"
>
> I replied: "I don't know—she has been doing well for a year, and the new combination of medications seems to be working."
>
> Josh said: "I don't know what to do."
>
> I clarified his dilemma for him: "Josh, we have been here before: When she is sick, you want to leave, and when she is well, you want to stay. She is well now, but given the natural progression of the illness, it is likely that at some point in the future, she will have another episode. Over the last 5 years she has been getting sick about every 18 months. This is the best indication of what may come in the future."
>
> Josh was still indecisive: "Let's wait and see what happens."
>
> I responded by pledging my support: "OK, let us hope she continues to be well. I will certainly do my best to help."

In the third case, although the fiancée's feelings for her boyfriend initially interfered with her ability to see the reality of their situation, after recognizing that the future was likely to be very turbulent, she decides she wants to leave. In this case the best approach is to refer the couple to a couples therapist who can help them negotiate the breakup.

> Natasha was proposed to by Vlad, a young man with bipolar illness and some behavioral addictions. They have been living together for

a year and have broken off the engagement twice amid frequent conflicts and fighting. Natasha wants to leave but does not know how to do so without hurting him.

Natasha said: "We have been fighting a lot and I am afraid of what could happen in the future."

I answered: "Well, nobody can see the future, but you can usually tell a lot from the past. Your imminent past has been turbulent and you have been fighting frequently."

She continued exploring options: "Is there anything that can be done, maybe medications?"

I responded: "He has been taking medications and he is much less irritable than before. I have also been suggesting couples therapy but both of you have voiced reluctance."

Natasha then indicated she wanted out of the relationship: "I have never had a relationship like this before: I love him so much but we are fighting all the time. We are living together and are engaged, but I would rather marry somebody with whom I have not been fighting for years and with whom I do not need ongoing couples therapy. How can I leave him? He will not survive without me."

I then validated her fears and her decision: "Yes, you have been very angry, depressed, and critical of each other for a long time. Here is the telephone number of an excellent couples therapist who mediates separations. He is very well known and respected."

WHETHER TO STAY WITH A BIPOLAR SPOUSE

This question most often arises when one of the spouses becomes ill with bipolar disorder after the wedding, often after many years of marriage, and frequently when the children are no longer small. The transition is often gradual and imperceptible. It can be heartbreaking when talented, emotional, exciting, and hardworking individuals gradually become grandiose and irritable, lose their judgment, and wreak havoc in their lives and the lives of their families. For instance, bipolar people often become involved in catastrophic financial situations or sexual escapades. The healthy spouse, standing in the middle of this wreckage, often wants to leave the marriage for his or her own protection and for the protection of the children.

During these times, the ill spouse may or may not be in the hospital. The clinician is often left to talk to the hurt, desperate, and angry caregiver alone. The doctor's task during such a meeting is to remind the caregiver that the illness is treatable and that in several weeks he or she may get his or her old partner back or at least have a spouse who is rational, reasonable, and apologetic. Whether the harm done can be corrected is a matter to be discussed when the patient is in a less acute state. It is usually not difficult to convince the caregiver not to make any rash and hasty decisions while the patient is in the hospital.

Throughout acute episodes caregiver spouses often think (and say) that as soon as the ill spouse gets better, they will be getting a divorce. As I mentioned earlier, the divorce rate for bipolar individuals and their spouses, although high at about 50%, is not so different from that of the general population. This means that after resolution of an acute episode, couples again become compatible and viable. Therefore the best strategy is simply to emphasize that much depends on the response to treatment, and the need to be patient and to understand the degree of residual disability before making a rational and informed decision.

Dear Jane, it seems he is not behaving rationally and the way he is behaving is consistent with being manic: His recent promotion has brought on an increase in responsibilities and new projects; this has lead to a lack of sleep and irritability. His inability to understand his own behavior is at this stage part of the illness. He feels like his usual self and does not have a reference point. He does love you very much and would hate to lose you. You are telling me that you cannot go on like this and may leave. If this is the case, he needs to be made aware of your feelings in no uncertain terms. As such, you must tell him: "If you do not get treatment, I will leave." You have to mean what you say and you cannot bluff or be manipulative with such statements. But if this is where you are going, you must tell him loud and clear. Most likely he will hear you and go to a psychiatrist. Once he is properly treated, there is a good chance that he

will start behaving more rationally. Furthermore, if he stays
on medications, there is a good chance he will continue to
stay well. Subsequently, you will be under much less stress
and will be in a clearer frame of mind to make your decision.

WHETHER TO HAVE CHILDREN
WITH A BIPOLAR SPOUSE

The discussion about whether or not to have children with a
bipolar spouse is relatively straightforward for the physician but
anything but straightforward for the spouse. In my experience, in
heterosexual relationships, the ill spouse is most frequently the female partner in the relationship. Both partners want to know the
risks of their potential children developing bipolar disorder and
the risks of the bipolar mother having a relapse. Often of particular concern to patients is the possibility of postpartum depression.

The physician's job in this case is to present the family with appropriate statistics from relevant research studies. It is important to
emphasize that statistics were obtained from epidemiological data
on families who are not consciously trying to reduce the chances
of their children developing bipolar disorder. Nor were these
families trying to minimize the risk of postpartum psychiatric
symptoms. When discussing the risks, you will need to emphasize
that risks can be altered by both medication management and
changes in stress and the home environment.

The pertinent epidemiological data show that 10% of children
with one bipolar parent develop bipolar illness and about 50%
have other psychiatric problems such as ADD, anxiety, or depression (Singh et al., 2007). Studies on bipolar mothers show that in
general they have fewer manic and depressive episodes than bipolar women without children. However, they are at a higher risk
(8–20% greater) of having a manic episode (not depression) during
a postpartum period (days 10–19) than at any other time (Munk-
Olsen et al., 2009). In a large Danish study, 25% of bipolar women
had a postpartum mood episode. Postpartum mania is a much
more common reason for admission to a psychiatric hospital than
depression (Munk-Olsen et al., 2009). Interestingly, some people

will feel that 25% risk is small, and others will feel it is unacceptably high.

The statistics are simple: For you, the postpartum period is a dangerous time and the risk of having a manic episode increases at least 10-fold, probably because of hormonal changes and postpartum euphoria. Twenty-five percent of bipolar mothers have a postpartum manic episode. Thus we'll need to be careful and more aggressive with medications during this period. Yes, you may be more sedated than you want to be for ideal bonding with the newborn, but if you develop a manic episode, you will probably miss the first month or two of his life. Your children are at a somewhat higher risk of developing a bipolar disorder. There are three groups of risk factors for developing bipolar illness: genetic, social, and psychological. Your children will have the genetic risk. However, you have some control over the other two factors. In terms of the second factor, you can try to reduce the stress on yourself and your family by working a predictable, steady job rather than an unpredictable, exciting, but insecure job. And psychologically, you can maintain a home environment low in hostility, criticism, and pressure to succeed and high on acceptance, structure, and sleep!

EPILOGUE

When you present a symposium proposal for the annual meeting of the American Psychiatric Association, you are asked to submit its educational objective, beginning with "At the end of this presentation the participant should be able to appreciate . . ." and then you fill in the rest. In the same vein, what should the reader be able to appreciate after reading this book?

As its title implies, the main goal of this book is to help doctors feel at ease discussing mental illness with the relatives of those with psychiatric disorders. This book provides tools for meaningful clinical discussions of the most common psychiatric symptoms and diagnoses and the ways they may affect the lives of both patients and their family members. It is my hope that this text will be used as a reference guide akin to a dictionary. Its organization should allow a clinician who is unsure of what to say to pause during the conversation, pick up the book from the shelf, find the relevant section, and resume the meeting with confidence in 20 seconds.

The book is also written for the families of mentally ill individuals. I have written it for those courageous individuals who choose to marry persons they love despite their mental illness, who go on to have and raise children, who choose to stay with them through the good and the bad times, as they say they will in their marriage vows. This book is intended to help them live happier lives, to prevent crises, and to help those around them deal with them in the most advantageous and rational manner possible, should crises occur. In short, I hope this book will help both family members and their mentally ill loved ones live happily and healthily ever after.

After reading this book, the reader should appreciate that nearly everybody has a mentally ill relative or friend. On more social occasions than I can count, after telling somebody that I was a psychiatrist and having a short conversation about what I do, I have heard in response, "My brother is bipolar," "My mother has depression," "My grandfather was in a psychiatric hospital," or "My mother-in-law is a borderline." Slowly but surely, people are coming out of the mental illness closet. The process is gradual. At first they become comfortable talking about their mentally ill friends, then their distant relatives, then their close relatives, and finally themselves. I hope that this book will help accelerate this process.

Another aim of this book is to heighten readers' awareness of the stigma of mental illness. Stigma occurs within families when relatives do not talk about each other's mental problems and treat depression and anxiety as personal flaws. From inside families, it spills over into friendships, the workplace, business relationships, and the media. Thus one of the aims of this book is to help reduce stigma. This should be done both in the office, if you are a doctor, and at home, if you have a mentally ill relative.

Finally, as both a psychiatrist and a human being, I sincerely hope that this book will help us save families. Too many families of mentally ill people break up because they are unaware of the tools that could allow them to reduce the burden of mental illness, improve its course, and reduce the chances of their genetically vulnerable children developing a mental disorder. At times of crisis, the temptation to walk away can be very strong. The sirens of the legal profession are always ready to get you hooked on the divorce process with promises of a windfall. The reality of a divorce is never pretty and looks more like a wreck than a rose garden. We are social beings, and families are a cornerstone of our existence. After all is said and done, all we have is our relationships: families and friends. They need to be cherished and protected.

Creating happy families and keeping them intact is an important issue for everyone, not just for those with mental illness. Many healthy people without mental illness lack the skills needed to find the right person and stay with him or her through the trials and tribulations of life. Although this goes a little beyond this scope of this text, maybe one day these concerns will be the subject of another book.

REFERENCES

Akiskal, H. S. (2007). The emergence of the bipolar spectrum: Validation along clinical-epidemiologic and familial-genetic lines. *Psychopharmacology Bulletin*, *40*(4), 99–115.

Akiskal, H. S., & Benazzi, F. (2006). The DSM-IV and ICD-10 categories of recurrent [major] depressive and bipolar II disorders: Evidence that they lie on a dimensional spectrum. *Journal of Affective Disorders*, *92*(1), 45–54.

Allen, D. M., & Farmer, R. G. (1996). Family relationships of adults with borderline personality disorder. *Comprehensive Psychiatry*, *37*(1), 43–51.

American Foundation for Suicide Prevention. Retrieved from http://www.afsp.org/index.cfm?fuseaction=home.viewpage&page_id=050FEA9F-B064-4092-B1135C3A70DE1FDA on April 18, 2010

American Foundation for Suicide Prevention. Retrieved from http://www.afsp.org/index.cfm?fuseaction=home.viewPage&page_id=050CDCA2-C158-FBAC-16-ACCE9DC8B7026C#depression on April 18, 2010

American Foundation for Suicide Prevention. Retrieved from http://www.afsp.org/index.cfm?fuseaction=home.viewpage&page_id=050fea9f-b064-4092-b1135c3a70de1fda on July 6, 2010

American Foundation for Suicide Prevention. Retrieved from http://www.afsp.org/index.cfm?page_id=fed822a2-d88d-4dbd-6e1b55d56c229a75 on July 6, 2010

Answers.com. (n.d.). *Stress: Top ten stressful life events.* Retrieved from http://www.answers.com/topic/stress-top-ten-stressful-life-events on April 18, 2010

Altman, S., Cohen, L. J., Ten, A., Barron, E., Galynker, I., & DuHamel, K. H. (2006).

Predictors of relapse in bipolar disorder. *Journal of Psychiatric Practice, 12,* 269–282.

Andreasen, N. C. (1999). A unitary model of schizophrenia: Bleuler's "fragmented phrene" as schizencephaly. *Archives of General Psychiatry, 56*(9), 781–787.

Arseneault, L., Cannon, M., Witton, J., & Murray, R. M. (2004). Causal association between cannabis and psychosis: Examination of the evidence. *British Journal of Psychiatry, 184,* 110–117.

Barrowclough, C., & Hooley, J. M. (2003). Attributions and expressed emotion: A review. *Clinical Psychology Review, 23*(6), 849–880.

Birmaher, B., Axelson, D., Goldstein, B., Monk, K., Kalas, C., Obreja, M., . . . Kupfer, D. (2010). Psychiatric disorders in preschool offspring of parents with bipolar disorder: The Pittsburgh Bipolar Offspring Study (BIOS). *American Journal of Psychiatry, 167,* 321–330.

Blanchard, V. L., Hawkins, A. J., Baldwin, S. A., & Fawcett, E. B. (2009). Investigating the effects of marriage and relationship education on couples' communication skills: A meta-analytic study. *Journal of Family Psychology, 23*(2), 203–214.

Bond, F. W., & Bunce, D. (2000). Mediators of change in emotion-focused and problem-focused worksite stress management interventions. *Journal of Occupational Health Psychology, 5*(1), 156–163.

Borderline Personality Disorder and Insanity Defense. Retrieved from http://www .4degreez.com/disorder/forum/borderline-personality/48-borderline-personality-disorder-and-the-insanity-/thread.html on April 23, 2010

Botella, L., Corbella, S., Belles, L., Pacheco, M., Gómez, M. A., Herrero, O., . . . Pedro, N. (2008). Predictors of therapeutic outcome and process. *Psychotherapy Resource, 18*(5), 535–542.

Bourgeois, M., Swendsen, J., Young, F., Amador, X., Pini, S., Cassano, G. B., . . . Meltzer, H. Y. (2004). Awareness of disorder and suicide risk in the treatment of schizophrenia: Results of the International Suicide Prevention Trial. *American Journal of Psychiatry, 161*(8), 1494–1496.

Brown, G. W., & Rutter, M. (1966). The measurement of family activities and relationships: A methodological study. *Human Relations, 19,* 241–263.

Buccino, G., & Amore, M. (2008). Mirror neurons and the understanding of behavioural symptoms in psychiatric disorders. *Current Opinion in Psychiatry, 21*(3), 281–285.

Butzlaff, R. L., & Hooley, J. M. (1998). Expressed emotion and psychiatric relapse: A meta-analysis. *Archives of General Psychiatry, 55*(6), 547–552.

Centers for Disease Control and Prevention. (n.d.). *Web-based injury statistics query and reporting system (WISQARS).* Retrieved from http://www.cdc.gov/ ncipc/wisqars on August 23, 2009

Chatters, L. M., Bullard, K. M., Taylor, R. J., Woodward, A. T., Neighbors, H. W., & Jackson, J. S. (2008). Religious participation and DSM-IV disorders among older

African Americans: Findings from the National Survey of American Life. *American Journal of Geriatric Psychiatry, 16*(12), 957–965.

Covey, S. (2004). *The 7 habits of highly effective people.* New York: Simon & Schuster.

Craddock, N., Kendler, K., Neale, M., Nurnberger, J., Purcell, S., Rietschel, M., . . . Thapar, A. (2009). Dissecting the phenotype in genome-wide association studies of psychiatric illness. *British Journal of Psychiatry, 195*(2), 97–99.

Craddock, N., & Owen, M. J. (2010). The Kraepelinian dichotomy—going, going . . . but still not gone. *British Journal of Psychiatry, 196*(2), 92–95.

Creswell, J., & Thomas, L., Jr. (2009, January 24). The talented Mr. Madoff. *New York Times.* Retrieved from http://www.nytimes.com/2009/01/25/business/25 bernie.html

Cross-Disorder Phenotype Group of the Psychiatric GWAS Consortium (2009). Common polygenic variation contributes to risk of schizophrenia and bipolar disorder. *Nature 460,* 748-752

Deisenhammer, E. A., Ing, C. M., Strauss, R., Kemmler, G., Hinterhuber, H., & Weiss, E. M. (2008). The duration of the suicidal process: How much time is left for intervention between consideration and accomplishment of a suicide attempt? *Journal of Clinical Psychiatry, 70*(1), 19–24.

Dilsaver, S. C., Chen, Y. R., Shoaib, A. M., & Swann, A. C. (1999). Phenomenology of mania: Evidence for distinct depressed, dysphoric, and euphoric presentations. *American Journal of Psychiatry, 156*(3), 426–430.

D'Souza, D. C., Sewell, R. A., & Ranganathan, M. (2009). Cannabis and psychosis/schizophrenia: Human studies. *European Archives of Psychiatry and Clinical Neuroscience, 259*(7), 413–431.

Eisenberg, D., Aniskin, D., White, L., Stein, J. A., Cohen, L., & Galynker, I. (2009). Structural differences within negative and depressive syndrome dimensions in schizophrenia, organic brain disease, and major depression: A confirmatory factor analysis of the Positive and Negative Syndrome Scale (PANSS). *Psychopathology, 42*(4), 242–248.

Farrell, J. M., Shaw, I. A., & Webber, M. A. (2009). A schema-focused approach to group psychotherapy for outpatients with borderline personality disorder: A randomized controlled trial. *Journal of Behavioral Therapy and Experimental Psychiatry, 40*(2), 317–328.

Fassaert, T., van Dulmen, S., Schellevis, F., & Bensing, J. (2007). Active listening in medical consultations: Development of the Active Listening Observation Scale (ALOS-global). *Patient Educational Counseling, 68*(3), 258–264.

Fazel, S., & Grann, M. (2004). Psychiatric morbidity among homicide offenders: A Swedish population study. *American Journal of Psychiatry, 161*(11), 2129–2131.

Fineberg, N. A., Sharma, P., Sivakumaran, T., Sahakian, B., & Chamberlain, S. R.

(2007). Does obsessive-compulsive personality disorder belong within the obsessive-compulsive spectrum? *CNS Spectrum, 12*(6), 467–482.

Fornaro, M., Gabrielli, F., Albano, C., Fornaro, S., Rizzato, S., Mattei, C., . . . & Fornaro, P. (2009). Obsessive-compulsive disorder and related disorders: A comprehensive survey. *Annals of General Psychiatry, 8,* 13.

Gabbard, G. O., & Horowitz, M. J. (2009). Insight, transference interpretation, and therapeutic change in the dynamic psychotherapy of borderline personality disorder. *American Journal of Psychiatry, 166*(5), 517–521.

Galynker, I. (2007). *Four months after the massacre, lessons to be learned.* Retrieved from http://www.ABCnews.go.com on August 30, 2007

Galynker, I., Cai, J., Dutta, E., Serseni, D., Finestone, H., Ongseng, F., & Rosenthal, R. (1998). Hyprofrontality and negative symptoms in major depressive disorder. *Journal of Nuclear Medicine, 39,* 608–612.

Galynker, I., & Harvey, P. (1992). Diagnostic value of neuropsychological testing in the psychiatric emergency room. *Comprehensive Psychiatry, 33,* 291–292.

Galynker, I., Ieronimo, C., Perez-Aquino, A., Lee, Y., & Winston, A. (1996). Panic attacks with psychotic features. *Journal of Clinical Psychiatry, 57,* 402–406.

Goodwin, R. D., & Hamilton, S. P. (2001). Panic as a marker of core pathological processes. *Psychopathology, 34,* 278–288.

Goodwin, R. D., & Hamilton, S. P. (2002). The early-onset fearful panic attack as a predictor of severe psychopathology. *Psychiatry Resources, 109*(1), 71–79.

Gorwood, P. (2004). Generalized anxiety disorder and major depressive disorder comorbidity: An example of genetic pleiotropy? *European Psychiatry, 19*(1), 27–33.

Green, M. F., & Nuechterlein, K. H. (1999). Should schizophrenia be treated as a neurocognitive disorder? *Schizophrenia Bulletin, 25*(2), 309–319.

Gunderson, J. (2008). *Borderline personality disorder: A clinical guide* (2nd ed.). Washington, DC: American Psychiatric Publishing.

Häfner, H., & an der Heiden, W. (1997). Epidemiology of schizophrenia. *Can J Psychiatry, 42*(2), 131–132.

Hall, W., & Degenhardt, L. (2008). Cannabis use and the risk of developing a psychotic disorder. *World Psychiatry, 7*(2), 68–71.

Hirshfeld-Becker, D. R., Biederman, J., Henin, A., Faraone, S. V., Dowd, S. T., De Petrillo, L. A., . . . Rosenbaum, J. F. (2006). Psychopathology in the young offspring of parents with bipolar disorder: A controlled pilot study. *Psychiatry Resources, 145*(2–3), 155–167.

Hodge, J. G. (2007). Protecting the public's health following the Virginia Tech tragedy: Issues of law and policy. *Disaster Medicine and Public Health Preparedness, 1*(1 Suppl.), S43–S46.

JobBank USA. (2006). *Top 10 most stressful professions; work stresses and col-*

league irritation. Retrieved from http://www.jobbankusa.com/news/business_human_resources/top_10_most_stressful_professions.html on April 18, 2010

Kato, K., Galynker, I., Miner, C., & Rosenblum, J. (1995). Cognitive impairment in psychiatric patients and length of hospital stay. *Comprehensive Psychiatry, 36,* 213–217.

Kendler, K. S., Aggen, S. H., Czajkowski, N., Røysamb, E., Tambs, K., Torgersen, S., . . . Reichborn-Kjennerud, T. (2008). The structure of genetic and environmental risk factors for DSM-IV personality disorders: A multivariate twin study. *Archives of General Psychiatry, 65*(12), 1438–1446.

Kendler, K. S., Gardner, C. O., Fiske, A., & Gatz, M. (2009). Major depression and coronary artery disease in the Swedish twin registry: Phenotypic, genetic, and environmental sources of comorbidity. *Archives of General Psychiatry, 66*(8), 857–863.

Kessler, R. C., Chiu, W. T., Demler, O., & Walters, E. E. (2005). Prevalence, severity, and comorbidity of twelve-month DSM-IV disorders in the National Comorbidity Survey Replication. *Archives of General Psychiatry, 62*(6), 617–627.

Kilbane, E., Gokbayrak, S. M., Tross, C., Cohen, L., & Galynker, I. (2009). Panic as a risk factor for suicide in bipolar mood disorder: A review. *Journal of Affective Disorders, 15*(1–2), 1–10.

Lal, R., & Kremzner, M. (2007). Introduction to the new prescription drug labeling by the Food and Drug Administration. *American Journal of Health-Systems Pharmacy, 64*(23), 2488–2494.

Lapierre, Y. D. (1994). Schizophrenia and manic-depression: Separate illnesses or a continuum? *Canadian Journal of Psychiatry, 39*(9 Suppl. 2), S59–S64.

Leising, D., Sporberg, D., & Rehbein, D. (2006). Characteristic interpersonal behavior in dependent and avoidant personality disorder can be observed within very short interaction sequences. *Journal of Personality Disorders, 20*(4), 319–330.

Linehan, M. (1993). *Cognitive-behavioral treatment of borderline personality disorder.* New York: Guilford Press.

Mark, T. L., Levit, K. R., & Buck, J. A. (2009). Datapoints: Psychotropic drug prescriptions by medical specialty. *Psychiatric Services, 60*(9), 1167.

Maselko, J., Gilman, S. E., & Buka, S. (2009). Religious service attendance and spiritual well-being are differentially associated with risk of major depression. *Psychol Med, 39*(6), 1009–1017.

Matza, L. S., Buchanan, R., Purdon, S., Brewster-Jordan, J., Zhao, Y., & Revicki, D. A. (2006). Measuring changes in functional status among patients with schizophrenia: The link with cognitive impairment. *Schizophrenia Bulletin, 32*(4), 666–678.

Meltzer, H. Y. (2001). Treatment of suicidality in schizophrenia. *Annals of the New York Academy of Science, 932,* 44–60.

Merikangas, K. R., Akiskal, H. S., Angst, J., Greenberg, P. E., Hirschfeld, R. M.,

Petukhova, M., & Kessler, R. C. (2007). Lifetime and 12-month prevalence of bipolar spectrum disorder in the National Comorbidity Survey Replication. *Archives of General Psychiatry, 64*(5), 543–52.

Miklowitz, D. J. (2004). The role of family systems in severe and recurrent psychiatric disorders: A developmental psychopathology view. *Developmental Psychopathology, 16*(3), 667–688.

Miklowitz, D. J. (2007). The role of the family in the course and treatment of bipolar disorder. *Current Directions in Psychological Science, 16*(4), 192–196.

Moreno, C., Laje, G., Blanco, C., Jiang, H., Schmidt, A. B., & Olfson, M. (2007). National trends in the outpatient diagnosis and treatment of bipolar disorder in youth. *Archives of General Psychiatry, 64*(9), 1032–1039.

Mueller, T. I., Leon, A. C., Keller, M. B., Solomon, D. A., Endicott, J., Coryell, W., . . . Maser, J. D. (1999). Recurrence after recovery from major depressive disorder during 15 years of observational follow-up. *American Journal of Psychiatry, 156,* 1000–1006.

Mullen, R., & Linscott, R. J. (2010). A comparison of delusions and overvalued ideas. *Journal of Nervous and Mental Disorders, 198*(1), 35–38.

Munk-Olsen, T., Laursen, T. M., Mendelson, T., Pedersen, C. B., Mors, O., & Mortensen, P. B. (2009). Risks and predictors of readmission for a mental disorder during the postpartum period. *Archives of General Psychiatry, 66*(2), 189–195.

Nadort, M., van Dyck, R., Smit, J. H., Giesen-Bloo, J., Eikelenboom, M., Wensing, M., . . . Arntz, A. (2009). Three preparatory studies for promoting implementation of outpatient schema therapy for borderline personality disorder in general mental health care. *Behaviour Research and Therapy, 47*(11), 938–945.

National Institute of Mental Health Web site. Retrieved from http://www.nimh.nih.gov/science-news/2006/targeted-therapy-halves-suicide-attempts-in-borderline-personality-disorder.shtml on April 18, 2010

Nayani, T. H., & David, A. S. (1996). The auditory hallucination: A phenomenological survey. *Psychological Medicine, 26*(1), 177–189.

Nelson, B., Sass, L. A., & Skodlar, B. (2009). The phenomenological model of psychotic vulnerability and its possible implications for psychological interventions in the ultra-high risk ("prodromal") population. *Psychopathology, 42*(5), 283–292.

Nesse, R. (2000). Is depression an adaptation? *Archives of General Psychiatry, 57,* 14–20.

Nestadt, G., Di, C., Samuels, J. F., Bienvenu, O. J., Reti, I. M., Costa, P., . . . Bandeen-Roche, K. (2010). The stability of DSM personality disorders over twelve to eighteen years. *Journal of Psychiatric Research, 44*(1), 1–7.

Nierenberg, A. A., Akiskal, H. S., Angst, J., Hirschfeld, R. M., Merikangas, K. R., Petukhova, M., & Kessler, R. C. (2009). Bipolar disorder with frequent mood episodes in the National Comorbidity Survey Replication (NCS-R). *Molecular*

Psychiatry. Advance online publication. doi:10.1038/mp.2009.61. Retreived from http://www.ncbi.nlm.nih.gov/pubmed/19564874 on April 23, 2010

Nock, M. K., Borges, G., Bromet, E. J., Cha, C. B., Kessler, R. C., & Lee, S. (2008). Suicide and suicidal behavior. *Epidemiology Review, 30,* 133–154.

O'Connor, R.C., Sheehy,N. P., & O'Connor, D. B. (1999). The classification of completed suicide into subtypes. *Journal of Mental Health, 8*(6), 629–637.

Oquendo, M. A., Barrera, A., Ellis, S. P., Li, S., Burke, A. K., Grunebaum, M., . . . Mann, J. J. (2004). Instability of symptoms in recurrent major depression: A prospective study. *American Journal of Psychiatry, 161,* 255–261.

Panksepp, J. (2007). Neuroevolutionary sources of laughter and social joy: Modeling primal human laughter in laboratory rats. *Behavioral Brain Research, 182*(2), 231–244.

Perahia, D. G., Gilaberte, I., Wang, F., Wiltse, C. G., Huckins, S. A., Clemens, J. W., . . . Detke, M. J. (2006). Duloxetine in the prevention of relapse of major depressive disorder: Double-blind placebo-controlled study. *British Journal of Psychiatry, 188,* 346–353.

Perlick, D. A., Rosenheck, R. A., Clarkin, J. F., Maciejewski, P. K., Sirey, J., Struening, E., & Link, B. G. (2004). Impact of family burden and affective response on clinical outcome among patients with bipolar disorder. *Psychiatry Services, 55,* 1029–1035.

Perlick, D. A., Rosenheck, R. A., Miklowitz, D. J., Kaczynski, R., Link, B., Ketter, T., . . . Sachs, G. (2008). Caregiver burden and health in bipolar disorder: A cluster analytic approach. *Journal of Nervous and Mental Disorders, 196*(6), 484–491.

Pertusa, A., Fullana, M. A., Singh, S., Alonso, P., Menchón, J. M., & Mataix-Cols, D. (2008). Compulsive hoarding: OCD symptom, distinct clinical syndrome, or both? *American Journal of Psychiatry, 165*(10), 1289–1298.

Pescosolido, B. A., Martin, J. K., Link, B. G., Kikuzawa, S., Burgos, G., & Swindle, R. (2000). *Americans' views of mental health and illness at century's end: Continuity and change.* Bloomington: Indiana Consortium of Mental Health Services Research.

Pluchino A, Rapisarda A, & Garofalo C. (2010) The Peter principle revisited: A computational study. *Physica A: Statistical Mechanics and its Applications, 389* (3), 467–472.

Posner, K., Oquendo, M. A., Gould, M., Stanley, B., & Davies, M. (2007). Columbia Classification Algorithm of Suicide Assessment (C-CASA): Classification of suicidal events in the FDA's pediatric suicidal risk analysis of antidepressants. *American Journal of Psychiatry, 164*(7), 1035–1043.

Poyurovsky, M. (2010). Acute antipsychotic-induced akathisia revisited. *British Journal of Psychiatry, 196*(2), 89–91.

Rogstad, J. E., & Rogers, R. (2008). Gender differences in contributions of emotion to psychopathy and antisocial personality disorder. *Clinical Psychology Review, 28*(8), 1472–1484.

Rozmarin, E., Muran, J. C., Safran, J., Gorman, B., Nagy, J., & Winston, A. (2008). Subjective and intersubjective analyses of the therapeutic alliance in a brief relational therapy. *American Journal of Psychotherapy, 62*(3), 313–328.

Rubino, T., & Parolaro, D. (2008). Long lasting consequences of cannabis exposure in adolescence. *Molecular Cell Endocrinology, 286*(1–2 Suppl. 1), S108–S113.

Ryan, S. Freud and the meaning of work in Gerhard Roth's Winterreise seminar: A Journal of Germanic Studies. University of Toronto Press, *31*(2) 19950037-1939 (Print) 1911-026X (Online).

Sackeim, H. A., Prudic, J., Nobler, M. S., Fitzsimons, L., Lisanby, S. H., Payne, N., . . . Devanand, D. P. (2008). Effects of pulse width and electrode placement on the efficacy and cognitive effects of electroconvulsive therapy. *Brain Stimulation, 1*(2), 71–83.

Schiffman, J., Walker, E., Ekstrom, M., Schulsinger, F., Sorensen, H., & Mednick, S. (2004). Childhood videotaped social and neuromotor precursors of schizophrenia: A prospective investigation. *American Journal of Psychiatry, 161*(11), 2021–2027.

Sheffield, A. (1999). *How you can survive when they're depressed: Living and coping with depression fallout.* New York: Three River Press.

Sheffield, A. (2003). *Depression fallout: The impact of depression on couples and what you can do to preserve the bond.* New York: HarperCollins.

Shor, J. (1992). *Work, love, play: Self-repair in the psychoanalytic dialogue.* New York: Brunner/Mazel.

Sims, A. (2002). *Symptoms in the mind: An introduction to descriptive psychopathology.* Philadelphia: W. B. Saunders.

Singh, M. K., DelBello, M. P., Stanford, K. E., Soutullo, C., McDonough-Ryan, P., McElroy, S. L., & Strakowski, S. M. (2007). Psychopathology in children of bipolar parents. *Journal of Affective Disorders, 102*(1–3), 131–136.

Skegg, K. (2005). Self-harm. *Lancet, 366*(9495), 1471–1483.

Solomon, D. A., Keller, M. B., Leon, A. C., Mueller, T. I., Lavori, P. W., Shea, M. T., . . . Endicott, J. (2000). Multiple recurrences of major depressive disorder. *American Journal of Psychiatry, 157*(2), 229–233.

Steele, A., Maruyama, N., & Galynker, I. (2010). Psychiatric symptoms in caregivers of patients with bipolar disorder: A review. *Journal of Affective Disorders, 121*(1–2), 10–21.

Thase, M. E. (2005). Bipolar depression: Issues in diagnosis and treatment. *Harvard Review of Psychiatry, 13*(5), 257–271.

Thase, M. E. (2007). STEP-BD and bipolar depression: What have we learned? *Current Psychiatry Reports, 9*(6), 497–503.

Tsuang, M. (2000). Schizophrenia: Genes and environment. *Biological Psychiatry*, *47*(3), 210–220.

van der Vegt, E. J., van der Ende, J., Ferdinand, R. F., Verhulst, F. C., & Tiemeier, H. (2009). Early childhood adversities and trajectories of psychiatric problems in adoptees: Evidence for long lasting effects. *Journal of Abnormal Child Psychology*, *37*(2), 239–249.

Vaughn, C., & Leff, J. (1976). The measurement of expressed emotion in the families of psychiatric patients. *British Journal of Social and Clinical Psychology*, *15*, 157–165.

Velligan, D. I., & Alphs, L. D. (2008). Negative symptoms in schizophrenia: The importance of identification and treatment. *Psychiatric Times*, *25*(3),

Williams, M. & Ahlberg, J. (Producer), Morris, E. (Director). (2003). *The fog of war: Eleven lessons from the life of Robert S. McNamara* [Motion Picture]. United States: Sony Picture Classics. http://www.errolmorris.com/film/fow_transcript.html

World Health Organization. (2004). *The world health report 2004: Changing history*. Geneva: Author.

Yassen, Z., Johnson, M., Fox, S., & Galynker, I. (April, 2009). *Construct validity of a suicide trigger state*. World Psychiatric Association Annual Meeting, Florence, Italy.

INDEX